The Politics of Northern Ireland

The Politics of Northern Ireland is written by one of the leading authorities on contemporary Northern Ireland and provides an original, sophisticated and innovative examination of the post-Belfast Agreement political landscape. The Agreement was a model of democratic ingenuity and political inclusion, and intimated the emergence of a new style of politics based on the principles of consent and mutual responsibility. It had the potential to transform Northern Ireland from a political culture of conflict to a political culture of accommodation. However, the implementation of the Agreement has been plagued by the mistrust of people in Northern Ireland and the imaginative institutions of government have had a fitful existence, operating in a permanent atmosphere of crisis. This book explains the experience of hope and frustration through a systematic analysis of the ambiguous political legacy of the peace process. Written in a fluid, eloquent and accessible style, the book explores:

- how the Belfast Agreement has changed the politics of Northern Ireland
- whether the peace process is still valid
- the problems caused by the language of politics in Northern Ireland
- what conditions are necessary to secure political stability
- the inability of unionists and republicans to share the same political discourse
- the insights that political theory can offer to Northern Irish politics
- the future of key political parties and institutions.

This text is an outstanding contribution to the literature on contemporary Northern Irish politics and history and is essential reading for students and scholars in these areas.

Dr Arthur Aughey is Senior Lecturer in Politics at the University of Ulster at Jordanstown. He is a member of the Northern Ireland Advisory Committee of the British Council and the management board of the Institute of Ulster-Scots Studies.

The Politics of Northern Ireland
Beyond the Belfast Agreement

Arthur Aughey

Routledge
Taylor & Francis Group

LONDON AND NEW YORK

For Sky

First published 2005
by Routledge
2 Park Square, Milton Park, Abingdon, Oxon OX14 4RN

Simultaneously published in the USA and Canada
by Routledge
270 Madison Ave, New York, NY 10016

Routledge is an imprint of the Taylor & Francis Group

© 2005 Arthur Aughey

Typeset in Sabon by LaserScript Ltd, Mitcham, Surrey
Printed and bound in Great Britain by
The Cromwell Press, Trowbridge, Wiltshire

British Library Cataloguing in Publication Data
A catalogue record for this book is available from the British Library

Library of Congress Cataloging in Publication Data
A catalog record for this book has been requested

ISBN 0–415–32787–3 (hbk)
ISBN 0–415–32788–1 (pbk)

Contents

11 Afterword 178

Acknowledgements

I would like to thank Professor Henry Patterson of the University of Ulster at Jordanstown and Professor Paul Bew of Queen's University, Belfast for their insightful comments on an earlier version of this work. I would also like to thank my Head of School in Economics and Politics, Carmel Roulston, who also read part of the manuscript and who has been very supportive of the project from its inception. Some of the arguments in this book are developments of ideas first given a public airing elsewhere. Chapter 8 generalizes a particular thesis on post-Agreement unionist politics presented in the second edition of M. Cox, A. Guelke and F. Stephen (eds) *A Farewell to Arms? From 'Long War' to Long Peace in Northern Ireland* published by Manchester University Press in 2004. Chapter 9 expands an interpretation explored tentatively in an article in *Irish Political Studies* in 2002. I am grateful to both sets of editors for their kind permission to reproduce aspects of those arguments in this work.

1 Introduction

The historian A. T. Q. Stewart once observed that the political divisions in Northern Ireland are not the result of a misunderstanding between unionists and nationalists. Rather, the divisions are a consequence of unionists and nationalists understanding each other all too well. Both communities are adept at the translation and interpretation of the other side's messages.

> Instead of extremists, who can be managed in a democracy, government (wherever it resides) has to deal with two hostile populations who cannot agree on definitions. Words like 'democracy', 'liberty', 'rights', 'esteem' become porous, and the parrot-cries of party no longer offer any guide to truth. And no one involved in the situation can really be impartial.

This, Stewart argued, was 'the labyrinth out of which the politicians must find a way' (2001: 180). The Northern Ireland problem, then, can be defined as a profound division over the ends of politics as well as the means to achieve them. These have been questions that political argument in Northern Ireland has been unable to resolve by reasoned debate. Equally, it has not proved possible to resolve them by political violence. Hence the 30-year impasse. Nevertheless, it has been the consistent objective of the British and Irish Governments – as it has been the consistent assumption of liberal opinion – that it is indeed possible to reach agreement on these questions. The Talks about the future of Northern Ireland, from which issued the Belfast Agreement, were based on a number of such expectations. Political negotiations on an inclusive basis would establish a new platform of tolerance from which progress could be made and would provide a form of political therapy through which a rational consensus on principles could be reached. Lasting political bargains would be struck in a satisfactory balance of gains and losses and on those foundations the Agreement implied the emergence of a new and stable political dispensation.

Recent works on Northern Ireland such as Ed Moloney's analysis of republicanism (2002) and Dean Godson's study of David Trimble (2004) have provided enormously detailed and insightful accounts of the peace process, based on intimate acquaintance with the main actors. There is little to be added by going over that ground again. However, there is further space for an examination of the disputed ideas that have contributed to the peace process as Richard Bourke (2003) and Adrian Little (2004) have shown and that is where this study attempts to make a contribution. Anxiety and expectation appeared to sum up the paradoxical experience of Northern Ireland after the Belfast Agreement. To explain that experience it is important to understand how current expectation has informed political anxiety and how current anxiety has informed political expectation. Both anxiety and expectation, of course, derive their substance from different readings of the past. The book is divided into three parts, each part consisting of three interconnected chapters. Each chapter follows a similar pattern. Alternative ways of interpreting political possibilities are stated and their respective merits considered in terms of the ambiguity of changing political relationships, an approach that is designed to reveal how old and new styles of argument interpenetrate. The motif is the motif of paradox and the chapters take as their guide Schopenhauer's aphorism: 'This would be a glorious world in which the truth were in no way paradoxical; for then indeed beauty would be recognized at once and virtue would be easy' (1988: 371).

In Part I, 'Conditions', three chapters examine the Northern Ireland question in terms of recent historical, imaginative and political under-standings, understandings that made any settlement of that question problematical. Chapter 2 examines two historical understandings that assert either that all politics is fated or that all politics is willed and open to choice. The first implies a tragic view of politics where action is compelled by the situation and the second implies an ethical view where responsibility for action is paramount. This chapter looks at these narratives of fate and choice and how they have woven themselves through the political condition of Northern Ireland. Chapter 3 assesses the view that politics in Northern Ireland has suffered from a lack of imagination, a lack that has fostered the negativity that so often is taken to define its condition. It argues that, contrary to that impression, Northern Ireland has suffered from the opposite condition, from an over-imagination that frequently borders on the fantastic and that these fantasies, or disconnections between means and ends, helped to sustain political violence for 30 years. Chapter 4 examines the politics of winning and losing. It considers the simplicity but also the difficulties of this style of thinking about politics and its consequences for long-term stability. The chapter argues that a substantial factor in the recent Troubles was the determination of unionism to avoid losing this time and the determination of nationalism to win this time. In both cases fate – the 'end' of history – played a large part in their respective calculations of political means.

In Part II, 'Modifications', three chapters look at the Belfast Agreement in terms of changing ideas, structures and circumstances and the extent to which the Agreement modified the Northern Ireland condition. Chapter 5 explores the contribution to politics in Northern Ireland of new ideas about democratic participation and reviews recent re-evaluations of the potential for inclusive transformation made by advocates of dialogic democracy. It compares this idea of democratic transformation with the more familiar concept of a historic compromise between communal blocs. Chapter 6 is devoted to the archaeology of the Belfast Agreement itself and assesses its institutions in the light of previous attempts to deliver stability. Chapter 7 considers the extent to which that Agreement provided the basis for a new beginning, a sort of re-foundation of Northern Ireland politics, and the extent to which it (more modestly) modified the circumstances in which traditional styles of politics continued to be conducted.

Part III, 'Consequences', surveys the implementation and effect of the Agreement since 1998. Chapter 8 is an appraisal of the anxiety and expectation the Agreement provoked amongst unionists and nationalists. It assesses the ambiguous interaction of both anxiety and expectation within and between the two political communities and the impact they had on the strategies of the political parties. Chapter 9 looks at the effect of the politics of 'constructive ambiguity' on the fortunes of the Agreement. Constructive ambiguity was that noble lie that would, it was hoped, secure the new condition of peace. Unfortunately, it could also be judged a calculated stratagem to betray and often it was difficult to distinguish between the two. This chapter reassesses the course of post-Agreement politics in terms of alternative readings of the noble lie. Chapter 10 attempts to summarize the new condition of Northern Ireland, the consequence of the modifications brought about by the peace process of the 1990s and the fitful experience of executive devolution after 1998. It re-examines the oppositions explored in the book and identifies no harmonious resolution but only the unavoidable paradoxes of Northern Ireland politics. A brief Afterword reflects on the prospects for resurrecting the institutions of devolution given the polarization of party politics by 2004.

Edna Longley has been critical of those who throw theory at Ireland, hoping bits of it will stick. Perhaps this book may be judged to suffer from that particular defect. Nevertheless, it has been written on the assumption that such theoretical throwing is a task worth doing not only to make sense of complex events but also to stimulate or provoke the work of others.

Part I
Conditions

2   Fate and choice

The Owl of Minerva, according to Hegel, spreads its wings only with the falling of dusk. We come to a fuller understanding of the character of a political era once its way of life has grown old (1952: 13). Any such exercise in the periodization of history – when does it start, when does it end? – is a very imprecise art and is open to all sorts of reservations and qualifications. In particular, the historian will be reluctant to put too much intellectual weight on the neatness that such periodization presumes. The enterprise is not without its utility, however, in that it can draw attention to what was distinctive, if not entirely representative, of a form of politics. There has been a tentative consensus amongst students of Northern Ireland politics that the Belfast Agreement of 10 April 1998 may be taken to mark the end of a particular era that began with the civil rights campaign in 1968 (see Holland 1999). These 30 years are popularly known as 'the Troubles' or 'the recent Troubles' in order to distinguish them from the political violence which attended the partition of Ireland in the early 1920s. There is greater reluctance to go further and to conclude that what the expression 'the Troubles' designates – widespread political violence – cannot be entirely rejuvenated. Nevertheless, contemporary judgement echoes J. C. Beckett's observation on the end of the earlier Troubles:

> Though the settlement left a legacy of bitterness, issuing occasionally in local and sporadic disturbances, it inaugurated for Ireland a longer period of general tranquillity than she had known since the first half of the eighteenth century.
>
> (Beckett 1966: 461)

In very different circumstances and for very different reasons, the Belfast Agreement appeared to provide the potential for greater tranquillity in Northern Ireland than at any time since 1968. Political reflection started to engage with the question of endings and beginnings and academic analysis turned its attention to what might be meant in this situation by the notion of 'the end of Irish history' (Aughey 1998; Ruane 1999). In other words, as it became possible to understand the Troubles as part of the past, understanding of these years was correspondingly modified. The very notion of closure (however arbitrary that closure may be) gave to the last 30 years a shape that permitted a more detached assessment, what Hegel called a portrait of 'grey in grey'.

This enterprise is both a necessary and a dangerous one. It is necessary because contemporary events affect the coherence of our view of the past and, in this sense, Zhou Enlai's celebrated judgement on the meaning of the French Revolution – that it is too early to tell – is less a witticism and more an historical truism. It is also dangerous because of the possibility of 'presentism', a reading of the past that already assumes the present, a notion that invites political manipulation. What common sense assumes is that the past is a realm of fact but in truth it inverts that assumption. Presentism makes the past into a realm of imagination, of half-truths and fabrications, of folk wisdom and, when politicized, folk wisdom then becomes a partisan narrative of necessity. In order to justify what we want to do in the present this is what the past *must* have been like. The greyness of the 'first draft' of history paints over the lurid and passionate colours of folk wisdom and of political necessity for the objective is to reconsider some of the dominant modes of thought that gave to this period its political shape. From the Owl of Minerva's perspective, we can now cast a cold eye on the Troubles and, from our contemporary vantage point, re-examine what were commonly held to be its realities and to reassess that period in a manner that may help to illuminate the possibilities but also the limitations of politics in Northern Ireland after the Belfast Agreement. This is not a 'Whiggish reading' of the Belfast Agreement (Jackson 2003: 260). It is more of an anti-Whiggish reading that emphasizes the contingency of situations and the consequences of choice. This is important since a particular notion of history (even the 'hand of history') is thought to inform the necessary character of the Agreement.

The Agreement's significance, it has been argued, lay not only in institutional structures but also in addressing the 'legacy of history' or even overcoming 'the burden of the past'. It was supposed to be, in this grander sense, a turning point, a new beginning, an opening to the future. Yet as Pridham has argued in another context, politics is never 'born of immaculate conception'. Changes of the extent intimated in the Belfast Agreement can also be 'an occasion for reconsidering the uncomfortable past as well as looking to the future' (Pridham 2000: 29–31). Pridham's main concern was the transition to democracy of Central and Eastern European countries during the 1990s. Those conditions and circumstances are very different from the situation in Northern Ireland, although one cannot miss a certain existential correspondence, a correspondence acknowledged by some of those engaged in negotiating the Belfast Agreement (Mansergh 1996: 209–10). For example, as it became clear that the negotiations were coming to a positive conclusion, David Ervine of the Progressive Unionist Party (PUP) told television reporters that the Agreement was the local equivalent of the fall of the Berlin Wall. In terms of world historical significance this was an obvious exaggeration yet it is worth pursuing the analogy a little further in order to clarify this chapter's intent.

In a poignant essay written in October 1989, the German novelist Christa Wolf recounted the difficulty that people in the former German Democratic Republic have had in finding a narrative, personal and collective, to make sense of their new situation and the problem of giving voice to their condition. For Wolf the task involved a difficult balance. It involved trying to make sense of 40 years of life without wiping out 40 years of history. Discovering a suitable narrative, she thought, would involve reviewing 'the basic assumptions and the unfolding of this history stage by stage, document by document, to evaluate its results and see how it meets the demands of the present day' (Wolf 1993: 301). Wolf was reminded of Chekhov for whom the intellectual task was to 'squeeze the slave out of himself drop by drop' and she thought that there were positive signs in East Germany that people were indeed beginning to squeeze the slave out of themselves. Squeezing out the slave meant recovering a sense of intelligent choice and this depended on laying aside the temptation to think of history in terms of a law, of national destiny or of necessity. A healthy politics could only grow, she concluded, if 'everyone takes active responsibility for society in cooperation with everyone else' and history, when confronted honestly, would form part of that healthy narrative (Wolf 1993: 302). Above all, what needed to be confronted was a dismal culture of historical fate that seemed to justify everything and to explain nothing. In a rather different context, this was also the subject of W. G. Sebald's ironically titled *On the Natural History of Destruction*. Armed destruction is anything but 'natural' for it requires the active organization of destruction, and naturalizing its history is a way to escape responsibility for its effects and to suppress experience of it (Sebald 2003: 64). And we suppress experience by relaxing into the arms of fate. The central question here concerns the appropriate form of historical narrative, for how we remember the past is constitutive of our present identity and it also says much about how we can imagine our future. This is where history and politics unavoidably overlap and where, as Seamus Heaney put it, 'hope and history rhyme'.

These observations on Germany would, at first sight, appear to have little relevance to the condition of Northern Ireland. Who would say that its citizens do not know how to talk of their condition when 'giving voice' has been one of the most dynamic, publicly funded growth industries of the last 30 years? And, unlike Germany East or West, surely Northern Ireland has been mightily conscious of its past? Has not the historian, rather than the philosopher, been king? Has not politics in Northern Ireland been conducted in the idiom of historical justification and justification by history? Have unionists and nationalists not sought to allocate historical blame rather than to seek present compromise? This has produced a distinctive style. Self-pity (we have been grievously wronged by partition –

the nationalist position; we have been grievously wronged by political subversion – the unionist position) and self-righteousness (our struggle is sanctioned by history – the nationalist position; our resistance is morally correct – the unionist position) fostered a discourse of grievance, a style of politics that has a long pedigree in Irish politics. For example, Stephen Gwynn thought that the Irish problem lay in 'generations of political passion without political responsibility' and that condition, replicated in the last 30 years and compounded by political violence, provides an insight into the condition of Northern Ireland (Gwynn 1924: 197). And seen in that light, Wolf's German question does not seem so far removed from the Northern Ireland question and from the challenges facing contemporary politics. In the Northern Ireland of the early 1990s, as Longley noted, 'the lid blew off as tightly sealed a society as any in eastern Europe: one sealed off by the introverted codes of its communities'. As a consequence, a rather paradoxical situation developed in which 'social change has been at once impelled and retarded by the exigencies of living in that explosion' (Longley 1994a: 1–2). The large and difficult questions that a generation of violence has bequeathed may never be properly addressed and even if they are addressed the result may not be a happy one. But certain things may be explored by way of a beginning. One of the major questions is also one of the simplest questions: To what extent were the Troubles a matter of fate or to what extent were they a matter of choice?

Fate and choice

It is not at all convincing that the outworking of Northern Ireland's recent past was either inevitable or that it was the consequence of some terrible fate. This remains the case even if, in the contest between fate and choice, most people are disposed to accept a pessimistic interpretation of the Troubles and, by contrast, to take a more optimistic view of contemporary possibilities. If something was inevitable one might assume that it was also expected. This was not the case. For example, reviewing public assumptions and expectations on the eve of the Northern Ireland crisis, Hugh Kearney has argued that the general impression was one of improvement and it was expected that old antagonisms were moving towards resolution. The violence of the next 30 years, then, 'was a future quite unforeseen in the 1960s' (Kearney 2001: 115–16). Equally, a young historian studying the premiership of Terence O'Neill has written of the shock when surfacing from his immersion in the documents and papers of the period 1960 to 1969 'to recall the disaster that overtook Northern Ireland in the years following' (Mulholland 2000: xi). Not only do the following years take a shape that seemed inconceivable in the period that preceded it; the violence of those years also appeared incommensurate with the nature of the antagonisms that constituted 'the Northern Ireland Question' of its day. As has often been pointed out, the civil disturbances of the late 1960s repeated patterns of disorder elsewhere in Europe and the United States. Few had expected that political contestation about civil rights would give way to the sustained political violence of the next 25 years. In Cox's view, the condition of the persistent paramilitary campaigns promoted its own fatalistic inversion. Very rapidly indeed, he argued, 'the Troubles had assumed their own deadly logic, and few now believed they would ever come to an end'. Political violence became a natural way of life and people learned to live with it (Cox 1997: 672–3). The expectation that things could not be otherwise has its own history and there was a sorry experience of failed political initiatives to confirm the popular view of the problem's intractability. Functioning constitutional politics, which assume a capacity to bargain over and to reach an accommodation between the claims of continuity and change, seemed ill-suited to the culture of Northern Ireland polarized further by paramilitarism. There had always been intractable constituencies within nationalism and unionism that denied the possibility of a trade-off between reform and stability, and these constituencies had become hardened by the continuation of political violence. There were sufficiently extremist constituencies within loyalism and republicanism that were now determined (and had the capability) either to frustrate change or to promote instability. But one should not confuse the determined campaigns of these paramilitary minorities with historical determination. It is important to recall how large were the constituencies prepared to accept the virtue, if not always the detail, of political accommodation. Opinion polls showed that power-sharing was widely and consistently acceptable to both unionist and nationalist voters, even if it was not necessarily their first choice (Whyte 1991: 82).

It became very easy, then, to accept a tragic vision of the conflict, a vision that was not without its own consolations. It was a vision that, for some, confirmed the exceptional nature of life in Northern Ireland and thereby contributed to their own sense of importance and self-worth. Instead of its accustomed provincial languor, Northern Ireland was now the focus of intense world attention. This fed the pretensions of those who considered themselves to be on a mission of historical redemption and of those who, like the Khan of Tartary, mistook their own world for the known world (Montesquieu 1993: 99). Furthermore, and exaggerating both importance and self-worth, there existed a pervasive feeling of victimhood, real and imaginary, that has been common to the cultures of unionism and nationalism (see Kennedy 1996: 182–223). Emotionally, this condition served to displace responsibility on to others. Politically, it encouraged a helpless attitude of going with the flow, an acceptance that the history of destruction all around was indeed 'natural'. The alternative to this tragic vision was a moralistic one, preaching the virtues of cooperation and the value of compromise that, in the circumstances of determined political violence, it was unable to deliver either. As a consequence, the moral vision tended towards a self-indulgence that was none other than the alter-image of the tragic vision. Indeed, it depended for its very existence on the depth and extent of the popular sense of the tragic and it should come as no surprise that these two visions could sometimes become comfortably interrelated in a self-serving discourse. A public body like the Community Relations Council made it into an art form. The apparent hopelessness of this condition often became an excuse for not thinking about it at all. The temptation was strong for individuals and families to escape into a politely privatized existence, one secured by the high level of public expenditure in Northern Ireland. However, in retrospect (and also in prospect) it is worth posing what Andre Gorz considered to be the most disturbing questions of all. Given this condition, was another choice possible? And given this choice, another condition? (cited in Marcus 1992: 117). The tragic vision answers 'no' to the first question and the moral vision answers 'yes' to the second. The problem with both answers is their certainty and dismissal of contingency. These are questions about history (rather than historical questions) that have been the subtext of most thoughtful work on Northern Ireland and they are questions that require a subtle examination. In short, what role does history play in divided society?

On that point, academic attention has been focused mainly on the revisionist controversy in Irish history (see Boyce and O'Day 1996). There has been another debate, less noticed, less celebrated but no less significant, on the role of Irish history in contemporary politics. Its central concern has been to assess the competing claims of continuity and change and out of that debate one may construct an idea of political limits. In that debate, A. T. Q. Stewart has been an eloquent advocate of one particular view. In *The Narrow Ground* he argued that Winston Churchill's famous remark about the 'integrity of their quarrel' came close to defining the 'essential character of the Ulster problem'. As Stewart understood it, 'people simply assume the political attitudes of the community into which they were born. They rarely choose their political attitude after mature deliberation.' Moreover, since each community 'identifies itself from the myth it takes from Irish history', then each side 'wastes its breath in trying to persuade the other to adopt its view of the situation' (Stewart 1977: 179–80). This does not mean that things never change. Society is changing constantly. Nevertheless, there are underlying patterns that are resistant to abstract moralization and wishful thinking (Stewart 2001: 161). Underneath all those momentous events (and the Belfast Agreement is no exception) 'the fundamentals of Irish history remain largely unchanged'. Challenging the fashionable view that dialogue is the only way to foster mutual under-standing, Stewart argued that Catholic and Protestant in Northern Ireland do not 'need to get to know each other better. They know each other only too well, having lived alongside each other for four centuries.' In short, the Northern Ireland problem 'is not just a clash of cultures; it is a culture in itself, a point overlooked by most observers' (Stewart 2001: 185; see also Akenson 1991: 127–79).

If Stewart's profound intellectual scepticism can be traced to any particular source it would be to his original research on that subject of great hope for republicanism, the United Irishmen. The eighteenth-century enlightened idealism that professed emancipation, equality and national fraternity encountered the earthy conditions of Irish culture. Indeed, in part that idealism was itself an earthy stepchild of a Protestant prejudice that assumed, as Wolfe Tone himself assumed, that 'the Irish Catholic was at last being emancipated from the thraldom of priests'. Enabled to think for themselves at last, Catholics would join hands with Protestants in the cause of 'the Rights of Man and the rights of Ireland' (Stewart 1993: 152–3). The error of the United Irishmen was not an error of stupidity. It was an error of intelligence. In Stewart's view, such errors of intelligence have a habit of repeating themselves and the Belfast Agreement may be another example. These errors repeat themselves by abstracting idealism from earthy circumstance and by assuming that circumstance is merely incidental while idealism is fundamental. Indeed, one may suggest that there is an ironic inversion of the original United Irishmen idealism in a contemporary nationalist view that Ulster Protestants need to emancipate themselves from the thraldom of a backward ideology and move forward into the light. If the original idealism mixed spiritual truth and material advancement, so the current idealism mixes material prosperity (Celtic Tiger) and cultural fecundity (West Belfast Festival). History, in other words, has delivered its judgement on unionist superiority but unfortunately it appears to have substituted a nationalist version of superiority.

Errors of a rather different sort have been explored by another historian, Brian Walker. In a series of popular articles and academic books, Walker has tried to show that even in 'given' Irish conditions other choices are always possible. The thesis of his *Ulster Politics: The Formative Years 1868–86* (1989), for example, is that 'the upsurge of sectarian politics was neither predetermined nor inevitable' but was the consequence of contingent political and economic developments in the second half of the nineteenth century (1989: xiv). Sectarian politics is not an immutable force of history over which it is impossible to exercise control and the close link between religion and politics is not set in stone. Walker's message is one of practical intent, reminding people that when they try to deal with the 'very real problems confronting them, they do so without the unnecessary and harmful burden of "history's tune"' (Walker 1996: 158). This enlightenment is critical, for history's tune in Northern Ireland plays a fatalistic note and frustrates the possibility of choosing compromise and peaceful coexistence. It 'creates a fatalistic sense of continuous conflict that undermines trust between communities' (Walker 2000: 121). Like Mairead Nic Craith's brilliant formulation of the problem, we can remember our past so well that we get it wrong, selectively 'forgetting to remember' what suits our present purposes (Nic Craith 2002: 41–5). Unlike Stewart, the message is that not only does the context of the Ulster question change but so too does the nature of the problem. It is possible to re-define and to re-structure political relationships in a more dynamic manner than Stewart suggests, if only because the contingencies of history provide a space for freedom. This intellectual objective of relieving people of the nightmarish 'burden of history' implies that real historical knowledge will give political leverage to the moral vision in its contest with the tragic. It can enable people to see that it is not an impossible dream to accept a shared heritage or for unionists and nationalists to enjoy their differences in a non-threatening fashion (Nic Craith 2002: 201). Stewart's considered response to the 'burden of history' argument has been curt. He has accepted that what it proposes is a comforting thought, he has acknowledged that the arguments are generally sincere and that the intention is good. Unfortunately, he still believes that the quest is hopeless. Efforts to promote reconciliation, at least those efforts that envisage political harmony emerging out of difference, 'are singularly futile' (Stewart 2001: 182–5). This response is not attributable to a personal disposition. It is an intelligent historical view in which the assumption of some 'end' to Irish history – in the liberal sense that one side finally comes to accept fully the 'other' in a mode of deep reconciliation – either ignores or 'distorts everything that has gone before' (2001: 4).

Here, at first sight, are two very different views of fate and choice based on solid scholarship and an intimate knowledge of Irish history. While remaining faithful to the sources, both appear to abstract from that history very different practical lessons. It is tempting to call these lessons pessimistic and optimistic, though it is better to understand them otherwise. The difference of emphasis in the interpretation of history is a differential emphasis upon continuity (Stewart) and change (Walker and Nic Craith). The practical message can be either optimistic or pessimistic but the common concern is to be realistic about the 'role of history' in political argument. What the first view stresses is the recurring patterns of behaviour founded in the characteristics of and relations between two embedded world views. What the other view stresses is the shifting patterns of behaviour influenced by changing circumstances and by changing self-understandings. Both views are partially true and together they constitute the complex historical unity of Northern Ireland. How can we grasp the character of this complex unity? It may be useful to briefly shift focus from history to literature. In his essay *A New Refutation of Time*, Jorge Luis Borges argued that time is a river that sweeps us along but that we are also the river; that time is a fire that consumes us but that we are also the fire. He concluded by noting that the 'world, unfortunately, is real; I, unfortunately, am Borges' (Borges 1999: 332). To put that otherwise: the history of Northern Ireland, unfortunately, is real; the people of Northern Ireland, unfortunately, are real and they are intimately connected to that history, even in ways of which they are not aware. Like the fire and the river our fate is our choice and our choices our fate. This is not necessarily a depressing doctrine. Like Oakeshott's reflections on the nature of tradition, what it excludes are hopes that were false in the first place. If we are deprived of 'a model laid up in heaven' we are not led necessarily into a morass of amoral fatalism (Oakeshott 1991: 158). This has not prevented Stewart, for example, being taken to task for having, rather like Schopenhauer, a 'misanthropic view of political relations', actively promoting division and desiring to prevent fraternity (Porter 2003: 268). Such a reading is quite perverse, confuses understanding with recommendation, limitation with inevitability, and reveals the historical ignorance at the heart of the moralizing vision. Some may think, like Porter, that Stewart's reading is 'unfortunate', but it is only unfortunate in the sense that people must try to struggle against comforting illusions and falsehoods about Northern Ireland and even more comforting illusions about themselves. It cautions against wishful thinking but it would be wrong to assume that to deprive us of wishful thinking is tantamount to proposing that we are fated always to succumb to murder and mayhem. Stewart's own historical researches reveal otherwise. On the other hand, and within these historical limits and when a lot of mythology is discarded, we bear responsibility for our acts, can make our own destiny, and that is the essential message of Walker and Nic Craith. Both insights together constitute neither fate nor choice in their simple alternatives but reveal practical history – how we presently understand our past – as a common predicament. Such an understanding compels attention to that predicament when sometimes, even for the best of reasons, it is more convenient to ignore it. In his masterpiece of research on the early Troubles, Richard Rose actually discovered that a widespread sense of fatalism was lacking and found amongst his respondents little consciously articulated awareness of the past. However, he was also aware of the limits of such social scientific results when all around the evidence of conflict obliged him to believe otherwise. He thought that ideologies of historical discord survive 'because they are relevant to the present as well as to the past' (Rose 1971: 353–4). This was not all that could be said, however. Though confronted with such problems, Rose thought that political leaders could not avoid the burden of their situation. It was not the burden of history that was at issue but a very immediate burden of choice, and every politician 'has the freedom and responsibility of deciding which choice will be his fate' (1971: 396). To choose, of course, is not necessarily to choose wisely or for the best, and 'fate' is often a convenient excuse for bad choices.

In so far, then, as the Belfast Agreement has assumed a self-liberating act of political choice as an alternative to a self-defeating fate of sectarian strife (even if one accepts that the choices open to the parties are limited by recent experience), the possibility of that act in itself compels some reassessment of historical justifications for violence and intransigence. In retrospect, these justifications become suspect in so far as they appeal to fate or necessity *alone*. It is no longer so respectable to protect oneself 'against the eerie experience of contingency' or to argue that it is futile to contest historical necessity (Gkotzaridis 2001: 125). The change in context changes perspective. At the beginning of the peace process, this changing perspective was well captured by Bernard Crick. On his many visits to Northern Ireland he used to be told by all sides: 'You've got to understand what it's like on the ground'. The implication of this mantra was twofold. The problem is 'grounded' in a manner which inferred that only those who had grown up in it can know what it really meant; and the problem was such that it is fated to work itself out in a manner which defies liberal, rational criticism. Crick confessed that he once found that interpretation persuasive and that he used to repeat it 'in a voice throbbing with realism' against those who would argue otherwise. However, this was not so much an argument as a self-justification. It took Crick ten years to answer back: 'Yes, but; you've got to lift your heads and look at the context which can help you, crush you or abandon you, but cannot solve your problems for you'. In other words, there was as much choice in accepting one's fate as there was in trying to seek another way. Yes, one can accept the fact of Northern Ireland's difficult history, but there are possibilities. Crick got just about right the historical balance between fate and choice and he was realistic enough to admit that there was no guarantee that looking at the problem by way of a larger context would necessarily make things any better (Crick 1994: 373–4). And one cannot avoid thinking, as Crick eventually did, that accepting the old mantra was both patronizing and ingenuous. It revealed a complicity between English disdain – 'What else would you expect of these people?' – and liberal guilt – 'We've got to make allowances for these people' – while it indulged the worst sort of behaviour in Northern Ireland. Like Borges's river, the Troubles were not a force of nature because people were also the Troubles. If there is no escape from ourselves there is perhaps a liberation of sorts in the idea that we are also our own fate. The political consequences of recognizing this are worth stating.

It would, to take one example, alert us to the self-serving claim that Irish republicans have been simply trapped in history. As O'Doherty has observed in his brilliant study (1998), if republicans were trapped in anything they were trapped in their own tradition. In that tradition they were active participants and not passive victims. The contrast with the view of other nationalists and former nationalists is quite instructive. Lord Fitt, for example, campaigned vigorously against the old Stormont system and was willing to engage in extra-parliamentary protest. It was completely consistent to hold the view that Catholics were disadvantaged, to consider civil disobedience an appropriate response, but to deny that a campaign of political violence was legitimate and, indeed, to sympathize subsequently with unionist victimhood. The substance of the criticism of republicanism made by the Social Democratic and Labour Party (SDLP) in an exchange of papers with Sinn Fein in 1988 stressed not only that violence was immoral but that it was also dysfunctional (see the summary in Hennessey 2000: 38–48). In O'Doherty's words, republicans 'had always made choices and they had often made bad or inappropriate choices'. Most of what the IRA did was calculated, tactically and strategically, and O'Doherty was horrified by the thought of his children being taught in school that 'the IRA campaign was a necessary phase in the readjustment of the constitutional anomaly created in 1921'. He was sufficiently realistic to allow that, for the purposes of ending republican killing, it might be wise to argue that the need for violence has passed 'rather than there was never a need for it' (O'Doherty 1998: 200–1). That, however, is a concession to pragmatism, not to fate, and no blind faith for long can hold against the reason informing that sort of pragmatism. At least it alerts us to the fallacy and helps us confront a certain (fatalistic) interpretation that has recently emerged which holds that 30 years of paramilitary violence was necessary in order to achieve peace in Northern Ireland. For example, the Labour MP John McDonnell claimed that 'without the armed struggle of the IRA over the past 30 years' the Belfast Agreement 'would not have acknowledged the legitimacy of the aspirations of many Irish people for a united Ireland. And without that acknowledgement we would have no peace process' (McDonnell 2003). A wrong-headed reading of history and strange means, one would have imagined, to achieve *that* specific end. This is 'presentism' at its worst and it also shows how resilient and adaptable are the forces to which Stewart draws our attention.

To take another example of self-justification masquerading as historical sociology, the refrain from loyalists in the 1990s, especially in the PUP, ran as follows. Northern Ireland was (and remains) a uniquely 'abnormal society'. Therefore abnormal behaviour and paramilitarism was just one inevitable product of that condition (Ervine 2003). Yet comparative politics has shown that the problems of Northern Ireland are far from unique and that a contest of allegiances is far from exceptional (McGarry 2001). For some this was clear from the beginning (see Rose 1971: 17–21). If there was (and remains) anything abnormal about Northern Ireland it was the choice and the sustained determination by paramilitary groups to address those problems with guns and explosives. It may be a politically pragmatic choice to permit paramilitaries an honourable escape from their past but only so long as violence justified by necessity becomes dishonoured as an excuse, for, in truth, the Agreement was not arrived at because of violence but in spite of it (Dickson 2003: 28). What is at stake in the engagement between fate and choice was also clear to David Trimble, particularly in the debate within unionism over the dynamic of the Agreement. His political position was based on an intellectual conviction that rejected the idea that 'things are inevitable, that things are set up, that history runs in a certain pattern' and which he owed to the philosophy of Karl Popper (O'Farrell 1998: 11–12). For Trimble, this was a calculated, if risky, challenge to the fatalistic strain in unionist politics (Aughey 2001). As he put it at a Young Unionist Conference shortly after the Agreement, the 'most difficult thing to cope with, the most difficult things to deal with are events'. Leaders may hope to shape events or to create them but no one is ever totally in control for everyone is, at the same time, at the *mercy* of events. If you want to shape events you also have to bear in mind that you are not the only actor and must cope with what happens elsewhere. For Trimble, fate is as much a consequence of passivity as it is of activity and he concluded that there 'are no historical inevitabilities' for history 'does not operate on fixed lines' (Trimble 2001: 40). Even so, there was no guarantee that things would work out smoothly. And they did not.

Iron cage and self-construction

The idea of fate has recently attracted the interest of students of politics. It has been argued that while politics cannot dissolve fate (understood as limits on activity), it 'can prevent fate turning into iron cages of constraint'. It is the very contingency of politics which allows us to see that our fate 'is in part constructed by us' (Gamble 2000: 16). Like the history debate about fate and choice, the politics debate is really about where to place the emphasis, whether on the iron cage or on self-construction. A consistent exploration of the former can be found, for example, in the work of Ruane and Todd. Dixon has categorized their account as a 'strong structuralist' one that draws the conclusion that the Northern Ireland conflict is beyond the ability of politicians and governments to control (Dixon 2001: 29). The argument of Ruane and Todd, however, is rather more complex and subtle than that.

They identified two approaches to the Northern Ireland problem which involved distinctive pre-suppositions. The first approach, which they call the 'cultural', assumes that the cause of division and conflict lies in the 'expectations, values, norms and attitudes of the two communities'. The second, the 'structural', believes that the source of the conflict lies in the 'institutional and structural context, in the way in which that context locks the two communities into conflict' (Ruane and Todd 1991: 27). It is these structural conditions, they argued, such as state power and institutionalized dominance, dependence and inequality, rather than the cultural peculiarities of Protestants and Catholics, that have driven the conflict. Like Stewart, Ruane and Todd thought that such cosy liberal values as tolerance and understanding offer no way of resolving fundamental conflicts of interest. It is structural asymmetries that make conflict so difficult to avoid (Ruane and Todd 1991: 39). There is much to this argument and it is well made. Nevertheless it has been difficult to sustain the coherence of this position simply because it is impossible to maintain an absolute distinction between 'culture' and 'structure'. To paraphrase Borges again, if the structures contain us we are also the structures. And if the transformation of the conflict required by Ruane and Todd's analysis is to be realized, not only does the structure need to be transformed but also the political culture. And here one might refer to Kant's proposition that all such good enterprises (like the Belfast Agreement) which are not grafted on to a receptive public mind 'are nothing but illusion and outwardly glittering misery' (Bubner 1997: 65). In the development of their argument, Ruane and Todd have been astute enough to acknowledge that proposition and have modified their analysis accordingly. What qualifies Dixon's interpretation of strong structuralism is their incorporation of an 'emancipatory' dimension (Todd 1995; Ruane and Todd 1996). The exposition of that emancipatory approach may be in part elusive, in part suggestive, and in part questionable. Nevertheless, it encompassed a wider range of possibilities than the iron cage of structuralist constraint may suggest. It allowed for self-construction and this made it more adequate to the complex realities of political change in Northern Ireland. Indeed, the notion of 'emancipation' helped to capture the radical interpretation some have placed on the Agreement that emerged a few years later. What such an agreement would require, they suggested, is 'a process by which the participants in a system which determines, distorts and limits their potentialities come together actively to transform it, and in the process transform themselves' (Ruane and Todd 1996: 15). Though this was perfectly logical, the thoroughness of emancipation required was a product of the depth of their structural analysis, and one interpretative absolute may be only compounded by attaching to it yet another absolute. This may expect too much of politics and exaggerate both the 'fatedness' of structures and the opportunities for choice. However, the reservation they entered that there was no guarantee of 'emancipation', that there was no security that people would transform themselves sufficiently and that the constraints of the iron cage might not be so easily diminished, was one of the virtues of their modified approach.

Of course, one difficulty with the use of the term 'structures' is the implication that the problem is to be found exclusively in the culture and operation of public institutions or what might be called, in more loaded terminology, 'the system'. Whether intentionally or not the perspective then becomes selective and this is something, Smith has argued, that limits the contribution of much of the political sociology approach to Northern Ireland. Once a theorist has become convinced that the conflict is a product of systemic conditions, then political violence is understood as merely an epiphenomenon, a reaction to the constraints of an unjust iron cage (republicanism) or the result of false consciousness (loyalism). What if the problem, though, lies not in the constraints of the system alone but in the intelligent (meaning consciously chosen) strategies of those committed to violence? This is an argument according to self-construction and this is a view of reality that comes at the problem from the opposite direction to Ruane and Todd (the value of whose assessment Smith acknowledged but of which he was critical for its ignorance of what he called the 'strategic dimension'). In this case, the attention paid to the system obscured the strategic mechanics of anti-system violence (Smith 1999: 91–2). Does the emphasis matter? Smith was convinced that it did because it had potentially severe consequences not only for how we judge the history of political violence in Northern Ireland but also for how we assess the justice of present political demands. The reason for this is that ideas do have consequences. Developing the principles of O'Doherty's re-examination of the IRA, Smith argued that 'there is nothing remotely involuntary about the violence perpetrated by the paramilitaries' and the danger to the Agreement lies in acting on the premises of an analysis which accepts that violence is a 'reflex to systemic conditions' whether against the state on the part of republicans or against the IRA on the part of loyalists. Here is another iron cage. It is not the iron cage of structures but the iron cage of limited mental flexibility (the sort of inflexibility that came to frustrate Crick). Smith's strategic approach calls attention to the deliberate intent of paramilitary campaigns when other, non-violent, options were available. It also calls attention to a possible consequence of building a peace process on the view that violence is the product of systemic forces. The danger is that it can lead not to 'a more just and equitable society, but potentially to the creation instead of a paramilitary state' (Smith 1999: 96; see also Chapter 10). This is a valuable corrective to the determinism of some commentary that is all the more insidious because it is implicit rather than explicit (Smyth 1995).

A similar encounter between determinism and freedom is also noticeable in the debate about identity. If we can accept that political activity is not inevitably trapped within the iron cage of structure we are not compelled to accept that everything can be otherwise or that we are entirely free in what we may choose. Equally, just because our identity is not a completely fixed thing, solid and eternal, does not mean that it is entirely unfixed or entirely evanescent (Barker and Galasinski 2001: 41–7). Therefore while it is important to acknowledge the decent intent of Fintan O'Toole's remark that, after the Belfast Agreement, the people of Northern Ireland were in the extraordinary position of being 'free to be anything they can agree to become', it is wise to be sceptical. That scepticism appears justified when he also suggests that unionists and nationalists 'have escaped from nations' (cited in Hazleton 2000: 35). The question of identity, in Northern Ireland as elsewhere, is a tricky one and this question can sometimes best be explored by 'outsiders'. Take, for example, Jean Amery's reflections on the meaning of 'home' in *At the Mind's Limits* (1999). Home, for the Jewish outsider and exile Amery, meant security, full command of the 'dialectics of knowledge and recognition, of trust and confidence'. At home, 'what is already known to us occurs before our eyes again and again, in slight variants'. Amery admits the possibility that at some point in the future – the point O'Toole thought Northern Ireland had already reached – one might get along without the idea of nation. However, experience of the absolute marginality of the persecuted European Jew obliged him to believe one simple fact: 'it is not good to have no home' (Amery 1999: 41–61). Take a very different example, Andre Gorz's meditations on identity in *The Traitor* (1989). For Gorz, the defect of all existing identities is their particularity, what he called that 'great flabby body' of nationality whose incarnation cannot be deduced by reason. Everything is 'permeated by the smell of wine, vodka or beer'; everything is contingent and promotes 'only particular, fragmentary truths caught in the lime of historical density'. The intellectual's critical quest is to fashion an identity 'relieved of the contingency of existing and the "metaphysical fault" of finitude' (Gorz 1989: 196–9). Both Amery and Gorz illustrate lucidly the two extremes of identity politics even though they were aware of the absurdity of both and committed to neither. The first of these illusions is the illusion of authenticity in which the local sustains its purity *against* the world. The second is the illusion of abstraction in which the local is exchanged *for* the world. The former suffers from the anxiety of alien corruption and the latter from the anxiety of local identification. The former holds that only insiders are privy to real knowledge of community, of whom we are (fated to be), the latter that such communal knowledge is not worth knowing anyway and that one is what one chooses to be. The cult of authenticity is the soul of parochialism and the cult of abstraction is the soul of cosmopolitanism. However, a moment's thought will show that there is none so parochial as the self-conscious cosmopolitan and none so cosmopolitan as the self-conscious parochial. Cosmopolitanism has the unfortunate habit of always being elsewhere and the cosmopolitan finds that elsewhere is not an escape because we have to take ourselves and all our particularisms along with us. Parochialism has the equally unfortunate habit of discovering its equivalent wherever it goes and the parochial soon discovers that everyone has the same idea of their own distinctiveness and everywhere else is special (for a literary exploration of these matters, see Longley 1999). Thus the authenticity of West Belfast communalism and the abstract Irish diaspora one finds in republican and nationalist discourse and the authentic people of the Shankill and the abstract British kith and kin one finds in loyalist and unionist discourse are intense examples of these common dispositions. They are hardly the basis for intelligent policy.

So, in some ways the identity debate has confused the real political question (see McDonald 1997). In a critical review of Seamus Deane's *Strange Country*, the literary scholar Edna Longley challenged his false conclusion that the choice today was between 'apocalypse or boredom'. In the terms used here, apocalypse and boredom are both varieties of nothingness, cosmopolitan nothingness or parochial nothingness. Longley proposed what she called the genuine choice for Northern Ireland: 'We must love one another or die' (Longley 1997: 38). A *jeu d'esprit*, perhaps, but the message is clear enough. If Northern Ireland cannot escape from nations, Irish or British (there is an iron cage), and one cannot be free to be anything (there are limits to self-construction), then it may be worth thinking through a wider sense of belonging within which most people can come to feel at home (see Elliott 2001: 482). The 'realities on the ground' may prevent that happening, the strategic choices of paramilitaries may oppose it, the structures that emerge may become insupportable. Things may actually get worse. None of these things, however, is fated to happen.

Process and action

If the focus of this chapter has been on recent history, the real concern has been about the present. It has attempted to draw attention not only to the temptation of finding justification in the tragic vision but also to the temptation of finding satisfaction in the moral vision. Both are more politically therapeutic than politically persuasive. The point would not be worth making except for the fact the temptations have been all too frequently indulged and they have encouraged a sort of anti-political politics with their own recognizable narratives. The first of these narratives claims that history and political structures so confined choice that there was no alternative to violence. It also claims that compromise is betrayal since to make one ill-judged compromise could be fatal. That position has been challenged by a second which has as its subtext the notion that if only nationalists would stop being nationalist and unionists would stop being unionist, then things would improve. In large part the instability of politics in Northern Ireland can be traced to the inherent instability of both these tragic and moral narratives. Their very one-sidedness means that they easily turn into their opposites. As a result of constant disappointment, the moral vision can transform itself into a bitter denunciation that is just as practically unconstructive (because of its lack of realism) as the style of politics it condemns. This was the substance of Trimble's criticism of those, like Porter, who dismissed the messy, tension-filled business of political compromise in favour of high-minded purity (Trimble 2003a). It can encourage apathy and disenchantment as it turns away from politics in order to preserve its righteousness. In other words, the moralistic narrative becomes yet another version of the tragic. Likewise, the tragic narrative can be transformed into a rejection of all limits, a transgressive force of ingenuity and dedication that attaches its fortunes to the judgement of history. Like Hölderlin's Society of Nemesis, those who hold this view consider their own subjective wills to be identical with the objective course of history. Abandoned to fate they seek to achieve mastery over fate in a profoundly destructive way (Michaelis 1999: 240–7). This is something that will be explored more fully in the next chapter.

Moreover, Gamble has proposed that only politics provides the realm in which 'fate is determined by chance and contingency rather than by anything that is preordained' (Gamble 2000: 16). If true, this view challenges the old certainties of Northern Ireland in both its tragic and moralistic narratives (and it has been suggested that the two have a lot in common). It also challenges new liberal and constructive certainties, even those embodied in the Belfast Agreement (Canovan 1990: 8–9). In particular, it challenges the idea that politics is a 'process' in which outcomes are determined according to some inner logic. It confronts the unionist fear that everything is indeed pre-ordained as well as the nationalist expectation that everything will unfold according to historical 'inevitability' (Dixon 2001: 47–66). Then again, there is nothing necessarily benign about the outworking of post-Agreement politics. If that leaves political life in a condition of unpredictability (though not in a condition where everything is absolutely unpredictable), then that *really* is our condition. As Hannah Arendt has described it, this condition of unpredictability arises out of the basic unreliability of our guarantees for good conduct and the impossibility of foretelling the consequences of our actions. We can only try to relieve this 'two-fold darkness of human affairs' by acting in such a way as to form 'islands of predictability' and to 'erect certain guideposts of reliability'. Nevertheless, the unpredictability of human affairs on the one hand and our own unreliability on the other remain to trouble us. Belief in 'process', she thought, was like Adam Smith's belief in an 'invisible hand'. It conveniently writes out of politics the problem of choice (Arendt 1958: 244, 185). And as Arendt's interpreter, Margaret Canovan, has reminded us, politics, unlike process, is not a matter of moulding passive material and 'no one can predict its outcome'. Therefore, initiatives like the Agreement could well encourage a more enlightened and responsible politics but 'it could just as well provide opportunities for populist mobilization that might reinforce entrenched concepts of "us" and "them"' (Canovan 2000: 430). Indeed, it could do both things at once, delivering both improvement and deterioration (see Chapter 10). That these considerations are not merely abstract may be illustrated by a rather simple example. In a public debate held in West Belfast in 1999, Sinn Fein's Vice-President Pat Doherty argued that the combination of the Belfast Agreement and natural demographic change had set in motion a process that would inevitably bring about Irish unity within a generation. In reply, the Ulster Unionist Steven King asked: 'And if that doesn't happen, can we still have peace?' To secure peace would require an active commitment by republicans, irrespective of the processes of the Agreement, and King's question neatly encapsulated the unionist difficulty with republicanism's unpredictability on the twofold darkness of human affairs.

Conclusion

There are two extravagances, wrote Pascal: to exclude reason and to admit only reason. Arguments according to fate, iron cages and process tend to exclude reason because, as Arendt has argued, they are the modern equivalent of the Gods. Arguments that admit only reason pay insufficient attention to the limits imposed not by fate but by people like us. Some might see in the combination of these two extravagances a caricature of Northern Ireland politics, politics that often swing between absolute pessimism and absolute optimism. However, that would tend also towards self-indulgence. In short, the Agreement did not provide an opportunity to relieve the 'burden of history' or the 'legacy of the past'. What it did provide was an opportunity, and no more than an opportunity, to 'squeeze out the slave drop by drop' in the sense of overcoming an addiction to disabling narratives of fatalism and moralism. It intimated a transformation of the notion of fate for people in Northern Ireland – from being fated to struggle to the death to being fated to live together as civilly as possible. The notion of a 'community of fate' is a delphic one. It suggests that even if we may not *choose* to live together we are *compelled* to live (and die) together. This is the truth we found in Stewart's understanding of Northern Ireland's history and it is the truth we also found in Longley's understanding of its choice. It might just be possible to make that fate a reasonably tranquil one rather than a confrontational one and this is the proposition we found in Walker and Nic Craith. The structures of political association make it impossible to secure sweetness and light but that does not rule out the possibility of emancipation from the excesses of sectarianism. A community of fate identifies the reality that people in Northern Ireland share many experiences and problems even if there is often a refusal to acknowledge common obligations. Yet for some theorists such common obligations are undeniable. Even if the interdependence of citizens is largely involuntary, the character of the interaction between them is not insignificant and 'for good or ill, things that appear in public acquire a significance which affects the possibilities of its members' (Honohan 2002: 155). Since we already know the quality of the 'ill', the 'good' in a community of fate implies that groups should ensure that the possibilities of conflict between them are contained. The problem may not be best understood *exclusively* in terms of inter-ethnicity or inter-cultural division. As Schopflin has argued, there needs to be some minimum acknowledgement of common security. 'Easier said than done, but nevertheless possible' (Schopflin 2000: 63). In Northern Ireland it is certainly no easy task, for there has been little political reward in trying to do so. Nevertheless, it is not impossible. One of the reasons why it has appeared so impossible is considered in the next chapter.

3 Means and ends

The previous chapter examined one of the widely held impressions that politics in Northern Ireland was somehow fixed in the past and constrained in possibilities by an iron cage of history. Even those who wished to remove that supposed 'burden of history' implicitly deferred to the practical effect of fixity and constraint. While recognizing the limits that attend all political enterprises, that chapter challenged the idea that the Troubles were fated to happen. It argued that notions like fate, process and inevitability had diminished political capacity and made it much harder to conceive of political compromise. In so far as their influence continues, they make compromise that much harder to sustain. This chapter engages with another widely held impression of Northern Ireland politics. It is often thought, especially by liberals, that violence is the direct consequence of a failure of political imagination. The integrity of the Troubles has been commonly attributed to a bad infinity of predictability, a politics in which the parties have endlessly re-stated their settled positions but have never shifted from those positions. This is the politics of refusal or veto, a politics in which the object is not to be creative or positive but only to negate the claims of your opponents. It is the sort of politics, as one journalist put it, that 'had nothing much to do with the rest of the world' (Paxman 2003: 3). There may be something in these claims, but they are often exaggerated. Northern Ireland is not out of this world and the politics of refusal applies in part to all forms of politics and not just to Northern Ireland, even though it is commonly held to have had a distinctively frustrating application there. One of the consequences of this frustrating negativity, it has been thought, was violence (Moloney 2002: xv). As we argued in Chapter 1, this too is a gross simplification. However, given the fundamental character of the division between unionism and nationalism, there is some justice to the proposition that the art of persuasion appeared to be limited. Like Lichtenberg, few believed that they could convince opponents with arguments. The point of addressing the opposition was not to persuade but 'to annoy them, and to bestow strength and courage on our own side, and to make it known to the others that they have not convinced *us*' (Lichtenberg 1990: 70; emphasis in original). Though this aphorism does convey a certain truth about political behaviour, it is only one aspect of the Northern Ireland problem and it is the argument of this chapter that it was not the most important factor in promoting and sustaining political *violence*.

This chapter proposes that, contrary to impression, politics in Northern Ireland has not suffered from a lack of imagination. Nor has it suffered from a lack of possible solutions, for these solutions have been for years the stuff of critical academic analysis (see McGarry and O'Leary 1990; Whyte 1991). On the contrary, it is argued that politics suffered from the opposite condition, from *over*-imagination of the fantastic kind. This over-imagination issued in a form of politics that may be called 'endism', a politics in which ends became all too easily disconnected from means. There was nothing new in this. Writing of the rebellion of the United Irishmen in 1798, Stewart had concluded that, like contemporary Northern Ireland, 'there was much confusion between ends and means'. Moreover, there was a consistent habit 'to take what was said for what was actually achieved' (Stewart 2001: 105, 153). Here is a mythological imagination which tends either to *over*estimate the potential of one's own side – an exercise in hubris – or to *over*emphasize the demonic potency of the other side – an exercise in paranoia. Initially, how might such a style of politics be conceived? This can be called the *Miss Congeniality* syndrome. In that film comedy, Sandra Bullock stars as an undercover FBI agent at a Miss America beauty pageant. At the familiar point in the proceedings when the contestants are asked: 'What is the one most important thing our society needs?' each one in turn looks dreamily at the jury and replies: 'World Peace'. When it is Sandra Bullock's turn (in the guise of Miss New Jersey) she looks seriously at the jury and answers: 'Harsher punishment for parole violators'. There is a sharp intake of breath amongst the audience. She pauses, smiles sweetly and, to great cheers, continues: '... and World Peace'. A clichéd scenario and a cheap Hollywood joke, of course, but the message of *Miss Congeniality* is not without its significance for understanding Northern Ireland politics. For there is more to this scenario than just a quick laugh.

There is a philosophical insight in *Miss Congeniality* and it may be expressed in the following formulation. The grander the objective one seeks, the more fantastic it becomes. The more expansive the aim, the more likely it is to be a cliché, like 'World Peace'. On the other hand, being really imaginative is often a question of being practical, and only the simple-minded romantic would think otherwise. And being creative does not mean losing touch with experience, for the imagination springs from practical experience and must have knowledge of appropriate *means*. The joke in *Miss Congeniality* is this. The disconnection between the piety of 'World Peace' and the policy of harsher penalties for parole violators is the condition of absurdity. We laugh because we recognize the absurdity of what might be called the 'aspirational gap'. We also laugh at the sudden recognition that the sublime and the ridiculous can actually be one and the same. This is what often happens when one has only a vision of *ends* or can only envisage achieving those ends by incommensurate means and the joke alerts us to the absurdity of the positions that some people can hold with evident sincerity. The significance of the Belfast Agreement, then, may be considered in the following way. Acknowledging the aspirational gap in Northern Ireland politics, it represented an attempt to shift the focus of politics away from ends like a united Ireland – upon which there is no agreement between the parties – to means – that, whatever end one seeks it should be pursued by peaceful, democratic, inclusive and constitutional methods. The hope has been that such means of democratic procedure will then become ends in themselves and thus secure the local variety of World Peace. This would be one local equivalent of Wolf's objective to squeeze out the slave of irresponsibility drop by drop. It is an imaginative formula because it is at source a reasonably modest formula, even if the Agreement encouraged amongst some expectations of a fantastic kind that it could never deliver (see Chapter 8). This requires some consideration of how we can conceive the role of imagination in politics. It also requires some assessment of the relationship between means and ends, the disconnection between which the Agreement is designed to remedy.

Nostalgia and imagination

In Chapter 2 we discussed how the absolute dichotomy between fate and choice or between iron cages and self-construction is a misleading political assumption. It is equally important, when exploring the character of political imagination, again to avoid a simple dichotomous understanding. In other words, the commonsense view of political 'realism' ('how things are on the ground') would oppose it to political 'idealism' ('head in the clouds stuff'). As we noted, Crick's latterday reflections on 'how things are on the ground' realism in Northern Ireland revealed its one-sidedness and indicated just how counter-productive it could be. Moreover, he showed that the supposedly 'head in the clouds stuff' could sometimes suggest positive, practical opportunities. It is important to keep your feet on the ground but it is also important to look beyond the end of your nose. Getting around intelligently in the political world – the condition of being *realistic* – involves coordinating vision and direction. In the most systematic theoretical exploration of these matters, Robert Berki proposed that political realism is 'not anybody's subjective fancies or dreams, it is not a realm of infinite experimentation, and yet its overall opacity is ever broken up by the light of limited possibilities' (Berki 1981: 29). Political realism, in other words, should take people as they are but should not lose sight of things as they might be. To be realistic, he thought, you must avoid interpreting the world as a dichotomy of one-sided abstractions. One of these abstractions is an idealization of the past that asserts the supreme value of a fixed tradition. The other is an idealization of the future that asserts the supreme value of eliminating the present condition of things. Berki called the first the idealism of nostalgia and the second the idealism of imagination (Berki 1981: 30–1). A sense of tradition, of course, is not in itself pernicious. What is pernicious is the refusal to accept that if you want the important things to stay the same, other things will have to change (see Aughey 2001). Nor is imagination in politics pernicious. What is pernicious is the failure to recognize that change also requires that some things should stay the same. In the Northern Ireland case, it is tempting to identify unionism and loyalism with the idealism of nostalgia, and nationalism and republicanism with the idealism of imagination, the one wanting to maintain absolutely the status quo and the other wanting to transform it absolutely (Aughey 1993). In one sense that is a self-evident truth but in another sense it is only a misleading half-truth. It would be more accurate to say that nostalgia and imagination find active embodiment on both sides of the political divide. The critic might add that as a result neither has been particularly realistic.

For Berki, the idealism of nostalgia always fails to supply 'timely and relevant' explanations because, in its concern to maintain what is and in its habitual assessment of the future by the criteria of the past, it misjudges opportunity and potential in the present. It is good at detecting the imperfection in all proposals but nearly always confuses imperfection with the corruption of an ideal past. Sceptical of change, it can allow scepticism to become a denial of the requirement for change. The line of reasoning found in the idealism of nostalgia is usually correct in so far as 'no political change ever produces the big transformation' (and the Agreement would be another example). Nevertheless, it is almost always wrong 'regarding the actual necessity of particular change' (Berki 1981: 202). Scepticism is a valuable political commodity but scepticism as a mode of absolute resistance is nothing other than a dogma and it is a dogma that is likely to be inimical even to one's own best interests. Imagination in politics is also a valuable commodity. It can invent better ways of doing things, it can emancipate people from restrictive modes of thought. However, imagination completely detached from possibility is yet another dogma and one that can also be dogmatically inimical to the cause of improvement. The idealism of imagination, because of its fixation on the future, equally fails to assess possibilities and potential in the present. It too is good at detecting the imperfection in all proposals but for the opposite reason. It too confuses imperfection with corruption, only this time corruption of the ideal future. This ideal future must be different, genuinely new, for all that now exists has been a betrayal of destiny (Berki 1981: 233). In other words, what is at the heart of both forms of thought is alienation. The objective of politics in both cases is to remove alienation and to achieve either a future harmony (the imaginative goal) or a lost harmony (the nostalgic goal).

Here we can detect initially the dynamic within both idealizations, a dynamic that tends towards fantasy. It is a dynamic that is detectable in the politics of both unionism and nationalism. This observation does not condemn these responses to events as unintelligent. On the contrary, they have often exhibited high intelligence, subtle analysis and logical rigour (see, for example, McCartney 2001). It is not intelligence that is the issue here but the adequacy of such responses to the complexity of politics in Northern Ireland. For, when confronted by this complexity, there has been a temptation to resort to the dogmas of nostalgia and imagination. And it is precisely when nostalgia and imagination feed off one another that the result is the politics of fantasy. Used in this sense, fantasy does not mean an illusion that masks reality. Rather, it is fantasy which structures reality itself (Zizek 1996: 79). The 'moment' of fantasy is that interpretative leap in which fragments of disparate experience are made to conform to an ideological preconception. The moment of fantasy is also that transformative act in which the actual divisions encountered in politics dissolve into harmony, be it unionists in a united Ireland or nationalists in settled British Northern Ireland. In short, these solutions have frequently been escapist ones and their broad outlines can be discussed briefly.

For the last 30 years unionist politics has not been very good at delivering 'timely and relevant' explanations of events. Unionism has been consistently convicted by its critics of a nostalgic arrest, of being behind the game, of being unable to adapt to new conditions. Indeed, some have gone so far as to argue that 'pro-active unionism' had to await the arrival of David Trimble's leadership of the Ulster Unionist Party (UUP) in 1995 (Bew, Gibbon and Patterson 2002: 224). This particular reading, of course, is rather 'Whiggish' and implies a virtuous interpretation of the sort of 'timely and relevant' adjustments Trimble acknowledged in his negotiation of the Belfast Agreement three years later. This would not be a reading of events universally shared by unionists. There is no doubt, however, that unionism's detection of imperfection in British Government policy disposed it to a consistent policy of rejection. As a result, unionism has been generally perceived as entirely negative, its political vision captured by the slogan of the campaign against the Anglo-Irish Agreement of 1985: 'Ulster says no'. This is an unfair and one-sided impression and abridges a complex history and if we take the *end* of politics as our measure, unionist attitudes have been no more rigid or predictable than those of nationalists. There has been a degree of flexibility in the means to secure that end. Certainly there existed nostalgia for unionist majority rule and for the nostalgic certainties of the Stormont system before 1972, but there also existed, for example, an imaginative exploration of ideas of equal citizenship within a Northern Ireland fully integrated within the United Kingdom. Moreover, both the Democratic Unionist Party (DUP) and the UUP have been quite inventive in their elaboration of models for responsibility-sharing within a devolved assembly, an inventiveness designed to circumvent the taboo term of 'power-sharing' with nationalists. In 1979, loyalist paramilitaries associated with the Ulster Defence Association (UDA) came up with a perfectly rational proposal for an independent Northern Ireland. Independence was the only viable option, they argued, because it would express the 'rational character of the Common Good' (on these initiatives, see Aughey 1989). The difficulty with all such proposals was neither the intellectual effort expended on their explanation nor was it the sincerity with which they were canvassed. The real difficulty was that the assumptions built into them about what, *in the circumstances*, either nationalists would accept or what the British Government would do made them into fantasies. To the critical eye, these proposals revealed unacceptably one-sided interpretative leaps and incredibly naive transformative acts. A typical response, revealing the truth of Lichtenberg's aphorism, has argued that unionists, whatever the nature of their proposals, 'failed to provide Nationalists with a moral justification for the border' and that the 'Union with Britain has been defended not with reasons but with power' (O'Neill 1994: 375). It is untrue to argue that the Union has never been defended with reasons. Rather, reasons proposed by unionists either have been dismissed by nationalists or they have gone unnoticed because it is assumed that unionists, by definition, have no rational arguments to make.

On the other hand, commentators have been much kinder to nationalist politics in general and the SDLP in particular has been associated with a consistently imaginative approach to the Northern Ireland question. SDLP supporters can legitimately argue that the Belfast Agreement embodied many of the principles the party had for years been advocating and there was an understandable temptation to claim that the SDLP had to wait 30 years for everyone else to come to their senses (Farren 2000: 49–61). That, however, would also be an inaccurate abridgement of recent history. One could argue, for example, that the failure of the power-sharing Executive and the Council of Ireland agreed at Sunningdale in 1974 was as much a consequence of the SDLP expecting too much of the Irish dimension as it was of unionists refusing to accept change. In the opinion of Conor Cruise O'Brien, this nationalist failure cannot be attributed to a political miscalculation alone. It must be attributed to the fantastic suggestiveness of 'ancestral voices' whispering in the ears of Irish politicians and reminding them of their duty and their destiny (O'Brien 1994: 166–7). The lure of the end (Irish unity) served to compromise the means to stability (power-sharing). Furthermore, it has been suggested that the major failing of John Hume's strategic thinking was his inability to comprehend the nature of unionist objections (or if he did, his unimaginative discounting of them). As Hennessey has claimed, Hume failed to see that unionist negativity was not necessarily the result of an inherent unwillingness to compromise but a judgement that SDLP solutions involved fantastic assumptions about what was acceptable to the unionist electorate. 'This meant either rapid movement towards a united Ireland – by the Council of Ireland or Joint British/Irish sovereignty – or a united Ireland full stop, as with their proposal for a federal Ireland' (Hennessey 2000: 19). Moreover, as Cunningham has shown, Hume's apparently imaginative language on, for example, post-nationalism or European regionalism involved moments of fantasy which concealed a very traditional nationalist understanding, something which did not go unnoticed by unionists (1997; see also Kennedy 1994). An even more critical reading of the nationalist project is provided by Bew, who neatly reverses O'Neill's argument according to moral justification. He has argued that it contains 'remarkably little in the way of a positive vision'. You will not find in the bookshop 'even a slim volume telling you "this is why a united Ireland will be a better place"'. On the contrary, a lot of intellectual effort has gone into outmanoeuvring the unionists mainly as a way of 'expiating some kind of original historical sin' (cited in Lynch 1994: 12). Of course, allowance should be made for the ambivalence of all political communication. A more benign reading of these unionist and nationalist proposals would interpret the language of unionist equal citizenship, for example, as a preparatory education in the politics of acknowledging difference and ultimately parity of esteem, and the nationalist language of joint sovereignty as a polite way of accepting the impossibility of Irish unity. A retrospectively benign reading of these proposals would understand them to be partial staging posts on the way to the common ground of the Agreement, temporary positions on the path to political accommodation. Even with that allowance, however, the integrity of these arguments undoubtedly tended towards escapism and fantasy. To adopt a Rilkean metaphor, they produced two fruits: a child and death – a child of the imagination that would die in the rough and tumble of political reality.

Fantasy, in the technical sense employed here and also in the colloquial sense, was a defining characteristic of republican strategy and it drove the IRA's campaign of violence. If the unionist imagination was tortured by fantasies of a British Government 'sell out' (fantasies encouraged by the stupidity of British Government manoeuvring, especially in the early years of the Troubles), then the republican movement lived by such fantasies (also encouraged by the stupidity of British policy). This is where nostalgia and imagination rhymed in a culture of militant purity, a condition not unexceptional in secret organizations that interpret reality by contemplating their own hearts. Willie Whitelaw, Northern Ireland's first Secretary of State, discovered this in July 1972 at a secret meeting he held in London with republican leaders. Whitelaw dismissed the demands for immediate British withdrawal as absurd without realizing that the meeting itself might have inadvertently encouraged such absurdity (Arthur 1996a: 249). Indeed, in these early years of the Troubles some Provisional IRA members had incredible expectations of imminent victory (Kent 1998: 13). And it is no coincidence, perhaps, that the best academic book on the history of the IRA is *The Politics of Illusion*, a book critical of the 'fatalism' of traditional interpretations of political violence that 'unconsciously mimic the self-serving certainties of the republican world view' (Patterson 1989: 6). In this world view, not only were republicans nostalgic bearers of the real spirit of Irish resistance untainted by the compromises and the corruptions of constitutional nationalism, they were also (to use Declan Kiberd's term) 'futurologists of necessity' (cited in Connolly 2001: 302).

In Eire Nua, for example, the Southern republican leadership of Ruari O'Bradaigh and Daithi O'Connaill had originally committed the movement to a policy of federalism in the expectation that this would attract Northern Protestants to the cause of Irish separatism. In this futurology, Protestants would retain a degree of self-government in the north but within an independent Irish state dedicated to fulfilling the radical social objectives of the 1916 rebellion. This was a fantastic expectation, though one that was actually encouraged by the loyalist Ulster Workers' Council strike of 1974 against the power-sharing settlement sponsored by the British and Irish Governments. Protestants, it was imagined, were throwing off at last the shackles of unionist false consciousness. In the 1980s, the Northern leadership under Gerry Adams was realistic enough in its assessment that such ideological concessions could never win Protestant allegiance and that the policy was naively idealistic (Patterson 1989: 198–9). That only left republicans to indulge certain other fantasies. One of these was that violence could coerce the British Government into declaring an intent to withdraw and thus coercing unionists into accepting the moral justification for removing the border. As one critic has pointed out, the ideological fantasy which structured that particular reality for the IRA was at odds with a strategic analysis of its military capacities to inflict significant damage on British interests (Smith 1997). Indeed, as Moloney's study of the IRA catalogues, it was the over-imagination of the militant mind which prolonged a pointlessly murderous campaign, pointless in so far as the desired end bore little relation to the means to achieve it.

A few of Moloney's examples will suffice to make the general point. IRA leaders confidently expected that the ceasefire of 1974/75 would lead to a British announcement of withdrawal. When this did not happen, a spokesman responded by stating that the only time the IRA would talk to the British again was when the British Government came to 'ask our help to secure their immediate departure from Ireland'. Activists would seriously compare their struggle to that of Castro's insurgent campaign in Cuba. There was also a widespread belief that, with additional weaponry from Libya, the IRA would be able to conduct a 'Tet offensive' against the British army. There was also discussion about carrying out a 'night of the long knives' against loyalist paramilitaries (Moloney 2002: 141, 170, 327, 323). These were interpretative leaps and transformative acts of a quite different order from the political manoeuvres of unionist or nationalist politicians. As Moloney consistently shows, the sort of military action which inspired these fantasies was precisely the sort of military action the IRA was not only incapable of conducting but was actually unwilling to conduct. It would have meant taking serious casualties and there is no evidence – apart from bravado – that this was ever seriously contemplated. For instance, the Tet offensive fantasy of the mid-1980s would have entailed the IRA, like the

Viet Cong original, being given a 'bloody nose'. But when the IRA lost eight men at Loughgall on 8 May 1987 the organization went into deep shock. As one middle-ranking commander told Moloney, the IRA was simply not capable of conducting such a campaign and it would have been a disaster if it had tried (Moloney 2002: 327). More to the point, as O'Doherty has observed, the IRA campaign never escalated and 'merely sustained a consistent output of death and destruction, without increasing the threat against the British', although for years activists were fed on a mythological diet of victory just around the corner (O'Doherty 1998: 100). The final myth was the 'bombs in London' myth, the myth (accepted by some unionists) that bombs like that exploded at Canary Wharf on 4 February 1996, and causing damage estimated at £85 million, meant that the IRA had forced the British Government to the negotiating table. The truth was actually quite the reverse. Republicans had forced *their* way to a negotiating table and by the time they did so the central question was no longer one of British withdrawal but of IRA decommissioning. The irony is that contrary to the expectations of 1975, it was republicans who now needed to seek the assistance of the British Government to bring their own campaign to an end (for which, of course, they accepted no responsibility).

Conservatism and radicalism

In Chapter 1 it was further suggested that instability in Northern Ireland was due in part to the unstable distinction between the tragic and moral visions of politics. A similar claim is made here about the instability of the distinction between the idealism of imagination and the idealism of nostalgia. This is something that Berki also noted. At a fundamental level, he argued, 'the radical is conservative, without realizing it'. The reason for this is that radicalism is insufficiently critical of its own objectives and exempts its own ideals from the imaginative onslaught on the alienation of the present. In short, the radical may often be 'a realist regarding the present, but is a dogmatic idealist regarding the alternative' (Berki 1981: 238). To put that another way, there may ultimately be little difference between the imaginative and the unimaginative in politics. An absolutely radical position on the future may mean, ironically, an absolutely conservative position on the existing; and an absolutely conservative position on the future may mean an absolutely radical position on the existing. In local terms, for a nationalist to be fixed on the end of a united Ireland could mean lack of interest in any reformist means short of that end. Better that things should stay in an alienated condition if the alternative meant settling for less than the final goal. For a unionist to be fixed on 'Ulster says no' could mean actively destabilizing the political order in Northern Ireland. Better that things should fall apart if the alternative was compromise with tainted and corrupted means. From this acute angle, nationalists and republicans can appear rather 'unionist', and unionists and loyalists can appear rather 'nationalist'. To the eye of a harassed Westminster Secretary of State the distinction is probably minimal and they can both appear to be very 'Irish'.

Thus, unionists have sought an indestructible and permanent guarantee that Irish unity will never be achieved against their will. They are always looking for a 'final settlement' as Sir James Craig, the first Prime Minister of Northern Ireland, so felicitously put it. It was also argued in Chapter 1 that there can be no final settlements in politics and that everything is open to revision and change. Hence the instability in unionism so frequently noted by English critics. It appears at one and the same time to be completely loyal and completely rebellious, prostrating itself before the Union Jack and the royal family and yet willing to take to the streets with an almost anarchical fervour at the slightest hint of its loyalty being compromised by British politicians (Aughey 1989: 1–29). Loyalist paramilitaries, for example, used to understand one of their key functions to be that of keeping Britain up to the mark in its obligations to the 'people of Ulster'. To claim, in pursuit of that end by means of murder and mayhem, that 'their only crime is loyalty' is a notion not without its irony (see Bruce 1992: 268–90). Indeed, from the point of view of stable governance it is no wonder that British ministers may not see much to choose between unionist 'loyalty' and nationalist 'disloyalty'. Republicans, on the other hand, used to argue that Northern Ireland could never be reformed. Indeed, as English has shown in his analysis of Richard McAuley's prison writings, this view of the futility of reform went wider than an application to contemporary Northern Ireland. It was historically absolute. Writing in 1977, McAuley proposed that even Daniel O'Connell and Charles Stewart Parnell had not really succeeded in changing things substantially. The Southern state had done little with its freedom from British rule to improve the lot of the Irish people. In Northern Ireland, no reform 'in essence' was even worth the paper it was written on. It was an artificial state with no legitimate reason to exist. The conclusion was straightforward. The 'republican movement will not settle for anything less than British withdrawal' (cited in English 2003: 216–17). This essentialism was politically debilitating and was slow to change. To paraphrase Rilke again, it was a world view that produced only two fruits: the child of single-minded militarism and (literal) death.

If political stalemate in Northern Ireland can be attributed to the aspirational gap between ends and means, then *sustained* political violence in Northern Ireland can be attributed to the belief that force was the only and historically legitimate means to bridge that gap to a better future. It is important to grasp that political stalemate and political violence are only contingently connected. There is nothing inevitable about the first issuing in the second. The fantasies of loyalist and republican violence derived from military will disconnected from political circumstance, from the conviction that it was possible to force people to be free (or to see reason). From a wider philosophical perspective, Novak believes that these are the very convictions at the root of political nihilism. Nihilism holds that there are no moral constraints that the will should heed in pursuing its objectives. To be free in the cause of freeing others is to exercise pure will. 'Nihilism means never having to be judged, and in this it gives the illusion of total freedom and unfettered autonomy.' Since this total freedom is an illusion, the dissatisfaction it brings only encourages activists to indulge their fantasy further. For Novak, the consequence is that nihilists become slaves to their fantasy and 'lose touch with reality' (Novak 1997: 5–6, 22). For those republicans who wanted to 'wreck the place' and for those loyalists who wanted to 'terrorize the terrorists' the influence of nihilism is manifest, all the more so in the manner of their justifications and in their resentment at being judged (Stevenson 1996). To adapt Novak's interpretation of nihilism neither implies that republicans and loyalists were able to do exactly what they wanted (the security forces saw to that) nor that they were capable of carrying through everything that their nihilism permitted (public opinion and political calculation saw to that). It does, however, provide us with an interesting insight into the romantic character of political violence and its powerful attraction. This terroristic nihilism is not new and its attributes were identified by Hegel at the beginning of the nineteenth century.

In the introduction to the *Philosophy of Right*, Hegel had attacked Jacob Fries for promoting a world view that could justify violence and terror. His point was that Fries's simple motto – 'Give allegiance to your conviction of duty!' – which appeared at first sight to be the quintessence of virtue could very easily become the quintessence of evil. According to Fries, for the person who 'has attained to purity, conscience is *infallible*'. No more can be demanded of anyone than that they follow 'pure conviction' (cited in Wood 1990: 178–9). For Hegel, however, this was an incentive to the sort of nihilism described by Novak which, 'when it gives evidence of the pure selfishness of baseless pride, the word most on its lips is "people". But the special mark which it carries on its brow is hatred of the law.' Because it was intrinsically inimical to law, this attitude was really the justification of 'false friends and comrades of what they call the "people"' (Hegel 1966: 7). In practice, loyalist and republican paramilitaries have shared this contempt for the law as well as the pride that they alone can interpret the true wishes of their respective peoples. Purity and conviction of duty promoted a romantic identity that warranted its own morality. It was the morality of destructive fervour, dispensing death 'with no more significance than cleaving a head of cabbage or swallowing a draught of water' (Hegel 1966: 605). Moreover, Hegel did not share Edmund Burke's assumption that only evil men can engage in evil deeds, albeit evil deeds cloaked in the garb of noble ideals. For Burke, you could never separate the merits of any political question from the character of those who were involved in it. The good cause was only pretence soon to be thrown aside or perverted. Burke warned that 'The power of bad Men is no indifferent thing' (cited in O'Brien 1993: 391). For Hegel, though, the danger was not to be found in bad men (alone). Quite the contrary. The real danger is the deep conviction and sincere beliefs of men and women who are convinced that what they are doing is correct, who believe that they have a sacred duty or inviolable right that can set aside the law. The cause of Irish freedom or the cause of God and Ulster, these ideals that can dispense cruelty with profound self-righteousness, attract both the good and the bad (Aughey 1997a: 1–12; English 2003: 367). This was, perhaps, shown most dramatically at the time of the Hunger Strikes in 1981.

The Hunger Strike was an example of propaganda of the deed, an ideologically erotic mix of self-sacrifice and self-righteousness that, in the death of Bobby Sands, permitted the cult of victimhood to achieve its highest expression. It played on the profound ambiguity of popular attitudes towards violence. Respect amongst Catholics for the endurance of the hunger strikers and their fortitude in self-denial could easily confuse sympathy for the prisoners' demands with sympathy for the cause of armed struggle. The objective of the prisoners was a classic revolutionary move. It was to show that the morality of the established order was nothing other than vengeance. Once that truth was unmasked, 'their' justice would reveal its corruption and 'our' justice would reveal its purity and strength. The objective was also to challenge the narrative of constitutional nationalism and the Catholic Church that it was possible, indeed necessary, to make a choice between violence and non-violence. Here was the performance of the republican version of the national story, honourable men, of deep conviction and true belief, convinced of the justice of their struggle, demonstrating the virtue of personal sincerity in the pursuit of a legitimate cause. It was a sorrowful romanticism yet all the more powerful in its tragedy. There was no choice, only fate. And it had its effect, for, as Zamoyski has reminded us, that sort of romantic nationalism has inherited from religion 'not only crude fanaticism, but also a spark of divinity, for it is, ultimately, a kind of mission' (Zamoyski 1999: 450). As Father Des Wilson noted, it became possible to speak respectfully of the IRA. It also became respectable to vote for Sinn Fein, and the history of the next 20 years has been a rather ironic outworking of that respectability since the peace process of the 1990s represented a failure of the traditional militaristic republican narrative. Sinn Fein's contemporary respectability is now at odds with the brutal reality of its former 'armed struggle', if not with the romantic rationalization of it. This is not how it appeared in the aftermath of the Hunger Strike.

For example, commemorating the 1916 Rebellion at Easter 1984, *An Phoblacht/Republican News* proclaimed that the IRA's use of 'revolutionary force', the tradition of 'bloody and deadly violence', was necessary 'to achieve the national rights of our people' because the enemy was not susceptible to 'reasoned persuasion' (cited in Hennessey 2000: 35). The proclamation was nostalgic in its deference to republican 'martyrs', proud in its invocation of the 'people', virtuous in its commitment to struggle for 'the unborn generations' and imaginative in its invocation of an alternative reality. Not only was there a faint and eerie echo of Fries. There was an even stronger echo of Robespierre, who famously believed that the revolutionary requires both virtue and terror: 'virtue, without which terror is evil; terror, without which virtue is helpless' (cited in O'Sullivan 1983: 57). Republican paramilitaries may have shown greater skill in romanticizing their virtue and justifying their terror than loyalists. Nevertheless, loyalists were not entirely without their own justifications for virtuous terror (see Taylor 1999). To the critical eye there was little distinction between the self-conscious radicalism of the one and the self-conscious defensiveness of the other. And as Hegel cuttingly observed, the logic of the politics of conviction is also the logic of the politics of equivalence in that the maxims of the worst of criminals are put on the same level as those of the law. Whatever demands may arise these maxims claim 'the same level of value as what constitutes the interest of all thinking men and the bonds of the ethical world' (cited in Avineri 1972: 121). Or, in Novak's terms, if such thinking is actually encouraged it becomes a temptation to 'indulge whatever desires pull one's heart', another species of fantasy which dogged the implementation of the Belfast Agreement. The question of equivalence was indeed to become a major destabilizing issue for unionists, who felt that the criminality of terrorism, loyalist as well as republican, was being put on a par with the forces of law and order.

The Troubles, then, produced a certain 'character' common to both republicanism and loyalism and that 'character' was able to emerge from, and to sustain in turn, the political fantasies of a generation in which the end justified the means. On the republican side, there was the possibility of drawing upon a long tradition of the *spiritually* self-sacrificing revolutionary (most IRA activists were reluctant *physically* to sacrifice themselves), though as English remarked this character imputed to 'the wider Irish population views which were in fact characteristic of a small clique of radical republican zealots' (English 1996: 568–9). Loyalist paramilitaries were not connected to a similar ideological tradition but they were also in the habit of identifying their own interests with those of the people they claimed to defend. In both cases, those interests were not only politically motivated but also criminally motivated, and after 1998 it became increasingly difficult for people to tell the difference between criminality and politics. In varying degrees, militant republicanism and militant loyalism shared two myths. These two myths are the myth of military valour and the myth of rebirth and renewal. The first of these myths allocates special regard to those who have performed 'deeds of military value'. In Schopflin's interpretation, this myth diminishes the role of the individual and enhances the group 'because of the very particular demands and qualities of group violence' (Schopflin 2000: 94–5; see also Tudor 1972: 137–40). As a myth legitimizing the intrinsic virtue of violence, it defines reform as 'cowardly' and compromise as 'dishonourable'. In the words of the original leader of the Provisional IRA, Sean MacStiofain, even if the end of Irish independence could be won by constitutional means it would be 'in a thousand ways demoralising'. Freedom worth the name could only be achieved 'with difficulty and heroic sacrifice, in the face of perils and death' (cited in Clohesy 2000: 76). The character of the romantic in politics is always problematic and the militant romantic in politics is usually disastrous. This myth distorted Northern Ireland politics for three decades.

Schopflin's second myth is the myth of rebirth and renewal, a myth which can involve both the Christian theme of death and resurrection and the pagan theme of the phoenix rising from the ashes. With its Dublin Easter commemoration and its Belfast phoenix symbolism, the IRA self-consciously identified with that myth and with the idea of revolutionary 're-creation' (see English 2003: 346). In the prison Hunger Strike of 1981, both Christian and pagan themes were intimately bound together. This myth is less characteristic of loyalism but is not entirely absent and it has manifested itself in less iconographic manner in the recent politics of the PUP. If it is claimed that 'a renewal or rebirth has taken place' then it can also be claimed that the sins of the past have been shed. In this new start 'the awfulness of the past can be forgotten' (Schopflin 2000: 95–6). Loyalist leaders like David Ervine or Gary McMichael would refer to the ceasefire announcement on 13 October 1994 by the Combined Loyalist Military Command as the moment of their 'new start'. Republican leaders like Gerry Adams or Martin McGuinness would refer to the second IRA ceasefire of 20 July 1997. And what is characteristic of loyalists and republicans is the common dismissal of those who would question their good intentions even though, as Schopflin argues, for the myth of the new start to be fully effective the victims of the conflict must also accept its symbolism. This is not to question the sincerity of those who have acknowledged either the futility of their violence or, less categorically, the ineffectiveness of it. It is to indicate the continuation of a characteristic, vainglorious, privileged and mythological self-esteem. It was that destructive form of arrogance which exaggerated all the worst tendencies in Northern Ireland politics and allowed them to flourish, and it was such arrogance that the Agreement hoped to tame.

Conclusion

In his uniquely delphic manner, Baudrillard captured this destructive form of arrogance in both its pagan and its Christian genealogy when he wrote that to anticipate the end was 'to turn God from history and make him face up to his responsibilities'. What is terrorism, he asked, 'if not this effort to conjure up, in its own way, the end of history'? It hopes to bring nothing less than the 'conditions for the Last Judgement' and is impatient of time and constraint (Baudrillard 1994: 8). The nostalgia and imagination of the republican movement put it at odds with genuine Catholicism. The IRA's Easter message posed an eternal identity both in history and above history.

That eternal identity was the cause of national freedom. It was in history in the sense that IRA violence was necessary to bring to a conclusion the struggle for Irish liberation. It was also above history in that national freedom was its own end and its own morality. This, as O'Brien once described it, is 'God Land' and the Catholic Church was right to think it blasphemous (O'Brien 1988. See also Zamoyski 1999). Indeed, that is what the then Archbishop Cahal Daly told the Sinn Fein leadership in 1983. The requirement of republicans to give unambiguous support for an armed struggle defined as 'morally correct' was, in the eyes of the Church, 'morally evil'. The end did not justify the means (see Hennessey 2000: 34–5). This has also been the substance of Protestant criticism of loyalist paramilitaries (Eames 1992: 158–9).

Both sets of paramilitaries have found this sort of argument more irritating than discomforting and have usually dismissed it for its ignorance of what it is like 'on the ground'. Furthermore, loyalists and republicans have been contemptuous of unionist and nationalist politicians who have been either one-sided in their condemnations of violence or have been hypocritical about their own past. This contempt consolidated the righteousness of their world view. Not only does the (future) end justify the (present) means but the end, when achieved, would retrospectively justify those means. Who would then say that violence had not been effective? So, the IRA could point to 1916 and the later War of Independence and ask why their violence should be condemned by the Irish state which was itself a product of violence. Or, as Danny Morrison of Sinn Fein once put it, 'the people who will tell you that the most that force can achieve is nothing are the very people who have a monopoly of its use' (cited in Aughey 1988: 83–4). Loyalist paramilitaries could point to the establishment of Northern Ireland and claim that without the use or threat of force Protestants would have been forced out of the United Kingdom. They could also point to the willingness of unionist politicians to engage in extra-parliamentary activity when it suited them or to claim that paramilitaries had been encouraged by the rhetoric of certain unionist leaders. There is something in these responses and the horrors of violence are not, of course, absolutely divorced from political fantasies and sectarian animosities more widely shared. However, to acknowledge this fact can only give limited comfort to paramilitary legitimation and cannot justify the paramilitary world view.

As Arendt observed, there is a certain brutally realistic logic in the response that you can't make an omelette without breaking eggs. But she went on to argue that you should be fully aware of the inherently murderous consequences of a view that 'forces one to admit that all means, provided they are efficient, are permissible and justified to pursue something defined as an end'. In this sort of means–end morality the definition of an end is precisely the justification of the means. And she concluded that so long as we believe in means and ends in politics 'we shall not be able to prevent anybody's using all means to pursue recognized ends' (Arendt 1958: 229).

If Arendt may demand too much of our political vocabulary, and if we cannot help thinking in terms of means and ends, how could, to use Berki's term, the 'idealistic immorality of extremism' in Northern Ireland be addressed? Berki provided at least an intimation of what might be done when he argued that a realistic morality of moderation must begin by acknowledging 'the limits of political ends in the shape of their own opposites, in what the various political ends leave out of their visionary formulations' (Berki 1972: 79). What could that subtle dialectical under-standing possibly imply in the ideologically contested terrain of Northern Ireland? The following brief exercise is an attempt to specify what it might mean.

At the heart of nationalist politics, constitutional and republican, has been the imaginative *aspiration* to Irish unity. The nostalgic assumption of nationalist politics is that there exists a single Irish nation that has been denied its natural completion since its right to self-determination has been frustrated. The problem with this 'imagined community' of the Irish people, the shape of its own opposite and exclusion, is the fact that the unionist majority in Northern Ireland does not understand itself to be part of that nation. No imaginative rhetoric of goodwill or promises of future generosity have been sufficient to dispel the unionist suspicion that the political project of Irish nationalism – as formulated and reformulated by its ideologues – is ultimately designed to defeat, marginalize and to destroy them. In short, unionists simply refuse to be defined in nationalist terms. At the heart of unionist politics is the nostalgic *fact* of the United Kingdom. The imaginative *assumption* of unionism is that continued membership of the Union is necessary for the prosperity and good governance of everyone who lives in Northern Ireland and only within the Union can there be proper accommodation of cultural and religious diversity. In short, the stability of British statehood is the only guarantee of rights, liberties and public welfare. The problem for this unionist ideal, the shape of its own opposite and exclusion, is that the minority in Northern Ireland has never fully acknowledged the legitimacy of the state because the character of that state is held to be incompatible with its own sense of nationhood. On the contrary, Northern Ireland has been understood as a political form designed to sustain inequality of rights. It may never be possible to accommodate these divergent views. No agreement may be able to contain satisfactorily such expectations and fears and the Belfast Agreement may have been only a hesitation before some future disaster. However, a formula that could acknowledge 'the limits of political ends in the shape of their own opposites' might begin with the following propositions.

First, if nationalists are sincere about persuading unionists of the value of being fully part of an Irish nation (rather than forcing or manoeuvring them), and if they are sincere about an inclusive definition of Irishness, then one should expect them to be true to their own imagination. In other words, they should act on the basis that the harmony of the nation must be the pre-condition for the unity of the state. The key here remains the principle of consent, not as some abstract concession but as an operative political principle. Nationalists, though, would have to accept the possibility that unionists would never be convinced. Second, if unionists are sincere about the benefits of the Union, then one should expect them to be true to their own imagination. The pursuit of inclusiveness within Northern Ireland would depend on unionists accepting that their interests can best be secured within a framework sufficiently accommodating of nationalists. The key here would be equality. Unionists too would have to acknowledge the possibility that nationalists may never feel sufficiently accommodated. Respect for the principle of consent would qualify severely the nationalist aspiration for unity but the changes required within Northern Ireland would be far from congenial to traditional unionism. Yet on that basis it might be possible to conceive of institutions, transcending the conundrum of means and ends and depriving political fantasies, especially the fantasies of IRA violence, of their destabilizing power. As one nationalist commentator argued, government of the north by Northern Irish people could become an alternative that all could live with (Gadd 2004).

This is what the Belfast Agreement was groping towards and if it had a message it was that seeking the attainable was not the same thing as sacrificing political imagination. However, the Agreement may have expected too much of politics, demanded too much of democratic politicians and misjudged the acceptability of the means it proposed. The peace process may have produced an Agreement but no agreement about the ends of that Agreement. A sustainable and workable compromise in Northern Ireland would require something more of unionism and loyalism and of nationalism and republicanism than a reconsideration of means and ends. It would also have required the modification of the notion of winning and losing. This is the subject of the next chapter.

4   Winning and losing

Politics has sometimes been described as the great game and, like all games, the objective is to win or at least to avoid losing. This may appear to be a truism and therefore not worth stating. Yet politics, unlike, for instance, football, involves more complex objectives than beating an opponent. It is part of a web of purposes and expectations in which it is sometimes difficult to distinguish strategy and tactic, long-term and short-term aims, advantages and disadvantages or, as we have seen, ends and means. If this is so, then what is actually understood by winning and losing becomes more difficult to specify and we may suspect that the idea of winning and losing is one of the great ideological simplifiers, one which projects its simplifications into the future and into the past. In this regard, the Northern Ireland peace process shares much in common with popular historical interest in the Irish Home Rule crisis of 1912–21 and the fascination both exert is the spectator's fascination with the politics of winning and losing. That fascination is not just a scholarly one but also an ideological one. An ideological concern with the morality of winning and losing has the effect, as Oakeshott observed, of transforming the past into 'a field in which we exercise our moral and political opinions, like whippets in a meadow on Sunday afternoon' (Oakeshott 1991: 165). Popular understanding of the Home Rule crisis provides a clear example of the ideological whippets of unionism and nationalism chasing each other and sometimes chasing their own tails. This is because the origin of Northern Ireland is so important to their respective political identities and has defined the character of winning and losing and its legacy remains a key issue in the peace process. To take just one example, a familiar whippet runs through Flann Campbell's *The Dissenting Voice* (1991). Campbell's purpose in that book was to recapture the radical dissenting tradition of Ulster Protestantism and to use that tradition as an index by which to measure the failings of Ulster unionism. The partition of Ireland, according to Campbell, was a great victory for unionists but a great defeat for the Protestant radical tradition (Campbell 1991: 424–33). In other words, unionists were the winners but Ireland was an even greater loser. Campbell's argument is part of a narrative of dispossession that has been and remains a vital component of Irish nationalism. According to

Stewart, nationalists have been in the habit of saying that Ireland is 'their' country, not in the sense of it being their native land 'but in a strictly legal sense – they claim to be the real owners because it was once taken from them' (Stewart 1977: 45). In Campbell's case, the Ulster unionist victory in 1921 not only took the six counties of Northern Ireland but also dispossessed partitioned Ireland of the (authentic) dissenting protestantism of Wolfe Tone and the United Irishmen. The Irish lost their natural inheritance and the Protestants lost their true selves. That is double odium indeed.

The narrative of dispossession that is found in Campbell is matched by a unionist narrative of celebration, pioneered by Ronald McNeill's *Ulster's Stand for Union* of 1922. This narrative constituted what Jackson called unionist Whiggery, 'works which cast the founders of Northern Ireland and their actions in an heroic mould' (Jackson 1996: 129). In this version of history, unionists were winners, not in a simple partisan sense but in that much grander sense identified by Sir Thomas Sinclair. For Sinclair, unionist 'sympathy with the world mission of the British Empire in the interests of civil and religious freedom' meant that 'Ulster is entitled to retain her full share in every privilege of the whole realm' (Sinclair 1970: 173). The unionist position was not only for the Union but also for civilization and progress against barbarism and backwardness, a stand so important that it was vital not to lose. Of course, both the nationalist and unionist versions of this period are ideological rather than historical interpretations. The question of winners and losers becomes a question of right and wrong and history is called as a witness at the trial. Perhaps most people outside the history profession view the past in that very practical way. Nevertheless, the ideology of winners and losers applied to history is a questionable one. The foundation of Northern Ireland, understood in this simple and reductionist manner, tells us nothing of the decline in sympathy for Ulster in the rest of the United Kingdom and of the political consequences of this for unionism, especially after 1969. It tells us nothing of the continued insecurities of unionists after partition who, with the experience of the Home Rule crisis constantly in mind, could never be certain of the unqualified support of the British Government to guarantee their full share in the privileges of the realm. The ideological interpretation, though, has a polemical force and has informed argument about the legitimacy of partition. The difficulty of achieving political stability in Northern Ireland can be traced in part to the perspective of winners and losers. Republican violence after 1969 was driven by the expectation that the original sectarian defeat of the 1920s could be reversed and loyalist violence by a continued determination not to be on the losing side this time around. That expectation and that determination reflected a wider public mood.

This inheritance has been politically debilitating. The perspective of winners and losers has encouraged three related tendencies. The first tendency is a culture of non-negotiable demands, a collective assertiveness that resists the proposition that the ultimate demand ('we must win') can admit of any qualification. The second tendency is an intensification of partisanship because it becomes difficult to distinguish between negotiable and non-negotiable demands. The third tendency is a reductionist view of politics in which all argument is related to that ultimate and non-negotiable demand. This simplifies things immeasurably but it does not contribute imaginatively to the management of grievances. Like the gap between the means at our disposal and the end of 'world peace', the ideology of winners and losers opens up a dangerous gap between practical aims and final objectives. At the heart of it is a profound alienation expressed in the desire to redeem history, to transform the future or permanently to secure justice. The condition, of course, is not unique to Northern Ireland. Christa Wolf, reflecting on the collapse of communism, thought that the biggest task of the present generation was to discard a mass of dogmas, especially 'the dogma that history has "winners"'. The dogma 'winners of history', she thought, was a barrier to coping with the complexity and ambiguity of events (Wolf 1993: 301–2). Those who think of themselves as the (righteous) 'winners of history' stop confronting the truth about their own past and take refuge in the comforting arrogance of justification by history. On the other hand, those who think of themselves as the (wronged) losers of history are just as likely to avoid confronting the truth about the past and to take refuge in a compensatory grievance culture. Unionist politicians can actually embrace both dispositions – they are 'winners' who feel constantly that they have been wronged – and so can nationalist politicians – they are 'losers' who feel arrogantly justified by history. Indeed, these positions are interchangeable. The cynic's response to Wolf's plea is that it represents an appeal for mercy by one of the losers (or potential losers) in history. It is wishful thinking but not political reality. Politics is not a literary parlour game, it is not an academic seminar and Ireland is indeed not that much different from divided societies anywhere else. Political ideas have a fierce cutting edge in divided societies because they are not matters of abstraction. In the Irish case, they have been precisely about how 'to win, or lose, in a political world where winning and losing could bring with them the most dire consequences'. To lose any argument in this sectarian condition would have profound effect and that is why politics was and remains a serious business – though a serious business is not necessarily a violent business (Boyce, Eccleshall and Geoghegan 1993: 5). And it was the continuity rather than the change in that sectarian condition that struck one observer of the peace process in the 1990s. In Northern Ireland politics no one expected either mercy or return for the 'Irish problem, as historically defined, is not susceptible to a loserless ending' (Simon 1999). There was always the lingering menace of unfinished business that no amount of fine words could dispel. The room for genuine compromise, according to this view, was probably illusory.

And yet the Belfast Agreement *was* supposed to be a loserless ending to 30 years of Troubles. It *was* supposed to be a balanced settlement under which the political and cultural identity of everyone would be respected and protected. The 'new beginning' proposed by the Agreement's Declaration of Support intimated a shift from a politics defined by winning and losing to a politics defined by sharing risks and jointly managing uncertainties. Its promise was captured succinctly by Richard Bourke who, while admitting that democratic politics tends to be a game of winners and losers, argued that 'at least an *acceptable* version of the general interest' was intimated in the Agreement. It had been arrived at, admittedly, through 'a process of political contestation' but the Agreement appeared to oblige sufficiently 'the demand for equal treatment' for everyone (Bourke 2003: 8–9). This view matched the hopes of those who argued that, after the end of the Cold War, the old 'either-or' of politics that had driven the Northern Ireland conflict could best be settled 'in the context of a much more flexible and multiform agenda' (Christie 1992: 76). There was the expectation amongst some that a new language of politics in Northern Ireland would emerge now that the old one no longer appeared adequate to reality. This reflected a more general popular mood that the conflict had become tedious, a tedium journalists chose to call 'war-weariness'. There was also a desire at last to get beyond the condition of Sisyphus where political initiatives were rolled up the hill only to roll back down again for lack of collective support. There was a widely expressed wish – though it was difficult to calculate its depth – for the old ways to be renounced, a new collaboration to begin, one that acknowledged the constraint of others but that also acknowledged their rights (see Mosher 1983: 122). Unfortunately, experience of the integrity of the problem – someone had to lose and someone had to win – obliged people to believe that it would not happen, changes in the rest of the world notwithstanding. The old style of thinking seemed too deeply ingrained. Furthermore, popular attitudes were ambiguous and the wish for peace was not an unqualified aspiration. This is why the Belfast Agreement came as such a great surprise to so many.

Cox has shown, however, that the influence of these wider political developments on Northern Ireland was not entirely without their effect. His thesis was that the end of the Cold War made the IRA ceasefire much more likely because its 'war' had been rendered meaningless by changes in the wider international arena. In short, 'it made it far more difficult for the organization to legitimize a strategy which by the late 1980s had already reached a dead end' (Cox 1997: 677). Cox's thesis, originally controversial, has become conventional wisdom. Another commentator noted how in this period the political lexicon of republicanism had begun to draw on a pluralist language of dialogue (Bean 1995a: 37). Even by the late 1980s, ran another argument, the IRA already realized that while (militarily) it could not lose, neither could it win and had begun to look for a way out and the end of the Cold War helped to open the door marked 'exit' (O'Brien 1993). In 1992 the former Northern Ireland minister, Richard Needham, put it rather differently (and more accurately). The IRA, he wrote, 'know they cannot win but they do not know how to lose' (Needham 1998: 322). This was not the 'military stalemate' that republican sympathizers came to speak of. Stalemate *was* military defeat for the IRA but it was also an opportunity for political gains. At about the same time some loyalist paramilitaries were also considering alternatives, though there is a certain irony in Ervine's claim that it was the intensification of loyalist killing in this period that made the IRA accept that it could not win (Taylor 1999: 234). Despite the importance of these developments within terrorist organizations, one should also remember that the emerging 'peace' process had been preceded by the 'political' process of talks between the constitutional parties, initiated in 1991 by Secretary of State Peter Brooke and continued in 1992 by his successor, Sir Patrick Mayhew. These talks were a significant breach in the blockage caused by the Anglo-Irish Agreement of 1985. While they did not issue in agreement they did help to identify a framework within which agreement could be sought (McDonald 2000: 120). By the 1990s, then, one could define Northern Ireland politics, in the words of the American philosopher Richard Rorty, as 'a contest between an entrenched vocabulary which has become a nuisance and a half-formed new vocabulary which vaguely promises new things'. The entrenched vocabulary was the vocabulary of 'either-or', the vocabulary of winners and losers, and the half-formed new vocabulary was the vocabulary of 'and', a possible vocabulary beyond winners and losers. Furthermore, there did appear to be some willingness to 'ignore apparently futile traditional questions' and to substitute 'new and possibly interesting questions' (Rorty 1989: 9) and this is something we examine in the next chapter. Nothing of course is that simple. In the new circumstances that were emerging in the 1990s it was difficult to know how significant these changes really were. The two vocabularies existed side by side and there was a suspicion, particularly on the unionist side, that the new 'promising' vocabulary was a cunning repackaging of the old. Indeed, the large question was also the simple question: What could politics beyond winning and losing possibly mean? In Northern Ireland, was it even imaginable? There were good grounds to doubt that it was.

Insight and vision

What is imaginable to people depends upon what Rorty called their 'final vocabulary' or their ultimate convictions (Rorty 1989: 73). The final vocabularies of unionism and nationalism did not appear conducive to the sort of politics that would go beyond winning and losing. For most of the 1990s, academics remained pessimistic about the possibility of delivering a workable accommodation. Longley argued that the Brooke/Mayhew Talks had failed for lack of an adequate language (Longley 1993: 22). Others proposed that there was a need to think seriously about the vocabulary of communication, a refreshed 'linguistic world where, far from being lost for words', a new discourse of mutual understanding would emerge (Lee 1993: 25). The possibilities of achieving this new vocabulary seemed limited. For example, Todd's systematic work on ideological structures in Northern Ireland had convinced her that even moderate nationalists and unionists remained poles apart. 'Not only do these ideologies lead to sharply opposed interpretations of just about every political event, they also lead to sharply opposed criteria of what counts as a fair political compromise.' She concluded that this was the case despite the adoption by most political parties, as Bean had noted, of a common pluralist language. That realistic assessment of the win–lose character of politics was combined with an intimation of what a different sort of politics would look like – one in which the ideological conditions of conflict would be 'deconstructed', in which tendencies to polarization would be undone and commonalities as well as conflict within and between communities would be expressed (Todd 1995: 163–4, 176). When Todd was writing, that emancipation seemed rather fanciful because there was little awareness that anything had changed or any serious expectation that it would. The temptation to keep faith with the politics of winning and losing seemed, to informed observers, just too great to deliver any prospect of success (English 1997: 24–5). It appeared all the more unlikely when the republican commitment to peace after 1994 seemed to be more tactical than genuine and the behaviour of all paramilitaries to be no better than that of the 'protection racketeer' (O'Doherty 1998: 118).

The politics of winning and losing is about keeping one's attention fixed upon the single end of politics, and the circumstantial incentive seemed still to be one of pushing matters towards a conclusion. From this perspective talks about the future of Northern Ireland would indeed be about victory and defeat, about mastery and humiliation, for that was thought to be the true nature of politics in a divided society. And winning in this case could mean simply laying the blame for failure and proving that the other side was incorrigible. That is what political communication appeared to be about, not agreement but manoeuvring for advantage. It involved the employment of strategic means to immobilize opponents and to mobilize support (see Edelman 1988: 103–4; Edelman 1977: 23–5). Trimble admitted that there was some substance in the allegation that his party in the past had understood politics in terms of tactical engagement – because this is what it assumed the other parties were up to as well. This is what he remembered doing for most of the 1975 Constitutional Convention because no one thought there could ever be a consensus. The general disposition was to argue proposals through, 'not so much with intention of seeking agreement, but of convincing Government that we are the reasonable people'. When deadlock was reached, the expectation was that British politicians and officials would appreciate that unionists had been reasonable and act accordingly. That was also, Trimble suggested, the unionist approach to the Brooke/Mayhew Talks in 1991 and 1992. It nearly worked. The reason it failed was not because of unreasonableness on the part of unionists but because a purely tactical engagement was no longer sufficient. From 1993 onwards that tactical engagement had been trumped by the strategic engagement promised by nationalists and republicans in the guise of the peace process. This was a threatening turn of events that changed the framework for unionist politics. It was no longer possible for unionists to remain 'essentially passive' because the new republican approach had transformed the context (Trimble 2001: 44–5).

A stable and relatively consensual society can accept political manoeuvring within limits generally understood. Disagreement is communicated in the manner described by Arthur Balfour in his introduction to Bagehot's *The English Constitution*. It is expressed within political machinery that presupposes 'a people so fundamentally at one that they can safely afford to bicker; and so sure of their own moderation that they are not dangerously disturbed by the never-ending din of political conflict' (cited in Schwab 1985: xvii). To win or lose in that condition is not a collective disaster. In Northern Ireland things have been of a different order. People have not been at one and what moderation has existed was marginalized by the continued use of force outside the realm of formal politics, by what some chose to call the 'communicative dimension of political violence' (Arthur 1995: 185). If, as Arthur contends, the *original* justification for this communicative dimension of violence was the exclusion of Catholics from decision making, then the *sustained* IRA campaign had done little to modify that exclusion. Indeed, the strategic use of violence made inclusion impossible for two reasons. First, because republicans had been determined to include themselves out and second, because republicans had also been determined to prevent nationalists including themselves in short of Irish unity. This determination contributed to what may be called the 'positional logic' of winning and losing, positions that, as Todd so clearly showed, logically excluded the claims of others. How can one grasp this notion of positional logic? To a journalist observing it at close quarters in the 1970s, it was a politics that did not value style over substance. 'It was all substance and no style.' There were few niceties here and what Paxman meant by the triumph of substance over style was the reduction of politics to intense sectarian beliefs (Paxman 2003: 3). This was an exaggeration but as a political *potential* in times of violence it was all too accurate. The general problem of positional logic lay not so much in the bigotry of unionism and nationalism as it lay in the self-referential nature of their respective world views. This can be illustrated by the application of Berki's categories of 'insight' and 'vision' (1983).

Berki defined two faculties of 'seeing' the world which are relevant here. The first he termed 'vision' and the second, 'insight'. Vision and insight involve both knowledge and attitude, fact as well as value. Vision 'sees' a world different from the existing, a world that ought to be. Insight 'sees' more practical and prosaic priorities, ones that either act as obstacles to or provide opportunities for the realization of the vision. For example, the nationalist vision is a vision of an Ireland yet to be. It is a vision of destiny and political insight reveals why it has not yet been achieved – British interference, Protestant bigotry and unionist resistance to change. What partially has reconciled this painful insight of present division with the beautiful vision of future unity has been a deep sense of inevitability, that history is on the nationalist side. This nationalist cult of inevitability has actually made having to compromise with unionists much harder to accept and acknowledging their objections all the more frustrating and irritating (see Chapter 7). If you encounter an obstacle, you are likely to want to go around it or to remove it and not to reason with it. For most of recent history, nationalists have not thought it worth while reasoning with unionists but have looked to the British Government to encourage unionists to be amenable. Republicans have thought it legitimate to use violence to force the British to abandon unionists to their fate and this is merely the militaristic version of positional logic. On the other hand, the unionist vision of a stable, British, Northern Ireland has always existed in the shadow cast by nationalist politics. Unionist insight has perceived the stratagem of its enemies in every political act from interference by the Irish state, abstentionism by nationalists, the deadly hostility of republicans to the indifference of British Governments. What has partially reconciled this painful insight with the beautiful vision of British Ulster has been faith in unionist resilience. The cult of resilience has made compromise with nationalists all the more problematic if compromise, by accepting their difference, means weakening or threatening unionist solidarity. That has been the perennial debate within unionism between those who can see no point in compromise because a willingness to compromise will be interpreted by nationalists as a sign of weakness and those who seek a platform of cooperation between the two traditions as the basis for stability. The distinctive ideological relation of insight and vision in both unionism and nationalism has given rise to two recognizable and relatively consistent forms of argument. The engagement of these two forms of argument in the Brooke/Mayhew Talks process of 1991/2 revealed how difficult it was to conceive of a politics beyond winners and losers. Indeed, the formal statements revealed perfectly the resistant attributes of positional logic.

The purpose of talks about the future of Northern Ireland for the SDLP was to devise those structures necessary to reconcile two Irish traditions. The concept of 'parity of esteem' or the 'legitimacy of both traditions' was the logical spine running through its submissions at all levels of the talks and this comprised a set of interlocking propositions. First, there are two politico-cultural traditions on the island of Ireland. While the unionists assert that their tradition is British, nationalists know that their tradition is Irish. Second, those two traditions need to reach agreement on how best to share the island of Ireland (which would constitute Northern nationalists as part of the Irish majority). Third, each tradition has an absolute right of self-definition, and since nationalists define their tradition in terms of allegiance to the Irish state that had significant implications for the role of the Dublin Government in Northern Ireland's affairs. The nationalist approach intended to push beyond the boundaries of Northern Ireland and the fact of its existence as a political entity and the aim was to enhance significantly the 'Irish dimension'. For both of the unionist parties, the DUP and the UUP, the purpose of the talks was to devise those structures that would accommodate the interests of two states on the island of Ireland. Since they did not acknowledge the legitimacy of the 'two traditions' analysis (which would constitute them as an Irish minority) unionists wanted to create new arrangements for the governance of Northern Ireland as a region of the United Kingdom. As an integral part of the British state there would be some need for special arrangements to deal with peculiar and specific problems, like Irish culture internal to Northern Ireland and the shared land border with the Republic of Ireland. But these special arrangements would be limited and should certainly not weaken the status of Northern Ireland as a part of the United Kingdom. The relationship between North and South would be based on the constitutional, political and institutional integrity of the two separate jurisdictions on the island of Ireland. It should be inter-governmental and acknowledge the fact of separate jurisdictions. The unionist approach defended boundaries in order to confirm Northern Ireland's British statehood.

The difference in these forms of argument was not just a matter of words (Cunningham 1997: 20). It expressed a real division in politics that no form of words seemed capable of resolving, the one seeking to stabilize Northern Ireland within the United Kingdom, the other seeking to develop towards Irish unity. Thus the common unionist criticism of the SDLP in general, and of its leader John Hume in particular, was a familiar and long-standing one. Nationalists, it was argued, were very good at articulating a grand *vision* but were hopelessly without *insight* into what was practical or attainable. Indeed, unionists suspected that the desire to speak in visionary generalities so characteristic of Hume had little to do with intellectual grandeur and everything to do with avoiding a commitment to the specifics of making Northern Ireland work. They judged it to be a stratagem the purpose of which was always to raise the price for nationalist cooperation but without ever delivering that cooperation. The familiar nationalist response was to reverse that critique. In short, unionist *insight* was parochial and myopic and its *vision* non-existent. Unionism was trapped within a perceptual iron cage and its desire to speak only in limited particularities was simply a device to avoid acknowledging the Irishness of nationalist identity. It was part of a stratagem designed to reduce the costs of cooperation but without delivering anything of substance to Catholics. In the 'insight thing' unionists believed they had a practical advantage because it presupposed existing political structures. This would advantage a process of consolidation within Northern Ireland to the disadvantage of a process of development towards all-Ireland structures. In the 'vision thing', nationalists thought that they would always win and unionists would always lose because it presupposed a process of inevitable development towards all-Ireland structures that coincided with their objectives. Here were two diametrically opposed understandings. One desired a steady-state Union and the other desired a dynamic arrangement. One attributed to membership of the United Kingdom permanent worth and value and the other perceived it to be provisional and of diminishing significance. One wanted a settlement to be substantially British and only residually Irish and the other aspired to a settlement substantially Irish and only residually British.

Moreover, the disposition of unionist and nationalist voters was to confirm their own suspicions about the good faith of the other by using as benchmarks the most extreme or ill-considered remarks of their opponents. This was a version of *la politique du pire*, a politics of worse is better, which ascribed an eternal purpose and character to all political utterance, the devilish intent of which was all the more threatening when it was not immediately obvious. There was a logic here, of course, but it was a positional logic that could only lead in the long run to an absolute win or an absolute loss simply because there appeared to be no political incentive to accept anything in between. This linear thinking helps to explain the frequently noted dispositions of nationalist optimism and unionist pessimism, dispositions that appear unrelated to the outcome of particular events. Nationalist optimism is the joy of anticipation, a form of 'endism' in which the struggle for justice will be won and the wrong inflicted upon them finally righted. It is the joyful anticipation of political advance and of winning the political argument. Republicans adopted this as their slogan and, killing along the way, worked for the time when their day would come. It revealed itself consistently in the expectation of favourable demographic change with the threatening message to Protestants that Catholics 'are going to outbreed you so you better deal now before it's too late' (Moloney 1998a). Unionist pessimism, by contrast, is the melancholy of anticipation, another form of endism which reads into the course of events a relentless injustice, often connived at by the British Government, that conspires against them. There was an apocalyptic quality to this anticipation, a fear of cultural death.

These dispositions were not universally shared but they are distinctive of the unionist and nationalist traditions. Some interpretations of these dispositions misunderstand Northern Ireland politics by taking unionist pessimism and nationalist optimism to be of recent origin when, in fact, they are historical conditions. Moreover, they often bear no relationship to reality at all but constitute yet another political fantasy of the sort explored in Chapter 3 (see Porter 2003: 204–15). Their common problem is, in the words of Lord Keynes, that in the long run we're all dead. These dispositions are not particularly helpful if you are trying to make the best of present circumstances where a more constructive alternative to the politics of winning and losing may suggest itself.

For example, Conor Cruise O'Brien defined the logic of the traditional nationalist and republican code thus. Within that tradition, the 'object of negotiating with unionists', he argued, 'is not to get them off a hook, but to impale them on one' for the desired objective is the triumph of Catholics over Protestants. Of course, the desire may not be immediately achievable but there should be no doubt about the objective. The proper task of nationalist representatives was to squeeze unionists and to 'get others to squeeze them in the general direction of a united Ireland' (O'Brien 1994: 166, 193). By the very nature of their culture, and whatever the differences of interest, O'Brien thought that Northern nationalists and Southern nationalists could understand the world in no other way than that of winning against unionists. In such circumstances, it should be clear why unionists have sought to avoid being impaled on any nationalist hook. Every nationalist invitation to discuss political options, like the New Ireland Forum of 1982/3 and the Forum for Peace and Reconciliation after 1994, has been judged to be an invitation to unionists to participate in their own undoing. And that is why the Anglo-Irish Agreement of 1985 was such a calamity since it appeared to provide the Irish state and Northern nationalism with a mechanism to manoeuvre unionism into a permanently losing position.

When one considers the logical nature of the anticipated win and the calculated loss communicated by both traditions, what is interesting is how remarkably similar they are. What unionists have required of their opponents is that they become *patriotic*, exchanging their Irish nationalism for identification with the British statehood of Northern Ireland. What nationalists have required of unionists is that they too should become *patriotic*, ultimately exchanging their Britishness for allegiance to the (united) Irish state. In neither case has this proved persuasive, despite the respective common appeals to a transcendent identity, for what is being asked is what the other side feels it cannot give without absolute capitulation. This was something that continued to dog negotiations for the Belfast Agreement itself (de Breadun 2001: 186). When the majority behaves tribalistically and equates the state with its own culture, Levy has argued, it is no good 'counseling the minority to be patriotic rather than nationalistic'. The sort of positional logic traditionally articulated by unionists and nationalists, even when presented as a benign civic vision, represented 'a blind application of inappropriate categories, not a move towards cosmopolitan individualism' (Levy 2000: 43–4). The Catholic experience of 'tribal' Northern Ireland between 1921 and 1972 and the Protestant fear of a 'tribal' republic provide good reasons for both communities not to cave in just because they have been outvoted (for a theoretical examination of this issue see Goodin 2003: 141–6). That was the problem that proposals for Home Rule failed to solve, it remained an unsolved problem in Northern Ireland after 1921 and the likelihood is that it would remain the problem even if there were some day a majority in favour of Irish unity. In other words, the problem with positional logic is that it provided 'no way to get the virtuous cycle started' because no one could think beyond a final calculation of winning and losing (Levy 2000: 97). The difficulties for unionists intensified with the development of the peace process after 1993 especially when that process was called by republicans, for partisan reasons, the 'Irish peace initiative'.

When talks between Hume and Adams resumed in April 1993 a statement was released that spoke of an acceptance by the two leaders that 'the Irish people as a whole have a right to national self-determination'. This uncompromising nationalist demand was softened somewhat by the rider that 'the exercise of self-determination is a matter for agreement between the people of Ireland' and that 'a new agreement is only achievable and viable if it can earn and enjoy the allegiance of the different traditions on this island' (cited in Rowan 1995: 47–8). While the first part of the statement appeared to confirm the traditional nationalist claim of Irish self-determination as a non-negotiable demand, the second part of the statement implied some notion of unionist consent. However, as we noted above, these were really two parts of a common outlook. Together they proposed that the nationalist case was morally correct and that the solution to the problem lay in the British Government acknowledging it and acting upon that acknowledgement. As Adams argued, in removing the obstacle to a 'democratic solution' (by implication, unionist resistance) the British establishment had no bottom line and could be moved as far as political power might push it (cited in Rowan 1995: 49). The stalemate of positional logic could be changed by the application of (now political) pressure to the weakest link and final victory would be delivered. The unionist position, as we have also seen, was exactly the opposite and it was understandable if the 'Irish Peace Initiative' filled them with deep anxiety. Indeed, two forms of political communication seemed to be running together in a threatening babble. Suspicious unionists interpreted the language of Hume and Adams to combine the search for peace with the objective of nationalist victory. Here was a call for talks about Northern Ireland's future in which each party would come to the table without pre-conditions except that of moving towards Irish unity; in which no one would have a veto except the 'Irish people'; in which consent would be essential except when unionists needed persuading; and where coercion must be removed except when it was called persuasion. The British Government were being called upon to persuade unionists and if persuasion did not work it must persuade them again in a way they could not refuse. In other words, the British Government was required to act as the unionists' 'Sicilian uncle', a patron and mentor but ultimately a sinister and treacherous one (Sciascia 2001). The pluralist language of the Irish peace initiative that linked Hume and Adams conjured up a traditionally separatist strategy in which fundamental political distinctions would be resolved within a familiar nationalist shell. As one critic put it, the idea at the centre of the Hume–Adams proposals 'is to bypass the need to accommodate unionists qua unionists and present the British Government with a choice between a cessation of IRA terrorism or maintaining the union' (O'Leary 1993: 15). If the desire for a non-sectarian Irish Republic may be genuine and laudable, there remained the uncomfortable implication in the origin of the peace process that unionists were simply unreasonable in their failure to appreciate it. The crude implication was that unionists were to make restitution for the sort of odium identified by Flann Campbell. As Longley so neatly put it, Protestants were required to go back to 1798 and to get it right this time (see Richards 1991: 142–4). Arguably, this particular tendency intensified within Irish nationalism as a consequence of the peace process. It is a tendency to be impatient with the reality of the Union and with the expressed (and not imaginary) support of unionists for its maintenance. In other words, there developed a heightened expectation that Northern Ireland was in a process of transition and that it should be transformed in reasonably short order into part of the new Ireland. This tendency within nationalism, as much as unionist divisions, has dogged the course of the Belfast Agreement since 1998 (this is explored more fully in Chapter 7).

Transition and transformation

If the notion of Northern Ireland being at the crossroads has become something of a political cliché, by the early 1990s it seemed to have become quite an apt one. The key question for those genuinely seeking a settlement was straightforward enough. How could the choice of direction, how could the character of the 'transition' from political violence to political stability, be one that was not an absolute win for one side and an absolute loss for the other? This was indeed highly problematic. To what was the peace process a transition and what transformation was expected? It is no surprise that transition and transformation meant different things to nationalists and republicans, unionists and loyalists.

The character of politics during a period of transition and its consequent transformations has been explored by Ernest Gellner. 'The crucial power in transitions', he wrote, 'is the power to decide which turning to take, being at the wheel at the big and rare road-forks.' Since 'some crucial road-forks generally only appear once' there will be no opportunity for those not in control at that moment 'to reverse the mistake made "last time"' (Gellner 1964: 66–7). This is a very particular reading of transition for it defines a state of exception and not the normal occasion of liberal democratic politics. In a stable situation 'one can play for marginal advantages, and accept defeat, tolerate opposition, and refrain from pushing every advantage to its utmost in the knowledge that tomorrow is another day'. This is Balfour's comfortable din of political conflict. A transitional situation is far from stable and in this case 'tomorrow is not *another* day: it is an *other* day, altogether'. In this case, 'the game is played for the highest stakes' because each side knows that there can be no replay. That is why it is essential to be in control because who has control during the transition will determine the character of the transformations. The crucial power in a period of transition, then, 'is the power to decide which turning to take'. Gellner's specification of the distinctive character of the politics of transition captures much of the frenetic spirit of Northern Ireland politics in which the political culture of winning and losing is so pervasive (1964: 66–7).

On the one hand, unionists have always feared that they only have to be unlucky once, that they only have to make one significant error of judgement, and the pass to Irish unity would be sold. On the other hand, nationalists have sought to establish a dynamic towards Irish unity while republicans have been reluctant to engage in any sort of negotiation without some guarantee that the outcome has been prejudged in their favour. In such circumstances, everything can become a state of exception and the stakes are always high. Gellner's thesis needs to be modified in one important regard. He admitted that it applied only to what obtains 'during a fundamental transformation' (Gellner 1964: 66–7). This begs the question of how fundamental the transformation in Northern Ireland could possibly be. Republican propaganda suggested that the transformation would be absolute, and unionist critics of the peace process were disposed to accept that argument. In other words, the process of transition entailed the irreversible transformation of Northern Ireland's constitutional status. For unionists, the transition was one which paramilitaries had to make from violence to democracy as the condition for stability and accommodation between the communities. In the apt phrase of the then Irish Foreign Minister Dick Spring, how did the British and Irish governments attempt to 'square the circle' of unionist and republican views? They tried to do so in the tortuous phraseology of the Downing Street Declaration of December 1993.

That Declaration established the principled framework within which the future of Northern Ireland would be discussed. It conceded the abstract principle of self-determination to the Irish people (the nationalist position) but retained the operative principle of self-determination for the 'greater number' in Northern Ireland (the unionist position), a rather different construction from the Hume–Adams original (see Bew, Gibbon and Patterson 2002: 219–24). It none the less involved a considered ambiguity. Conceding the metaphysics of self-determination to the Irish people was immediately and practically qualified by the need for consent within Northern Ireland and this was the square circle the two governments had sought. But was it more of a square than a circle? Ambiguity on this matter – even the considered ambiguity of the Declaration – was ambiguity still. It had the potential to be what was later to become known as 'constructive ambiguity'. It also had the potential to become destructive ambiguity. For example, James Molyneaux, then leader of the UUP, thought the Declaration to be both comparatively safe and to have the makings of a betrayal. That was not confusion. It was political realism. Both these things were true from a unionist point of view. Equally, both were true from a nationalist point of view. On the one hand, if the British Government had conceded the principle of self-determination to the people of Ireland, whether that people be 'metaphysical' or not, it could be read as a fundamental concession to the aim of Irish unity. Everything else, for instance the stipulation that this right of self-determination should be exercised North and South, would be a mere temporary qualification of the governing principle. One could argue that unionist rights would now exist as a mere concessionary derogation from the rights of the Irish people as a whole and unionists would have become those who were temporarily unpersuaded of the value of a united Ireland. This would be an identity on a sort of sale and lease-back arrangement, acceptance of which would mean unionist defeat. This was the interpretation put on the Declaration by unionist critics and from it flowed their opposition to everything else that followed (McCartney 2001: 91–2). On the other hand, the acknowledgement by Irish nationalists of the principle of consent for constitutional change could be read as guaranteeing the unionist position indefinitely. If the statehood of Northern Ireland remained securely in the hands of the 'greater number', everything else in the Declaration became embellishment and detail. Self-determination would remain stubbornly partitioned and the right of democratic citizenship in Northern Ireland thereby strengthened rather than weakened. This was the argument of republican critics of the peace process. In this reading, unionist fears of the Hume–Adams initiative were actually misconceived for the peace process was not about removing the British state but about removing 'armed struggle'. This was the end of true republicanism because without the armed struggle constitutional nationalism would continue the great historical betrayal. Once 'the IRA is finished, constitutional nationalism and the British state can swing whatever way they please' (McIntyre 1994: 17). The subsequent politics of this period then came down to this. Who would have the biggest say in deciding which turning to take, whose hand would be strongest at the wheel at the road fork of inclusive negotiations which lay ahead?

The text of the Declaration certainly took many republican activists by surprise. For republicans, the purpose of the so-called pan-nationalist front, as Jim Gibney explained, was to link Sinn Fein, the SDLP, the Irish government and Irish American supporters into a 'nationalist consensus that a united Ireland was feasible' (cited in Schulze 1997: 97). When Sinn Fein sought clarification of the Declaration the purpose was to reinstate the role of the British Government as a 'Sicilian uncle', a role which would be reinforced by the mobilization of international opinion in favour of radical constitutional change. This was the 'winner' that had tempted republicans into the peace process in the first place (Patterson 1994: 14–17). As one commentator remarked, Sinn Fein was asking of the British Government: 'Why should we be a minority in their – unionists' – state when you can "persuade" them to be a minority in ours?' (Wilson 1994: 5; see also Breen 1994: 8). Republican disappointment lay in realizing that this was yet another fantasy. The general reaction of unionists to the text of the Declaration was one of relief mixed with profound anxiety, as Molyneaux's comment revealed. Few would admit to actually liking the Declaration but there was a feeling that, in the circumstances, it could have been much worse. There was relief, first, that no commitment had been given by the British Government to espouse the 'full legitimacy and value of Irish unity'; second, that the constitutional guarantee had been confirmed; and third, that the consent of the 'greater number' had been accepted as a governing principle for change. This had imparted sufficient confidence to encourage the loyalist paramilitaries to go on ceasefire in October 1994, announcing that they believed the Union to be 'safe'.

The fork in the road that seemed to point in the direction of Irish unity was not the Downing Street Declaration but possibly *Frameworks for the Future* published in February 1995. *Frameworks* set out a 'shared understanding between the British and Irish Governments to assist discussion and negotiation involving the Northern Ireland parties'. It proposed to cater for present and future inter-connections on the island of Ireland and intended that new North/South institutions should be created, leading to 'agreed dynamic, new co-operative and constructive relationships'. They would have executive, harmonizing and consultative functions (HMSO 1995). These institutions represented an acknowledgement of the SDLP's claim that there could be no exclusively internal solution to the Northern Ireland problem. This was the 'Irish dimension' that was recognized to be essential in any settlement. For republicans, whatever arrangements were to be put in place had to confirm the transition to Irish unity. This meant that nationalists should not only aspire to Irish unity but also that they must have a self-standing institutional structure that would 'facilitate' the achievement of that aspiration and 'transform the situation'. In that transformation, active unionist consent would not be necessary and the struggle would be as good as won. This was a triumph of vision over insight and another fantasy – like the expectation of British persuasion – though it was one that a substantial section of unionists also chose to believe (Donaldson 1995: 20). This strictly fatalistic and familiar judgement of matters actually concealed a more important reality. In moving centre stage in the political debate, republicans had quietly acknowledged and accepted that there *was* a choice other than violence and that it was a choice most of the leadership had already made. While they were assiduous in putting across their own interpretation of the consequences of that choice it was not the only one since republicans were becoming slowly integrated into constitutional politics (see Moloney 2002: 303–15 for the best analysis of this development). The big unknown was the effect of that integration, whether it would intensify ethnic resentment (a continuation of republican destabilization) or help to contain it (poachers becoming gamekeepers).

That was why the issue of cross-border institutions became the overwhelming focus of concern after the Frameworks Document, especially so since the Irish Government had given no firm commitment to change Articles 2 and 3 of its Constitution (which made a territorial claim on Northern Ireland). There was a deep sense amongst unionists that, if they were to lose their grip on the wheel on this fork in the road, there would be no way back. The fear was that the principle of consent would have no purchase on the transfer of power from Northern Ireland to all-Ireland bodies. Political effort was mobilized to prevent any dynamic that would (to use a phrase of 1974) trundle Northern Ireland into an all-Ireland state (see Chapter 6). Ultimately, the reality was that unionists would have to live with the fact that Irish unity could not be ruled out – actually they always had done so. The point was to make sure that it would not be ruled in against their wishes. If this could be done successfully and there was the possibility of securing a stable if reformed Northern Ireland, then the '20 years' to unity hoped for by nationalists would remain, as it always had done: sometime, maybe, never. This was to become the position adopted by the Ulster Unionists under Trimble. Such was not the view of the Democratic and UK Unionist Parties. The leader of the UK Unionist Party (UKUP) argued that the whole nationalist strategy of bringing in Sinn Fein was to 'undermine the strength of the Union and the quality and nature of their British citizenship' (McCartney 1995: xiv). The objective of Paisley was to prevent negotiations taking place on an agenda which would lead to 'the annexation of Northern Ireland by Dublin' (Democratic Unionist Party 1997). These conflicting views divided unionism down the middle, a division notably absent on the nationalist side. One critic, however, believed that on the issue of North–South cooperation it was possible to move beyond this sort of politics. For the past decade, he argued, parties had been playing a game of manoeuvre and counter-manoeuvre, trying to put their side in a winning position. In victory 'they would be magnanimous and give the vanquished a range of concessions to ensure they would not lose by too much. But this is the politics of obstinacy and dogmatism, of back-room dealing and low trust.' The new hope was that a more pragmatic style of politics beyond positional logic and beyond winning and losing was now in prospect (Teague 1994: 34).

Conclusion

Positional logic, in other words, is not always good politics. According to Minogue, logic claims to see through every deception because of the assumption that there must be a rational pattern to political activity. This logic can sometimes combine a complete cynicism about the motives of others with a complete innocence about one's own motives. As La Rochefoucauld proposed: 'We have not the courage to declare as a general principle that we have no shortcomings and our enemies no good qualities;

but when it comes to details that is what we are none too far from believing' (La Rochefoucauld 1959: 88). In Northern Ireland it would be more accurate to say the rule of thumb was that both as a general principle and on details enemies had no good qualities. Taken to its own conclusions such logic was counterproductive, for 'human affairs are marked by an element of contingency which sets limits to the range of any general doctrine, including any system of total cynicism' (Minogue 1996b: 8). The manipulative logic of winning and losing may sometimes – but not always – lose touch with reality. Possibilities for constructive and mutually beneficial change can be lost through politicians being too clever by half or too paranoid for their own good. An exclusive focus on the strictly logical pattern of an opponent's ideas may encourage rigidity rather than the flexibility required to make the most of new circumstances. There may be variations within patterns and revisions of positions that are missed by a strict logic that can see no way out (Todd 1999: 69). However, the intellectual resources available for delivering success were not as limited as most people thought who only followed the tortuous path of the peace process from the outside. A broader range of concepts were available to participants in the talks that had been under way since 1996 and that from September 1997 now included Sinn Fein (but from which the Democratic Unionist Party (DUP) and the UK Unionists had withdrawn in protest). This is not to claim that these concepts somehow 'made' the Agreement and that the parties were merely the vehicles through which they found expression. That really would be to stand history on its head. The argument is a very modest one. It is that these concepts had become part of the general, if contested, intellectual climate and this made the character of the debate in the 1990s quite different from Sunningdale in the early 1970s. There had emerged a larger sense of what an agreement should involve and once the major paramilitary campaigns had ceased, these ideas helped to frame (but did not determine) the context of deliberation about agreement. The next part of the book examines these matters in greater detail.

Part II
Modifications

5 New ideas and old arguments

M. L. R. Smith once made the provocative suggestion that Northern Ireland remained one of the most under-studied conflicts in the world. He did not mean that there was little published on the Troubles. Rather, he meant that the academic study of Northern Ireland had been insulated to a large degree, in his words 'intellectually interned', from the influences and debates at work in the wider academic community. Of course, he admitted that 'an intellectual establishment that is content to operate within traditional analytical frameworks is not something that uniquely affects Irish studies'. Nevertheless, since the outbreak of the Troubles he felt that there had been a reticence to expand the horizons of understanding. Smith argued that the literature assumed that 'the violence is entrenched and unchanging, the constant backdrop against which scholarly studies of Northern Ireland are drawn'. This is what he called the 'hardening of the categories', the cult of exceptionalism, that made it difficult to think of alternatives (Smith 1999: 78, 93) However, Smith argued that the Northern Ireland problem was not inherently complex. What made it distinctive was the violence of those prepared either to destroy or to defend the state. Edna Longley had similarly used Yeats's line that 'things thought too long can be no longer thought' to express a mood of dissatisfaction with the prevailing mode of political interpretation in Northern Ireland (Longley 1994a: 1). This criticism of the hardened categories of interpretation had also been anticipated by Cox, who complained that it was 'almost as if Northern Ireland existed outside of world history' for all the attention scholars had paid to wider currents of thought (Cox 1997: 676). The frustration on the part of both Cox and Smith was qualified by their estimate that in the 1990s things had begun to change, intellectually and politically. There now existed the possibility that 'real politics – the absence of which has been one of the most obvious casualties of the past 25 years – might once again take centre stage in Northern Ireland' (Cox 1997: 678).

These criticisms of the *inwardness* of prevailing reflection are perhaps a little too harsh and would need to be qualified in one significant respect. Important frameworks for analysis had been proposed by those working within the political science tradition. Lijphart's theory of democracy in plural societies, for example, was an early influence on scholars studying Northern Ireland, as was the pioneering work of Rose (Lijphart 1977; Rose 1971 and 1976). Later studies by O'Leary and McGarry were equally influential and helped a generation of scholars to think through and against their interpretations (McGarry and O'Leary 1995; O'Leary and McGarry 1996). Political theorists, on the other hand, seemed to have little to contribute. In his comprehensive survey of theories of the Northern Ireland conflict, a survey that accorded significant weight to the political science tradition as well as to unionist and nationalist interpretations, Whyte considered only Marxist analyses to have made a significant contribution to knowledge (Whyte 1991: 175–93). One of the reasons for this lack of interest in political theory may be attributed to the significance of literary criticism in Irish intellectual life. Many of the big arguments about politics have been conducted in that idiom and literary criticism has often been a vehicle for political theorizing. It has engaged the attention of the best minds and the best stylists and provoked the most stimulating and exciting exchanges. Given that the subject matter of politics was the rather dreary predictability of party politics and the nasty, repetitive violence of paramilitarism – the hardened categories of Smith's critique – interesting theoretical reflection appeared to take place elsewhere and elsewhere was often the literary review or the literary text. The contributions of intellectuals like Edna Longley and Declan Kiberd, John Wilson Foster and Seamus Deane, had a political significance and a public impact well beyond the academy. These were debates in which big ideas were recruited to fight old battles but in the course of which, with a sort of cunning of reason, the old battles became transformed into new ones (see Connolly 2001).

Both Smith and Cox located their hopes in the unlocking of new perspectives that accompanied the end of the Cold War. It was no longer possible to categorize Northern Ireland as a simple exception to the rule or to argue that it existed in a peculiar limbo outside the norm of left–right politics when, as theorists were arguing, politics had now gone beyond left and right (Giddens 1994). Hence the post-communist fashion to 're-invent', 're-think', 're-imagine' or 'revise' politics was not without its local impact for, as Cox also demonstrated, it coincided with new developments in Northern Ireland politics – either the hesitant shift away from violence on the part of paramilitaries or the need to respond to that shift on the part of democratic parties. This created a more receptive climate for ideas that tried to theorize a political space beyond the simplicities of majoritarianism, either actual or potential. At one extreme, majoritarianism was the means by which all politics should be legitimated (the positional logic of unionism) and at the other, the end pending which all judgement should be deferred (the aspirational logic of nationalism). The principle of the 'majority' has a history, as Maitland had argued, and can be a humane and civilizing route to settling differences. But majority rule may not be civilizing in each and every instance and in these instances a more acceptable way could and should be found. This seemed particularly appropriate in the Northern Ireland case (see Burns 2003: 85). To recompose that specific problem in Hobbesian terms, the cult of majoritarianism, unionist or nationalist, has been the condition of war, actual or potential. The way to a rational peace was the abandonment of the cult. The Belfast Agreement was supposed to provide the means of transcending the majoritarian impulse, implying a balanced settlement under which the democratic expectation of political equality would no longer be thwarted by the mechanisms of democratic government (see Bourke 2003). The appeal of 're-thinking' politics was based on the assumed freedom that such a historized view of behaviour provided. For, if we do not have a nature but a history, it should be possible to change what history had bequeathed. Of course, there was disagreement over precisely what history *had* bequeathed and what *was* open to change (see Chapter 2). Nevertheless, the obvious moral and political bankruptcy of the IRA's campaign, a bankruptcy now obvious even to most of its leadership, served to confirm the general proposition that 'people should act on the basis of persuasion rather than coercion' (Vernon 1998: 307). Much of the new thinking on politics was an attempt to flesh out the meaning of that for a society changing from conflict to peace. How might we characterize the changes taking place? Again, it was a literary critic who conveyed the moment best.

Inwardness and outwardness

In 1994 Longley tried to capture the new political mood by describing the moment as a Northern 'turn', a concept softer than Gellner's notion of 'transition' but the implications of which could be just as radical. 'The Downing Street Declaration offers a framework – not a process towards some further (nationalist) goal but an unfolding of itself – that could potentially undo all the political and cultural damage that was done in the 1920s.' It represented for her an exercise in 'trust-building activities as a long-term project, with no foreclosed outcome'. The politics of Northern Ireland appeared to have become unexpectedly fluid, unusual in the 'stagnant pool' of traditional attitudes. The rigid, she thought, was now being separated from the flexible in rather surprising ways. If things were really now moving towards 'endgame', the most profound consequence would be that 'all bluffs will be called' (Longley 1994a: 1–13). Yet what was the character of this Northern 'turn' and what did it mean to call all bluffs? At first glance the idea of a Northern 'turn' appeared to be at odds with one of Longley's most celebrated images, that of Northern Ireland as a cultural corridor open at both ends. One end of the corridor connected it to the rest of the United Kingdom and the other connected it to the Republic of Ireland. The image of the open-ended cultural corridor has been Longley's personal contribution to undoing the political and cultural damage that was done in the 1920s. The openness of the corridor was a criticism of those who wished to close it off – republicans and nationalists who wanted to seal off the British end and loyalists and unionists who wanted to seal off the Irish end. Either political project violated the 'multi-dimensional anthropological jigsaw that makes the North so interesting' (Longley 1994a: 12). The 'turn' itself would have to be multi-dimensional as well. In other words, what was envisaged could not be the return of inwardness that would mean sinking back into the stagnant pool. Anyway, terms like inward and outward, parochial or international, applied 'to states of mind, to imaginative and intellectual horizons, not to domicile or content' (Longley 1999: 85). It had been the politicization of one dimension or another that had contributed to the intractability of the Northern Ireland problem.

Outwardness, for example, had become politicized in the sense that nationalism had remained fixated on the prospect of dissolving Northern Ireland. It was a 'failed political entity' and so the very real internal problems of creating a just and stable society could not be properly addressed until Irish unity was achieved. The solution to these problems was externalized and the description of nationalists 'looking to Dublin' was therefore an accurate one. There was something of the politics of the desert island about this, the horizon being scanned constantly for the Southern ship of state to rescue its people from the 'nationalist nightmare'. That is why the Anglo-Irish Agreement of 1985 appeared to be such a brilliant coup because it was an externalization of executive authority, made all the more attractive by the fact that its negotiation had excluded unionists and its operation had marginalized them. The common interaction of Northern constitutional nationalism and the Irish state within that Agreement's logic 'definitively replaced the old strategy of engagement with unionism by a new approach going over unionist heads' and this had had 'disastrous implications for any future attempt to build relationships and trust' (Wilson 1997: 188). Indeed, nationalists and republicans believed that the inherent dynamic of the Anglo-Irish Agreement was towards joint authority between Dublin and London, evacuating entirely political responsibility from Northern Ireland. Because it promised to alienate and marginalize unionists even further, this prospect helped to entice Sinn Fein towards politics. It also found its supporters within the British Labour Party. That logic was positional logic, the logic of winning and losing and, if the British Government had been persuaded of its merits, it would indeed have had calamitous implications for the building of relationships and trust *within* Northern Ireland. The externalizing project lived on in what later became known as the 'pan-nationalist front', a strategy designed to bring outside pressure on unionists to submit to a nationalist agenda. Unionism, of course, had its own form of politicized 'outwardness'. Ironically, the Anglo-Irish Agreement helped to consolidate a tendency within unionism that had always looked favourably on the externalization of Northern Ireland's problem through direct rule from London. This was the objective of unionist integrationism and it proposed that only when

Northern Ireland was governed in exactly the same way as the rest of the United Kingdom would the conditions for peace and stability be created. In the 1980s this project at least appeared to complement the dominant priorities of Mrs Thatcher's conservatism that were equally hostile to devolution and it sought to reinstate Northern Ireland into the main currents of British political life. If the model for nationalism was the model of an idealized Irish Republic, the model for integrationist unionism was the model of an idealized British parliamentary democracy. If the critique of the logic of nationalist outwardness was its design to ignore unionists, then the critique of integrationism was its design to ignore nationalists, taking refuge in a beautiful illusion. By trying to transcend the Northern Ireland crisis in London rather than engaging with nationalists in Belfast, critics argued that integrationism was no better than dogmatic nationalism. Here was another politics of the desert island, seeking the good ship *Britannia* in order to escape from an uncomfortable reality (see Aughey 1989: 134–5).

Other externalizations also suggested themselves and one of these was Europe. The European Community (subsequently Union) appealed to some nationalists in the SDLP, especially its leader John Hume. The idea of European integration became a touchstone of the progressiveness of the SDLP as a political party but unionists suspected that it was an idea with a very traditional subtext, namely the removal of the border and the unification of the island. It represented yet another attempt to evade dealing with unionism within Northern Ireland. 'To an extent, therefore, the European dimension has been a divisive, not a cohesive factor' (Kennedy 2000: 11). A more imaginatively comprehensive proposal was developed by Kearney and Wilson, one that identified the central weakness of the Anglo-Irish Agreement. By prioritizing the relationship between the two governments in London and Dublin, they argued, that Agreement had failed to address 'the key feature of the conflict identified by the literature – the internal relationship between the "two communities"'. Moreover, it had promoted a sterile debate over the merits and demerits of exclusive models of outwardness – joint authority and integration – and had deserted the inner ground of politics. Their overall vision was of a federal 'Europe of the regions' in which Northern Ireland would take its proper place. This would have the double advantage of helping nationalists come to terms pragmatically with the entity of Northern Ireland and permitting unionists to become less fearful of a wider (European) integration process (Kearney and Wilson 1994: 51–69). Unfortunately, as critics pointed out, this model did not (yet) conform to any external European reality since Europe was a construction of member states (Christiansen 2000: 33). However, it did have one significant merit in that the model acknowledged the multi-dimensionality of the Northern Ireland problem and that is really the issue to which Longley was calling attention.

On the one hand, that inwardness of the Northern Ireland problem, as identified by Longley, Smith and Cox, no longer appeared either appropriate or persuasive. On the other hand, that outwardness of the problem represented by the Anglo-Irish Agreement, as identified by Kearney and Wilson, was equally defective. What they excluded or ignored had to be reconstituted and this was the project that Longley intimated. It should be neither inward alone nor outward alone but involve the interpenetration of the two. For her at least, the open-endedness of the Northern Ireland cultural corridor was neither an invitation to escape (outwardness) nor an invitation to resist (inwardness) but an invitation to accept the reality of a complex condition. The goal of the political imagination, to paraphrase T. S. Eliot, was to return to Northern Ireland and know it for the first time – as a place both distinct and connected, both British and Irish, and requiring that reality to be appropriately institutionalized. This would mean undoing the damage of the 1920s, not in the sense of undoing partition but in the sense of undoing the positional logic of unionism and nationalism. The outward and the inward dimensions needed to be re-integrated, where the stability of internal arrangements would be dependent upon the stability of external relations and vice versa. The intellectual appeal of such a view was its comprehensiveness and its sense of symmetry and the purpose was to 'help the North to relax into a genuinely diverse sense of its own identity: to function, under whatever administrative format, as a shared region of these islands' (Longley 1994b: 195). This was an attractive vision but was it practically attainable? If such arrangements were indeed imaginable (as suddenly seemed possible by the mid-1990s), then quite a few bluffs were indeed about to be called.

One of the bluffs Longley identified was Hume's 'post-nationalism'. What she detected was a traditional nationalist subtext and this had to be addressed seriously in any future negotiations. What substance could be given to the fine words in Hume's familiar speeches about 'sharing this island'? What definite political relationship with unionism would emerge from this tension between post-nationalist and nationalist conceptions? The idea of a post-nationalist turn appeared to accommodate a variety of political options and to be a way of escaping the 'zero-sum game of exclusive "national identities"', allowing the citizens of Northern Ireland to owe 'differing degrees of allegiance to an expanding range of identifications: from regional townland, parish or province to national constitution (British or Irish or both) and, larger still, to the trans-national union of Europe'. It was only with the triumph of 'and' over 'either/or', only when the two communities 'acknowledged that they could be "British or Irish or both", that they could be united once again'. This would not happen as a unitary national identity, but 'as a multiple post-national one' (Kearney 2000: 22–5). However, as Ruane has shown in the best analysis of post-nationalist discourse in Ireland, even the sophistication of Kearney's vision could not avoid a persistent national inflection. In his view 'a dialectical model is more appropriate than a unilinear one in interpreting the changing relationship between nationalism and post-nationalism in contemporary

Europe'. Both discourses can co-exist and continue as 'two contradictory tendencies within a complex and dialectically integrated whole'. This was only to be expected given the emotional power of an 'Irish ideology firmly set in a nationalist mould' (Ruane 1994a: 191). The significant question would be the emphasis within that dialectic and this would have consequences for Northern nationalism as well as for Southern nationalism.

Like all forms of political discourse, Hume's post-nationalism was ambiguous and was addressed to different audiences. It was directed at traditional nationalists and republicans in Northern Ireland, allowing them to identify with an idea that appeared at one and the same time sufficiently progressive to satisfy the requirement of modernity and sufficiently like the old cause to re-assure them of the continuity of the 'Irish ideology'. It was directed at an international audience that preferred a style of politics that was not ethnically exclusive, irredentist, illiberal or undemocratic. It was also directed at a unionist audience to suggest that the project of post-nationalism was less threatening and more accommodating than the old one (see McCall 1999: 95–122). Longley, however, suspected that Hume, with his all-Ireland and European options, was uninterested in internal Northern politics. In this form, post-nationalism was yet another externalization of the problem, a turning away from the North rather than a 'Northern turn'. Her suspicion was confirmed by Trimble's remark about the Brooke/ Mayhew Talks. The reason why there was no agreement in 1992, according to Trimble, was because Hume had told Jim Molyneaux, then leader of the Ulster Unionist Party, 'You must realize my problem Jim, I cannot agree to a system of administration in Northern Ireland based on an elected body' (Trimble 2001: 45). The irony was that Hume's later development of a common position with Adams threatened the central role that Hume had created for the SDLP in the 1980s. Under the Anglo-Irish Agreement it had, through Dublin, influence on policy making within Northern Ireland and it was no wonder that the advantages of this policy of 'outwardness' reminded some in the party that they had no ideological commitment to devolution. The embrace of the Sinn Fein leader helped to displace the SDLP and to move Sinn Fein centre-stage. Though the objective of both Hume and Adams may have been originally to strengthen the outwardness of Anglo-Irish structures towards joint authority, the practical requirements of the peace process brought devolution back into the frame.

Here was another delightful irony that Longley pointed out. The 'only place in Ireland where Sinn Fein had a chance of real political influence on behalf of its people (if violence is renounced, etc.) is in Belfast and in the UK' (Longley 1994a: 5). Once Sinn Fein recognized that, and if an elected body were to be established in Northern Ireland, then even the SDLP's electoral predominance within nationalism would be threatened. Again, as Longley observed, the fact that the SDLP could identify 80 per cent common ground between republicans and constitutional nationalists was not significant. 'It was ever thus. The remaining 20% is the hard bit.' This was the narrow percentile on which the bluff of both the SDLP and Sinn Fein would be called. If the IRA's military campaign had really ended was the consequence to be a constitutionalizing of republicanism or was it to be a republicanizing of constitutional nationalism? Or if, as was more likely, the new situation would bring forth some combination of the two would this modified politics encourage or undermine a stable agreement with unionism? The prospect was and remains uncertain.

The attitude of Southern nationalism, as Ruane has shown, also remained complex. However, new ways of thinking imaginatively about Northern Ireland had been in evidence since the predictable proposals of the New Ireland Forum in 1984. It has been argued that the project to reconstitute a sense of 'Irishness', exemplified by the cultural venture Field Day, was 'eloquent, if ironic, witness to the degree to which popular consciousness had become too fragmented and diverse to be reconfined within any type of national project' (Hazelkorn and Patterson 1994: 59). In her account of civic republicanism, Honohan captures in summary that sort of diversity in Southern politics. If the civic republican idea of recognition demanded an openness to the values and identity of others, she was conscious that in Ireland the politics of recognition had historically served to reflect and to reinforce 'existing shared values and identity' in an exclusive manner. Partition was not the cause of this but was its consequence (Honohan 2002: 258). In her view, civic republicanism offered an alternative to an individualistic liberal conception of politics on the one hand and to an ethnic nationalist conception on the other. Civic interdependence rather than cultural community would constitute the basis of political solidarity and so transcend the exclusive claims of Southern nationalism (Honohan 2002: 281–9). Here was an alternative to old-style nationalism that could make the South more open to the complexity of Northern Ireland politics. And this alternative was possible because old-style faith and fatherland, irredentist nationalism, no longer represented adequately public attitudes. In other words, Honohan was writing out of a Southern context in which, like Balfour's House of Commons, intense political debate on particulars could take place because of shared understandings. This has been an achievement of Irish democracy and, ironically, probably depends on the security of an Irish national identity within the boundaries of the Irish Republic (see British Council Ireland 2003). Those who complained about the partitionist mentality of people in the Irish Republic appeared to miss the point that this was an important condition of Southern stability. Intelligently mobilized, it had also the potential to secure stability in Northern Ireland.

Another important bluff to be called would be on the unionist side. Unlike post-nationalism there was little talk of 'post-unionism'. However, in the 1990s a 'new unionism' became voguish, especially in the ranks of the UUP. It had developed as a response to the Downing Street Declaration and recognized the potential it provided for unionism to get beyond the negativism that had resulted from rejection of the Anglo-Irish Agreement.

This new unionism involved a number of distinctions. A distinction was made between acknowledging an Irishness of place that could be shared by both Protestants and Catholics and a politicized Irishness determined to destroy the entity of Northern Ireland. A further distinction was made between self-government for the people of Northern Ireland, a general movement throughout Western European democracies to devolve power, and a process of Irish self-determination leading to an attrition of the British connection. Finally, a distinction was made between practical cross-border cooperation between the two parts of the island and cooperation driven ideologically by a nationalist agenda. Furthermore, three key propositions were invoked. The first was that the principle of consent should govern the political arrangements within Northern Ireland and those between North and South. The second was that nationalists must abandon the 'Sicilian uncle' option, the idea that the British Government should be a persuader for Irish unity. The third was that in order to secure the proper atmosphere for relationships on the island the Irish Government should remove the territorial claim in Articles 2 and 3 of its Constitution. Here was a genuine concern to reconnect the parts of the unionist location – to return democratic authority to Northern Ireland, to reconstitute cordial links with the British Government and to end what Trimble later called 'the cold war' on the island between North and South. Most of these points had been raised during the Brooke/Mayhew Talks of 1991/2 but they now took on a new importance (Seldon 1997: 412–15). As Trimble had admitted, the approach of the UUP to negotiations in the past had been tactical rather than strategic (see Chapter 4). Not only would this have to change – ultimately the bluff would be called if a deal seemed within reach – but the UUP leadership would itself have to call the bluff of their own opponents within unionism. These critics understood the emerging dynamic of the peace process to be far from a balanced accommodation between unionism and nationalism in Northern Ireland. Experience obliged them to believe that republicans certainly and nationalists probably did not want a stable settlement. On the contrary, they assumed that republicans, if they could not force unionists into Irish unity, and nationalists, if they could not manoeuvre unionists into Irish unity, desired only a dispensation that would erode further Northern Ireland's position within the United Kingdom. In this sense, there certainly could be no loserless endings. Someone had to give and it was suspected that for reasons of power politics – the IRA had the weaponry – the someone would be them. This played on the old notion of sacrifice that had such a powerful emotional resonance within unionist politics. The only problem was that it appeared to provide no way out of the stagnant pond.

How could a workable, institutional reconnection of the multi-dimensional aspects of Northern Ireland's politics be achieved? Two models suggested themselves. The first was a radical model of democratic transformation that attempted to draw upon new ideas of political association. The second was a more conservative model of historic compromise that continued to draw upon older ideas of political accommodation. The first of these models is given greater prominence here since the institutional outworking of the second is explored systematically in Chapter 6.

Democratic transformation

In a parody of Virginia Woolf's ironic claim that around 1910 human nature changed, John Dryzek proposed that around 1990 'the theory of democracy took a definite deliberative turn'. This was a shift from merely liberal concerns such as voting and the representation of interests to locating democratic legitimacy in the 'ability of all individuals subject to a collective decision to engage in authentic deliberation about that decision' (Dryzek 2000: v). Deliberative democracy, he thought, should involve a process of open and uncoerced participation of citizens in political debate with the objective of seeking consensus through collective discussion. However, it is the process rather than the consensus that is desirable. In other words, one of the recent concerns of democratic theorizing has been with 'process and procedure, not merely with substantive outcomes'. As Goodin explained, contemporary democratic theory is not interested in getting the right answer in the wrong way and, contrary to the concern of political science, the 'bottom line is not the be all and end all, from a democratic perspective'. In other words, there should be a qualitative rather than a quantitative emphasis in modern democracy for merely 'counting votes is a poor substitute for deliberating together about what really is the right thing to do'. There is a further aspiration to encourage 'communities of enlightenment', that mix of self-interest and interest in the well-being of others, that might successfully marginalize those 'communities of darkness', that mix of exclusive commitment and threat at the heart of political violence, actual or potential (Goodin 2003: 9–13, 46–7). The keywords of this democratic idea have been inclusion, deliberation, participation, empowerment and civic activism. This implied an historical shift from the quantitative democracy appropriate to an industrialized and homogenized society to the qualitative democracy appropriate to a post-industrial, post-national and pluralistic society. Cooke has possibly conveyed best and most concisely these sorts of aspiration by describing them as being congruent 'with whom we are' and related them to a new democratic self-understanding on the part of citizens. The new self-understanding demanded 'rational accountability' since political authority could no longer rely on deference or on customary respect (Cooke 2000: 967). Since we are, or think ourselves to be, better educated, better informed, more sophisticated, more critical and intelligent consumers of ideas than previous generations, then the activity of politics must be made to correspond with our sense of 'whom we are'. Cooke's explanation is a persuasive one, though accepting it does not mean that people, as individuals or as communities, feel any less powerless than they did before. Living in a world in which rational accountability and justification are primary public virtues may actually make people feel even more dissatisfied if the demand for 'rational accountability' cannot be adequately met because of lies, concealment, bad faith and 'spin' (see Chapter 9). None the less, the expectation remains and makes demands on politics.

These difficulties notwithstanding, the objective should be to include as many interests as possible in public deliberation, especially drawing upon politicized interests in civil society (Dryzek 1990: 18–19; Dryzek and List 2003). The radical motivation here is to develop what Young calls 'deep democracy', an engagement of citizens with one another 'in the attempt to win their hearts and minds, that is, their assent'. This should always be an active and self-critical struggle to widen the conversation. 'Fair, open, and inclusive democratic processes should attend to such disadvantages and institutionalize compensatory mechanisms for exclusion.' The democratic procedures proposed would distinguish between 'normatively legitimate outcomes' and those that result from 'the will of the powerful'. They would also help to distinguish between 'subjective preferences and more objective judgements of justice or rightness' (Young 2002: 50–1). The deliberative approach represents an attempt to make democracy operate explicitly on the basis of what it implicitly is for modern *people like us* and it is a theory with consequences.

This is an imaginative ideal and an important one but the difficulties with it are obvious even to its advocates. For example, Festenstein (2000) notes the political objection that such a process 'depends upon the existence of an attitude on the part of citizens which it is not plausible to assume'. Those citizens supposed by this model are paragons of political virtue who take other views seriously, are always considerate, think beyond their own interests, and are always willing to subordinate their paltry concerns to the common good. They are no longer self-centred but de-centred. To this objection, Festenstein admits he has only the feeble excuse that all democratic theory assumes some ideal of the citizen. However, not all democratic theories entail such rigorous requirements for inclusive discussion. As one critic observed, what is often 'left out of this decision-making model is the decision' itself and this implies a deficiency in the theory's grasp of politics (Scholz 2002: 747). In short, it threatens to be all process and no product, precisely the very problem of all deliberation on Northern Ireland in the past.

Moreover, it also assumes a reciprocal relationship of speaking and listening that is itself problematic. Deliberative theorists address the question of guaranteeing a free and equal expression of opinions. But guaranteeing everyone a voice is not the same as guaranteeing everyone a hearing (Goodin 2003: 178). Some may not be listened to, not because what they say is unimportant, but because what they say is not congenial to those who decide what *is* important. In other words, the politically incorrect can speak all they like but they will only be listened to when they say what is required of them. There is an even more fundamental difficulty. As Oscar

Wilde so sweetly put it: 'I delight in talking politics. I talk them all day. But I can't bear listening to them' (cited in Gambetta 1998: 19). That disposition is all the more likely in a culture that Gambetta describes as discursively 'machismo', where no one listens either because they already know what the other side has to say or because no matter what the other side has to say nothing can possibly be a surprise. Those who have spent a dispiriting hour listening to the discursive exchanges between listeners and host on BBC Northern Ireland's radio broadcast *Talkback* will recognize the truth of that observation. It was a problem at the very centre of the Saville Inquiry into the events of Bloody Sunday. A journalist with the *Derry Journal*, unaware of the irony, proposed that there was a huge chasm between the Saville Inquiry's 'view of the events of Bloody Sunday, and the view held by the people of Derry' (MacDermott 2003). In other words, the people of Derry knew the 'truth' and the purpose of the Inquiry was to confirm that 'truth'. When the Inquiry's truth was at odds with the version of the people of Derry, then it was better that it was not heard at all. Dialogic rationality may misunderstand matters by misdescribing one part of democratic politics as the whole of politics. No matter how essential that half may be in sustaining a legitimate order, to place too heavy an expectation on dialogue may actually foster public cynicism when dialogue (alone) cannot deliver. Dialogic rationality may overreach itself, claiming, as one critic observed, 'philosophical resources which turn out to be impotent in the resolution of conspicuous and divisive disagreement' (Knowles 2001: 341).

Indeed, in a penetrating critique of what she appropriately called 'the civic faith', Canovan observed that, ironically, there is at work an idea that is quite insensitive to modern conditions. Earlier civic republicans always thought of citizens 'as creatures of artifice' who were 'formed through patriotic education' and republicans 'were prepared to go to disconcerting lengths to achieve this'. Shared political principles and values must be agreed (to make authoritative decisions) and serious efforts are also needed to be made to ensure that all citizens respect them. Canovan concluded with the provocative remark that just as 'earlier generations of political theorists took for granted that states had an interest in the religious beliefs of their citizens, so the patriotic polity seems also to be envisaged as a kind of confessional state' (Canovan 2000: 420). The civic plea for tolerance, openness and inclusion may come at the heavy price of illiberal political manipulation and educational engineering. People in Northern Ireland, it seemed, would need to be 'transformed' through dialogue almost in the way in which Christians become 'born again'. In the new Northern Ireland people would 'not simply "influence" one another but rather "remake" one another' and in the process of remaking they would be deprived of 'any independent stance from which to disagree' with rational civic virtue. As Goodin concluded, that is not really what we think democracy is about (1998: 557). The danger is that our search for deliberative rationality may end up in the most crushing conformity and we find these tendencies in

Porter's *The Elusive Quest* (2003), a catechism of the civic faith. In his alternative Northern Ireland, politics does become a secular religion. After suffering on the cross of the Troubles, the people of Northern Ireland must be born again in the light of 'strong reconciliation'. Unfortunately, Porter can give no indication as to how the transformation he requires can be brought about and the argument dissolves into a sort of blessing on those deemed politically correct (republicans) and an anathema against those who are deemed to be politically incorrect (unionists). Political thinking, of course, can be at one and the same time a general theoretical argument *and* a move in a political game (Canovan 2000: 432). Porter's philosophical sophistication was such a political move and his strategy was part of a shadow game, conjuring a vision of democratic transformation that claimed an authority it could not substantiate. This is not unique to Northern Ireland and neither is it new. As Montesquieu once observed of such theorizing: 'It has been well said that if triangles had a god, they would give him three sides' (Montesquieu 1993: 124). This was also true of O'Neill's philosophical argument. He used the discourse theory of Habermas to argue, for example, that only joint British–Irish sovereignty provided equal recognition for nationalists in Northern Ireland and that the dispute over the Orange Order march at Drumcree could only be decided rationally in favour of the nationalist residents (O'Neill 2001, 2000). Like the triangle's God of three sides, here was a universal theory that in every particular spoke in favour of nationalism and against unionism, a point not missed by his critics (Newey 2002; Little 2003). In Porter's case, it begins in philosophy and ends in mysticism while in O'Neill's case, it begins in reason and ends in politics. To argue that your political opponents are wrong is one thing. To argue that they are unable to present their arguments in a fully moral or rational way is quite another (Hampton 1995: 309). Not only is this an exercise in philosophical hubris; it suggests, contrary to either Porter's or O'Neill's celebration of dialogue, that one responds to opponents not by reasoning with them but by re-educating them. To those who are on the other side or sides in the political game, who are deemed to be politically incorrect or who dissent, not from the values but from the ethical or logical conclusion, such use of reason is not only threatening but also has the whiff of authoritarianism about it.

Whether such civic theory is persuasive or not, it did serve very practical purposes in Northern Ireland. The inclusive principles of deliberation appealed to those who were active and employed by organizations in what is known as civic or civil society. By the 1990s those in this (albeit very diverse) sector in Northern Ireland had developed a self-confidence about 'who they are'. This self-confidence was directly related to the fact that civil society was *not* party politics and was *not* associated with traditional conflict and closed forms of morality. Civil society, by contrast, understood itself to be progressive, open and consensual. This phenomenon was observable in all developed states and had been the inspiration of the 'velvet revolution' in

Czechoslovakia. The righteous distinction between party politics and civil politics, however, was internal to the ideology of civil society rather than a distinction in fact (Tester 1992: 146). In the case of Northern Ireland this ideological distinction was all the more acute because party politics was judged to have failed. As a consequence, the self-esteem of civil society was enhanced by the benign myth – an elaboration of a partial truth – that the fabric of society in the Troubles had been held together by networks of community associations. It was these groups, so the argument went, that had for 25 years 'negotiated the politics of everyday life with non-elected, locally based officials' and it was these groups that had helped to persuade politicians to move 'from positions in which compromise was construed as weakness to a negotiated settlement' (Meehan 1999: 28). Of course, what this myth wrote out of the account was the vital contribution of policemen and soldiers to maintaining a sufficient level of order and security for 'the politics of everyday life' to function. That truth did not correspond with the ideological predispositions of some civil society advocates since it was the success of the police and army (and their agents) against republican and loyalist paramilitarism that really created the conditions for a negotiated settlement. The self-esteem of 'community politics' depended on ignoring the framework of legitimate force. Not only was this self-esteem a factor in the emergence of the myth. The size of this sector and its pervasiveness was also striking. There are 5,000 voluntary and community organizations in Northern Ireland employing about 35,000 staff with a gross income of £514 million. As one commentator put it, this institutional part of civil society is 'a heavy hitter, and it must be counted in with the big boys' (Nolan 2000: 30). Not surprisingly, there was a reluctance of those employed in it to see the traditional parties returning to power and usurping entirely the political role of civil institutions. This was intensified by the belief that their own values were more consistent with the sort of future most people appeared to want than the conflictual values of party competition.

As a consequence of its claim to have negotiated the politics of everyday life, civil society presented an idealized democratic, bottom-up alternative of power-sharing to the traditional elitist, consociational, top-down model of power-sharing. Moreover, the consociational model was open to criticism for lacking accountability, encouraging secret deals, for being rigidly divisive and inhibiting the emergence of alternative forms of social cooperation (Spencer and Wollman 2002: 186–7). In deliberative scope a civil society model seemed much more inclusive, inventive and dynamic than the predictable stand-offs of the parties. Many of the suggestions for 'reconstituting politics' around the dynamics of civil society were well considered and made a significant contribution to intelligent political discussion. For example, the potential of civic energy was proclaimed in the Opsahl Report on Northern Ireland, set up by the independent citizens' group Initiative '92. The objective of the initiative, as the chair of the commission, Torkel Opsahl indicated, was to give the people of Northern Ireland 'an opportunity to express themselves, to overcome their sense of impotence and helplessness after nearly a quarter century of political violence and deadlock' (Pollak 1993: 3). Between May 1992 and June 1993, the Opsahl Commission received 554 submissions from over 3,000 people and held public meetings across Northern Ireland. Many of the proposals set out in the Opsahl Report were controversial at the time but later became part of a wider political consensus. However, the recommendations went beyond the strictly political and constitutional and expressed what the Report called the 'hidden agendas' of social and economic concern. As one of the key thinkers behind Initiative '92 argued, no future political settlement could possibly stick if groups in civil society were not bound into the process (Wilson 1993: 5). That was a central proposition that motivated some of the more intelligent reflections on the weakness of Northern Ireland's political class and the case for a wider democratic input (Democratic Dialogue 1997).

However, the expectations of civil society were sometimes less inclusive than they seemed. They involved unspoken exclusions (no Orange Order for example) and the connection between partisan interest and common good was often conveniently elided (Dixon 1997). Furthermore, 'community deliberation' in some cases could mean political manipulation and all manifestations of community activity were not necessarily the virtuous engagements of an active citizenry (O'Doherty 1995: 12–13). In Northern Ireland, the boundary between civil and uncivil deliberation was sometimes hard to define, instances of paramilitary control were particularly insidious, and the outcomes did not always conform to the positive expectations of deliberative theorists (Whitehead 1997: 107). If we accept Cooke's proposition, then, who we are as a people can also, at the extremes, mean the crudest forms of communal assertion and sectarian confrontation. In this case, the principle of inclusion in Northern Ireland was indeed open to challenge for it implied a very different idea of deliberation – an offer that cannot be refused (a whole culture of Sicilian uncles). This was not a civic principle but a militaristic one where the demand for inclusion brought with it a veiled threat of violence. If one's mandate was the silence of the guns, the gun remained a central part of the mandate. This did not go unnoticed by critics and created a moral crisis at the very centre of the peace process and of the Belfast Agreement (McCartney 2001: 154). Inclusion, one of the aspirations of democratic transformation, was to become one of the difficulties of making the Belfast Agreement function (see Chapter 10).

Historic compromise

If antagonistic forces will not disappear in political life it may be possible to conceive of them being 'convertible' and developing a code of 'civility'. That notion designates a different model for Northern Ireland that can be called the model of 'historic compromise'. The idea of an historic compromise in Northern Ireland between unionism and nationalism starts from a very different understanding of politics than the model of democratic transformation and, as a consequence, has more modest expectations of what an agreement can deliver. The 'historic compromise' in Northern Ireland has been associated with the theory of consociationalism and the process of its achievement through inter-party talks. Consociationalism proposes that in deeply divided societies it is only realistic to accept group differences and try to construct stable institutions that can accommodate those differences (see McGarry and O'Leary 1995). The consociational model has been criticized for its elitism, basing its hopes on bargains between party leaderships; for its conservatism, being concerned to stabilize ethnic blocks rather than to transform them; and for its exclusiveness, ignoring the interests of those who do not fit or refuse to fit into the two communities' culture of Northern Ireland politics (Dixon 1997; Taylor 2001: 37–48). Its strength has been its understanding of agency. It is obvious to the consociationalist who is to deliver the deal, who is responsible for maintaining it and what sort of institutional arrangements are appropriate. Its weakness has been the problem of sustainability. Just as the model of democratic transformation makes large assumptions about the rationality of the parties to an agreement, so too does the model of historic compromise make large assumptions about the objectives of the parties to an agreement.

The idea of historic compromise begins by restoring that aspect of politics which deliberative democracy sometimes ignores but of which Johnson usefully reminds us by reference to a passage in Mannheim's *Ideology and Utopia*. For Mannheim, political argument seeks not only to be in the right but also 'to demolish the basis of its opponent's social and intellectual existence'. It involves a struggle for social predominance, an attack on the self-confidence of the opponent, even a dynamic towards psychic annihilation. Unlike the presumption of deliberation, here the process is nothing and the outcome is everything. Undermining your opponent's theories is the way in which you undermine your opponent's political position (cited in Johnson 1998: 165). It is, in other words, the familiar zero-sum game of winning and losing, of assessing the means according to the end desired. It is a view of politics as decision not as discussion. For example, Schmitt held the uncompromising view that a political decision is usually the outcome of a struggle between alternatives and one that could not necessarily be supported by 'reason'. Real politics actually starts where communication leaves off and the ideal of endless conversation is an escape from the requirement of political decision. The reluctance to decide in favour of the 'eternal play of potential outcomes' was an intellectual failing (Kelly 2000: 38; see also Slagstad 1988). For Schmitt, then, all political concepts have a polemical meaning and a 'word or expression can simultaneously be reflex, signal, password, and weapon in a hostile confrontation' (Schmitt 1976: 31). The 'peace process' itself is a good example. Unionists feared that the meaning of peace would be redescribed by the manoeuvres of republicans, nationalists and the Irish Government in terms that would undermine their position (McCartney 2001: 119–36). Republicans equally feared that the requirements for peace would be described in terms that would undermine or weaken their position (Moloney 2002: 455–79). In both cases, their fears were understandable ones. Neither wanted their political objectives to be re-defined in ways that disadvantaged them. It is possible to go quite some way towards interpreting the Northern Ireland problem in Schmittian terms, one in which the *political* relationship between unionist and nationalist communities is that of friend and enemy (Aughey 1997b). This relationship need not necessarily entail widespread inter-communal conflict. It need merely acknowledge that there does exist the possibility of such conflict and recognize that every political utterance is usually judged according to source – friend or enemy? – and according to purpose – friendly or hostile? The political intensity of the friend/enemy relationship explains why those who refuse to define themselves as either unionist or nationalist continue to find it difficult to get a hearing. More to the point, it helps to explain why disagreements *within* communities about the nature of the struggle *between* the communities tend to be so bitter, something that defined both the unionist and the nationalist response to the peace process. Schmitt reminds us that struggle is normal in politics and should not be seen as some failure of 'strong reconciliation'. His work warns against the hypocrisy that 'lies in seeking to de-politicize what is inescapably political' or in disguising a political move 'under the cloak of moral rectitude' (Bellamy and Baehr 1993: 181).

Therefore, once we accept the impossibility of a world without antagonism, then we need to think hard about those conditions that can sustain a pluralistic democratic order. The friend/enemy distinction in this sense means the emergence of a political community from political violence in which 'the opponent should be considered not as an enemy to be destroyed, but as an adversary whose existence is legitimate and must be tolerated'. The struggle of friend and enemy is displaced but not removed and is reconstituted within freshly negotiated rules of the game. Only those who do not accept these rules 'thereby exclude themselves from the political community' (Mouffe 1993: 4). The objective lies 'in finding a way of establishing the us/them discrimination which is compatible with the pluralist character of contemporary democracy' (Mouffe 2000: 126). This intimation of historic compromise has provided some interesting insights into the Northern Ireland problem. Little, for example, has argued in Northern Ireland's case for the local value of 'contingent, imperfect settlements rather than rational agreements'. If a consensus is at all imaginable under the terms of the Agreement it will be a 'conflictual consensus', one that 'leaves space for dissension about the outcomes' of the decision-making procedures. The real task is 'to think about how we manage and contain conflict rather than dreaming up impractical forms of resolving it' like those found in the literature of democratic transformation

(Little 2003: 386–8). Whatever our philosophical or moral understanding, the divisions in Northern Ireland are unlikely to vanish.

This is the sort of 'historic compromise' that John Gray has called *modus vivendi*, a limited style of politics in which toleration is valued as a condition of peace. He is critical of those strong reconciliators who condemn the sort of shabby compromises reached by political negotiation or who hold that the pursuit of *modus vivendi* is morally suspect. There is, he argues, no 'rational' solution and once that illusion is discarded, then we are confronted with a Hobbesian choice. 'There are better and worse compromises, and some that are thoroughly bad; but what all have in common is that they involve reaching an accommodation among opposed ideals and interests.' Gray's conclusion is an uncomfortable one for many people. 'If such accommodations are condemned by "morality" so much the worse for "morality"' (Gray 2000: 133–4; see also Gray 1998: 159–63). It can, of course, be so much the worse for 'accommodation' and 'historic compromise' if the settlement arrived at is such an offence to popular morality that support for common institutions is undermined. The appeal of historic compromise is its apparent realism. Unfortunately, that very realism can often be its undoing. And some would claim that has been the fate of the Belfast Agreement. Those claims are discussed in Part III of this book.

Conclusion

Old ideas, of course, have immense powers of survival and reconstitution. As Dryzek admitted in a critical aside on the Belfast Agreement, it had resulted from a process that was far from being a 'paragon of deliberation'. That was true. Nevertheless, Dryzek was confident enough to declare that 'the deliberative component is also undeniable, and one product of that is that traditionally hostile actors began to learn how to live together despite continuing deep divisions'. That was also true. In the manner of Hegel's remark that you could not learn to swim without getting wet, Dryzek concluded that the only way to learn civility was through the process of deliberation (Dryzek 2000: 41–2, 169). That is a properly modest judgement. Unfortunately, such reflections did not answer the Northern Ireland question but raised further ones. Was inclusion of fundamentally opposed political parties in government a practical strategy? Could one trust the integrity of political dialogue? Could functioning decision-making procedures endure a conflictual consensus? If the space for dissension about outcomes remained wide would there ever develop the trust required for agreement about outcomes? Could an historic compromise on such a basis be anything other than a fragile and unstable one? When the negotiations for the Belfast Agreement were reaching their conclusion those questions were as far from a clear answer as they had ever been. The negotiation of the Agreement at least provided new opportunities for old enemies to practise the political art of civility and the outline of that Agreement is the subject of the next chapter.

6 The Belfast Agreement: archaeology and exposition

At the beginning of the 1990s few expected that by the end of the decade there would be a formal agreement on the government of Northern Ireland. The obstacles rather than the paths to a settlement were much easier to identify (Evans and O'Leary 2000: 98; O'Leary 1989). Writing in 1992 O'Leary had reported on the bleak assessment of 'seasoned observers' who spoke of a 'third generation' of republican and loyalist paramilitaries willing to continue the violence of their predecessors. He had concluded that ethnic antagonisms 'are presently being reforged rather than resolved, and despair is widespread that the cruel conflict will continue, apparently with no end in sight' (O'Leary 1992: 170). O'Leary's article is interesting but not because of his widely shared pessimism about the prospects of agreement between even the constitutional parties. It is interesting for two reasons. The first is his reasonably accurate predictions about the broad shape that any eventual agreement would take. The second is the questions he then asked of that prospective agreement. O'Leary argued that the most likely constitutional package would include devolved partnership government in Northern Ireland, modification of Articles 2 and 3 of the Republic's Constitution and *two* Irish dimensions – continued British-Irish inter-governmental co-operation and new arrangements between Belfast and Dublin. This package he envisaged being put to the 'peoples' of Ireland, North and South, in two concurrent referenda. O'Leary then asked three subsequent questions. If this balanced constitutional settlement accurately expressed the limits of the attainable, was it really necessary to go through the elaborate motions of talks, and talks about talks, between the Northern Ireland parties? If the only acceptable outcome was known in advance, was it really wise to allow the parties themselves to negotiate proposals that they knew to be unacceptable and, as a consequence, to foster an atmosphere of political frustration and futility? Would it not be more sensible, as some local commentators had also proposed, for the two governments to outline the parameters of a settlement and to encourage the parties to negotiate within those parameters? O'Leary's article was written at that point when the Brooke/Mayhew Talks of 1991/2 were about to break up without success and just before that political process was to be absorbed into the wider peace process including Sinn Fein and the loyalist parties (O'Leary 1992: 169). This step change meant that O'Leary's strategic proposal became inconceivable for the political balance shifted even further along the negotiation axis and intensified the political and the assumed therapeutic significance of dialogue. However, he was not alone in his scepticism about the likelihood of inter-party compromise. As one insightful commentator put it, unionists and nationalists appeared to be locked into their 'competing communal majoritarianisms'. Since the local political leadership had failed only 'a proactive drive for a settlement by the two governments, mobilising what is left of sympathetic opinion in Northern Ireland, can offer any hope of success' (Wilson 1997: 192).

Nevertheless, O'Leary's point did touch on one of the crucial issues discussed in the previous chapter. Politics is about decision and not just about discussion. The rehearsal of alternatives from Irish unity to full integration into the United Kingdom might have been an interesting academic exercise, but it was no longer realistic or decisive politics (Cox 1991: 525–8). By the mid-1990s no one bothered any longer because there appeared to be 'only one game in town' and that was the peace process. It was vital, of course, for the parties (to use the jargon of the time) to 'feel ownership' of the process and to deliberate the content of any agreement. It was also vital for a decisive shape to be given to the process and a decisive impetus to be given towards a settlement. O'Leary had identified the only agents capable of doing this and they were the two sovereign governments. To understand the Belfast Agreement as the outcome of a deliberative process between the parties, then, would be only a half truth. Crucial strategic decisions were also made by the British and Irish Governments in the Downing Street Declaration of 1993, the Frameworks Document of 1995, the Propositions on Heads of Agreement of January 1998 and the Mitchell Document of April 1998 (see Hennessey 2000 and de Breadun 2001). These documents were not divorced from assessments of what the parties had discussed, but in each case they laid out the best guess of the two governments about what was acceptable and so fulfilled the O'Leary principle (if not quite in the manner he originally envisaged. His 'decisionist' strategy was directed mainly against the unionists and intended to compel them to come to terms. In the end the two governments acted in a more even-handed manner). In the British case, this represented a long-standing bipartisanship between government and opposition. In the Irish case, this represented a convergence of party positions on Northern Ireland over a number of years, a reappraisal of Northern Ireland policy that predated the negotiations on the Belfast Agreement of 1998 (Ivory 1999: 102). The positions adopted by London and Dublin reflected their respective public opinions. In short 'continued disinterest by British public opinion coupled with a new flexibility in Irish public opinion' had created the scope for a resolution of the Northern Ireland problem (Hayes and McAllister 1996: 80). To accept the interrelationship between sovereign initiative and party deliberation is simply to acknowledge political realism.

The archaeology of the Agreement

For example, in his assessment of theoretical contributions to understanding Northern Ireland, Burke accepted that while in academia a plurality of legitimate interpretations can be reconciled, 'in politics decisions have to be made'. In the case of the Belfast Agreement, 'a decision has already been made' and not only, as Burke assumed, as a consequence of deliberation but also as a result of prior decisions by London and Dublin (Burke 1999: 17). When reflecting on the Belfast Agreement, Dryzek was equally realistic. He asked himself whether deliberation uncovered limits that already existed or whether possibilities were created in the process of deliberation itself. He concluded that 'it is hard if not impossible to tell the difference; and quite possibly some mixture of discovery and creation occurs' (Dryzek 2000: 42). It would not be overly distorting the facts to suggest that the limits were the conclusions already reached by the British and Irish Governments and the possibilities were what the parties to negotiation were additionally able to extract. This political interrelationship had a long pedigree. As Seamus Mallon, former deputy leader of the SDLP, famously put it, the Belfast Agreement was 'Sunningdale for slow learners'. That celebrated remark could not possibly mean that 1998 was just like 1974, because the balance of political forces was so very different. A 'slowly learned' Sunningdale should mean a common understanding of what the principles and the purpose of partnership government involved. That there was such an understanding was far from clear in the period leading up to the Agreement and it has been far from clear ever since. Indeed, it was argued at the time that the Belfast Agreement could be less a case of 'Sunningdale for slow learners' as 'Sunningdale in slow motion'. In other words, despite the fact that in 1998, unlike 1974, all the threads of the political settlement appeared to be woven together, there was just as strong a possibility of things unravelling over time (Bew and Gillespie 1999: 403–8).

Indeed, in a critique of the peace process, English questioned the central deliberative principle that if the parties were talking, then understanding and progress would rationally emerge. He took the more sceptical view that talks were 'as likely to be a symptom of a conflict ending as they are to be the cause'. Unfortunately, he found it difficult to sustain the view that there existed any solution that could be implemented (English 1997: 24–5). English made a distinction between the intellectual and the political. On the one hand, he was not persuaded by arguments suggesting it was possible to resolve the Northern Ireland conflict. On the other hand, he left open the possibility that a political arrangement to manage the conflict could be reached. These two positions are not irreconcilable. There was no necessary connection between logic and calculated political moves. English's scepticism has proved to be well founded. Moreover, his observation that talks were more likely to be a symptom of the end rather than a cause implied that a settlement would probably be as much a product of decision as it would be one of deliberation, since the peace process already presupposed a willingness to end violence. There was certainly no inevitability about a positive outcome but the engagement itself made such an outcome more likely. And if such an outcome was now more likely, then its shape would be that of an historic compromise rather than that of a radical transformation. That appeared to be the dynamic within republicanism. According to Moloney, the peace process had already been 'precooked' and it was 'an exercise in management towards an already decided outcome' (Moloney 2002: xvi; see also McIntyre 1995: 113). There was less clarity about the dynamic within loyalism but a desire to find an alternative was also detectable (Schulze 1997: 97–100). Strategy may be defeated by tactics, however, and the incompatibility between contesting tactics and conflicting strategies sustained profound public scepticism about what was happening.

For example, that the IRA's first ceasefire lasted only from August 1994 to February 1996 confirmed the suspicions of unionist voters that republicans were not serious. It struck one nationalist commentator as rather ironic that 'those who had been engaged in the "Long War" of the previous quarter-century ran out of patience after only seventeen months of comparative peace' (Arthur 1996b: 430–1). Even when re-admitted to the process after a new IRA ceasefire on 19 July 1997, republicans contributed little of substance to the talks about devolution. This has been described in one commentary as 'self-exclusion' and in another as an 'inert role' because whatever proposals Sinn Fein did submit were irrelevant. Republicans appeared incapable of moving beyond maximalist requirements and that seemed to bode ill for any workable administration (Hazleton 2000: 31; see also Horowitz 2002: 202). Since republicans did not accept the principle of consent it was assumed that the purpose of Sinn Fein's role in the talks was a purely tactical move to divide further an already divided unionism and to weaken the position of the leader of the Ulster Unionists, David Trimble (McDonald 2000: 186). Moreover, the permanence of the IRA's ceasefire was ambiguous and it was believed by both unionists and republicans that physical force had been successful in securing Sinn Fein a place at the negotiations. If there had been a definitive move in which 'semantics will replace semtex' that was far from clear to Sinn Fein's opponents (Bean 1995b: 5–6). The talks for republicans, in other words, seemed not to be about getting an agreement but about laying the blame and proving to the world that unionists were 'afraid of peace' and were incapable of accepting change. And it was not only unionists who read republican intentions that way. O'Doherty feared that if the efforts to achieve agreement failed the IRA could claim Northern Ireland to be an 'untenable political entity' and increase the pressure on the British Government to make further concessions to the republican position, perhaps in the direction of joint authority (O'Doherty 1998: 118–19).

If this was how most unionists read republican intentions, then republicans were also suspicious of the sort of deal Ulster Unionists were trying to forge. As de Breadun discovered from his conversations with senior unionists, their desire was 'to cut a deal with the SDLP and leave Sinn Fein out in the cold' (de Breadun 2001: 109). This was an expectation that sustained Ulster Unionists' hopes to the final moments before agreement was reached. The reason for this hope lay in the fact that the SDLP and the UUP had developed 'a tacit alignment' during the course of the talks. The talks 'may have looked like a convention, but in the end they were really a *tête-à-tête*' (Horowitz 2002: 202). Unionists spoke of forging a democratic centre. If they thought that this would entice the SDLP from a further tacit alignment with Sinn Fein on the requirement for inclusivity, then they were mistaken. Furthermore, inclusivity was a principle to which the two governments also held (Bew, Gibbon and Patterson 2002: 236). One reading of the SDLP position is Hume's absolute determination to make republicans part of a new consensus and thereby to get them to accept, at least implicitly, the principle of unionist consent. In the course of the talks republicans still denied that unionists had a right to a veto over whether there should be a united Ireland. The price for a tacit, but practically significant, change in their position had to be the inclusion of Sinn Fein in the government of Northern Ireland (Guelke 1996: 15). Another reading is that the SDLP was incapable of doing a deal with unionists that would exclude Sinn Fein because it feared being punished by nationalists. Yet another is that it was unwilling to do so because inclusion of republicans maximized nationalist capacity, irrespective of party advantage, to weaken the unionist position. Given unionist fears of the subversive intent of the 'pan-nationalist front', this latter tacit alignment had the potential to undermine not only the UUP–SDLP *tête-à-tête* but also the talks process itself. The fragility of the UUP–SDLP understanding did not appear to be the sort of solid ground upon which to deliver a comprehensive political settlement. Even that fragile understanding was threatened by divisions within the UUP about the wisdom of the process and by the challenge to Trimble from unionists outside the talks (Aughey 2000). For all these reasons, most people responded to the Belfast Agreement with either surprise or scepticism. This was a more authentic response than either joy or alarm.

To examine the Belfast Agreement is rather like exploring an archaeological site in which the remains of past initiatives have been incorporated into it like functional layers in a new constitutional edifice. The Agreement contained within itself the reworked remnants of failures in the hope that their reworking would deliver success. In short, it can be read as a brief constitutional summary of the Troubles and was more than just 'Sunningdale for slow learners'. It was also rolling devolution for slow learners, the Anglo-Irish Agreement for slow learners, Brooke/Mayhew for slow learners and the Downing Street Declaration for slow learners. Some would regress further the Agreement to 'a much deeper substratum of Irish politics'. That substratum is the Government of Ireland Act of 1920, repealed under the terms of the Agreement, but the influence of which 'could not be lightly expunged' (Jackson 2003: 315–16). The historian can cast a wide interpretative net and haul in ironic references. The social scientist's net is not so capacious. However, acute observers of the process noted how the Agreement trawled up previous proposals of the last 30 years. In an insightful interpretation, Horowitz argued that it resembled 'the sum of all previous proposals'. It was these 'residues of history' that contributed a stock of ideas that were drawn on to design the institutional arrangements. 'Pieced together, these partial survivals from overall failures comprised a kind of immanent constitution of Northern Ireland, ready to be shaped and reshaped into a document that commanded acceptance.' The 'invisible actor at the table' had been recent history. The 'lessons of history' informed the behaviour of participants and 'the deposits of history' were incorporated into the Agreement (Horowitz 2002: 212, 219). History, of course, never repeats itself. As the Parisian radicals of 1968 used to say, it merely stutters. What at first we take to be repetition invariably turns out to be something different. That provides some hope for those deposits of history in the Agreement, for what failed in the past was not necessarily doomed to fail in the present. That had been the message of Walker's interpretation of Irish history. Unfortunately, it is less hopeful for those lessons of history. Having learned the supposed lessons of the past is no guarantee that even bigger mistakes will not be made in the present. In politics, blunders are frequently the result of intelligence and learning rather than of ignorance and stupidity (Fischer 1970: 158). That had been the message of Stewart's interpretation of Irish history.

The historical layers were also apparent to Hazleton who observed that the Agreement did not conform to the way devolution was normally described in legal texts. On the contrary, it 'is based partly on constitutional precedents, partly on theories of conflict management, partly on trial and error, and partly on sheer expediency' (Hazleton 2000: 34). The Agreement has been described, to change metaphors slightly, as a convergence of three planes of historic policy geometry. The first was the persistent determination of the British Government to devolve power to Northern Ireland. The second was 'the *idée fixe* of consociationalism'. The third was the need for an Irish dimension (Wilford 2001: 4–5). The shape and significance of these planes have changed so that while a comparison with Sunningdale 'is a beguiling attraction', the 1998 Agreement was more subtle (Wilford 2000: 579). In some ways it represented the putting together of the parts of Northern Ireland's complex identity that Longley had specified. Moreover, the Belfast Agreement was more comprehensive and much more ambitious than Sunningdale. The latter was a political arrangement. The former was not only a political arrangement but also a peace settlement (Hadden 2000). The policy geometry and the intersections of the planes varied depending on where you stood and on who you were and was thus a good example of political 'hyperopia'. The grandeur of the architecture in its postmodern pastiche seemed clear enough from a distance but the shape, operation and substance of it was fuzzier the closer you got (Heath 1995: 146). This fuzziness was thought to be one of the strengths of the Agreement. It was also one of its major weaknesses (Morgan 2000). The main institutions of the Agreement and their antecedents can be summarily described.

Institutions of the Belfast Agreement

There has been a lively academic debate about the definition of consociationalism and its appropriateness to the Northern Ireland problem. Some favoured the 'civil society' approach rather than the 'elitism' of the consociational approach. Their arguments seemed eminently reasonable given the widespread – and continuing – scepticism about the ability of party leaders to deliver their own constituencies to any prospective deal. 'How credible', asked one critic, 'is consociationalism's elite orientation in the "age of the masses"?' (Dixon 1997: 19). However, it has been argued that a 'consociation can be created without any explicit consociational theory to guide it'. Consociation is an association of communities – unionist, nationalist and 'other' – and whether explicitly theorized or not there was no doubt that the Agreement was 'the product of tacit and explicit consociational thought, or what is sometimes called "pacting"'. In short, at its political core was an historic compromise from which democratic transformation might flow. At the centre of all such consociational arrangements is an assembly and communal power-sharing (O'Leary 1999: 68–9). The Agreement made provision for a 108-member Assembly, elected by the Single Transferable Vote system of proportional representation. It was to have full legislative and executive authority in respect of matters devolved to Northern Ireland government departments. The Westminster Parliament kept control of non-devolved matters relating to security, taxation, foreign policy and the European Union, and the position of Secretary of State for Northern Ireland was retained within the Cabinet in London. There was the possibility of the Assembly taking responsibility for other matters like policing and justice reserved to Westminster and this provision embraced the concept of 'rolling devolution' enunciated by Secretary of State James Prior in the ill-fated Assembly initiative of 1982–6. Members elected to the Assembly were required to designate themselves unionist or nationalist or other. Key decisions were to be taken on a cross-community basis. This involved either parallel consent (a majority composed of a majority of unionist and nationalist designations present and voting) or weighted majority (60 per cent of all members including at least 40 per cent of unionists and 40 per cent of nationalists). Statutory committees of the Assembly were established and their role was broad: scrutiny, policy development and consultation with respect to government departments. They were also to have a role in the initiation of legislation. The chairs and deputy chairs of committees were allocated proportionately according to the party composition of the Assembly and membership was also to be broadly proportionate. When the six former Northern Ireland departments became ten this meant a total of 20 chairs and deputy chairs nominated by the parties (Wilford 2000: 581–4).

The executive authority of the Assembly was discharged by a First and Deputy First Minister and Ministers with departmental responsibilities. The First and Deputy First Ministers were elected by the parallel consent process. They were not responsible for choosing the Executive. Ministers were nominated by reference to the seats each party held in the Assembly (according to the d'Hondt procedure) and had full executive authority in their respective areas of responsibility. This procedure meant that departments could become autonomous party fiefdoms, a possibility encouraged by there being no requirement for collective responsibility in the Executive (O'Leary 1999: 72–3). On 15 February 1999, the Assembly approved ten executive departments covering all devolved matters in addition to the Office of the First and Deputy First Ministers. The allocation of these departments resulted in the UUP and the SDLP getting three each, Sinn Fein and the DUP two each. The Executive met without the DUP Ministers being present because they refused to sit with Sinn Fein while the IRA remained in existence. These arrangements for voting in the Assembly and for choosing the Executive were strongly consociational, indeed more inclusively so than the Sunningdale Agreement (Wolff 2001: 13). The Assembly procedures and the form of the Executive represented a deal hammered out between the UUP and the SDLP in the final days of the talks, with the former providing the latter with the reassurances it had demanded about inclusive government (Hennessey 2000: 168). In short, this was an unusual form of compulsory power-sharing, one that owed little to notions of executive efficiency or even credibility but much to notions of political expediency. The UUP had accepted it, making the calculation, wrongly as it turned out, that it 'would be easier to sell to their supporters than a voluntary form of power-sharing' (Bew, Gibbon and Patterson 2002: 237).

There is an interesting point here about Assembly procedure that merits some attention and it is the question of 'opposition'. The term in the United Kingdom and the Republic of Ireland has come to mean a distinction between opposing the state and opposing the ministers of the state. In the British and Irish case it has also meant a system of adversarial (if civil) politics and it is thought to be an essential attribute of a democratic society. 'Opposition is a relative term – but opposition to what?' (Parry 1997: 458–9). That is an essential democratic question. The problem in Northern Ireland was that there was no clear answer to that question and it had three elements. First, it was unclear in this case whether republican support for the Agreement meant continued opposition to the state. Second, the distinction between opposition to the Agreement and opposition to the implementation of the Agreement remained confused. Third, even what was meant by support for the Agreement was uncertain. All the large parties in the Assembly had been incorporated into government, so formal opposition would either take place within the Executive, and be invisible; or it would devolve to those small parties with insignificant strength outside the Executive, like the Alliance Party or the Women's Coalition, and be ineffective (Horowitz 2001: 104–5). Both forms of opposition operated and both were unproductive and this contributed to public cynicism about the role of the Assembly. The 'lack of a formal (let alone loyal!) opposition' underlined 'the uniqueness of the Northern Ireland case' (Wilford 2000: 585). Since the Democratic Unionists formally opposed the Agreement but took their Executive posts, they designated themselves a sort of internal opposition. This confused opposing the Agreement with opposing the Executive. The smaller parties felt like the hecklers of a steamroller, as Labour MP Austin Mitchell once described the practice of opposition. Moreover, their support for the Agreement moderated their opposition to the Executive. The question of institutional opposition was given little attention mainly because of the intensely fractious condition of the whole process. However, there is an historical irony that is worth noting. One of the pervasive nationalist grievances against the old Stormont was that opposition to the Unionist Government, even when constructive, failed to make any impact or to have any influence (Elliott 2001: 396–7). The absence of nationalist concern today about the impotence of formal opposition is a measure of how times have changed. It tends to confirm Jackson's observation that certain of the structures and attitudes of the old Stormont were perceptible within the new Assembly. The big difference was that 'all the parties now have access to official patronage' (Jackson 2003: 316). In truth, some had more access than others and the argument for strong opposition remained a concern of those on the margins of ethnic politics.

The Agreement established a North/South Ministerial Council (NSMC) to bring together in plenary and sectoral contact Ministers from the Northern Ireland Executive and from the Irish Government. The Council was to exchange information and consult, using its best endeavours to reach agreement on matters of mutual interest and concern. In addition six matters for cooperation were agreed that required the establishment of cross-border or all-island implementation bodies. The six implementation bodies agreed were Waterways Ireland, Food Safety, Inter-trade Ireland, Special EU Programmes, Language Body (Irish and Ulster Scots) and Agriculture and Marine. There was also established a public company, Tourism Ireland, designed to promote tourism throughout the island. Designated areas of cooperation included Health, Environmental Protection and aspects of the operation of the Common Agricultural Policy. This was the critical Irish dimension upon which Sunningdale had foundered in 1974 and upon which the Agreement almost foundered as well. The original scope for North/South cooperation set out in the Mitchell Draft Paper of 6 April 1998 had panicked the unionist negotiators. This was not Mitchell's draft at all but the work of the two governments. Whatever its provenance, it was impossible for unionists to accept and it was easy to see why (Hennessey 2000: 160–1). Of the 11 pages devoted to North/South matters in the Draft Paper, three annexes comprising seven pages detailed a wide range of functions to be subject to the Council. These functions were prescribed and the language was categorical. What was worse from a unionist point of view was paragraph 7. It specified that the two governments were to establish cross-border implementation bodies without any prior involvement of the Assembly. The paragraph stated that London and Dublin were 'to make all necessary legislative and other preparations to ensure the establishment of these bodies at the inception of the British/Irish Agreement or as rapidly as possible thereafter'. Frantic unionist re-negotiation resulted in the three annexes of functions being reduced to one. They also succeeded in changing the language from the prescriptive to the permissive. Paragraph 7 was reworked entirely and replaced with five paragraphs (7–11 in the Belfast Agreement). They specified an interim period between the election of the Assembly and the transfer of power to it in which a 'shadow administration' of the Assembly would identify and agree with the Irish Government the functions for North/South cooperation. In other words, the First and Deputy First Ministers were to be involved from the start and would have a significant say over the shape of cross-border activity. This secured a vital unionist principle for it meant that the North/South Council was not free standing but clearly derived its authority from the Irish Parliament and from the Northern Ireland Assembly and was to be directly accountable to both of them. For unionists this removed the old Sunningdale danger of a 'third government', an embryonic all-Ireland Executive (Moloney 1998b; Bew 2000: 44–6). It also secured a vital nationalist interest in that they were assured that functioning North/South bodies were not dependent entirely on unionist goodwill. This was certainly not the transitional structure for a united Ireland that republicans had demanded, the shape of which their leadership had claimed to detect in the Frameworks Document of 1995. However, it was not without its potential to develop in a 'confederalist' direction (O'Leary 2001a: 60–3). In short, for unionists to get the Assembly to function there needed to be cross-border cooperation. For nationalists to get active cross-border cooperation there needed to be a functioning Assembly. For republicans to be part of the process there needed to be tacit acceptance of the principle of consent.

In the event, the NSMC worked reasonably smoothly. Between 1999 and 2003 there were 65 meetings of the NSMC. There were 29 officials who worked in the Joint Secretariat, 650 were employed full time in the implementation bodies and there were 72 part-time board members. Up to the end of 2001 there had been expenditure on projects of £225 million. The indicative budgets for the years 2003–5 were set to increase from £85 million to £89 million per annum. Agendas at all meetings of the NSMC have been by agreement, with a balanced attendance of unionist and nationalist Ministers. The watchwords have been transparency and accountability and, as a consequence, the NSMC has bedded in with general cross-party support (for a different view see DUP 1998a). There have been some practical achievements such as common tourist promotion and the handling of the foot and mouth crisis in 2001/2. The principle has been Trimble's one of 'what matters is what works' and what seemed to work, on the basis of agreement, was practical cooperation for mutual benefit. Following the suspension of the devolved institutions in Northern Ireland in October 2002 and the return of direct rule from London, it was decided that decisions of the NSMC relating to implementation bodies and Tourism Ireland would be taken by the two governments but that the agenda of the NSMC would not be expanded beyond what had been already agreed prior to direct rule. This was justified on the expectation that devolved institutions in Northern Ireland would be reinstated.

The Agreement established a British-Irish Council (BIC) comprising representatives of the British and Irish Governments and the newly devolved institutions of Northern Ireland, Scotland and Wales together with representatives of the Isle of Man and the Channel Islands. The purpose of the BIC was to consult on a wide range of matters of mutual interest and suitable issues were identified such as transport links, agriculture, the environment and approaches to EU issues. The procedures were to be entirely consensual but members could either opt out if they so wished or they could develop bilateral arrangements. The BIC was to meet twice a year at summit level and more regularly in specific sectoral formats. The BIC was seen as an East/West balance to the North/South Ministerial Council and therefore a concession to unionist concern about the need for a British dimension to the Agreement. The UUP had long been interested in such an overarching Council of the British Isles and it had also been an idea that inspired British Conservatives like Sir John Biggs-Davison who had earlier coined the acronym IONA, Isles of the North Atlantic, for a similar vision. In this shape it represented an intellectual counter-attack against the familiar thesis of Irish nationalism that the demise of the Union was inevitable. The counter proposition was that the web of interconnections within the British Isles would actually become more complex and intimate in the post-devolution era. A new multilateral relationship would replace the old centre (London) and periphery (Celtic fringe) model and 'one of the vehicles for such multilateralism is likely to be the British-Irish Council' (Birnie 2001: 171). There was, however, a paradox. If the main motive for establishing the British-Irish Council was to reassure unionists of the importance of Britishness, its effect on the United Kingdom as a whole 'symbolizes the changing power relations within the Atlantic archipelago' between England and the other nations such that the BIC could have 'a centrifugal tendency' (Bogdanor 1999: 297–8). That probably overstated the importance of the BIC's role but it was, ironically, a possibility that nationalists seized upon to refute the unionist interpretation of strengthening connections within the United Kingdom (Nairn 2000: 305). If some had hoped the Agreement would foster a post-national mentality and provide an escape from the dichotomous narratives of unionism and nationalism (and not only in Northern Ireland), argument over the trajectory of the BIC showed profound continuity with traditional modes of thought (Walker 2001: 139).

Cooperation between London and Dublin was to continue in the shape of a new British-Irish Intergovernmental Conference (BIIC) dealing with 'the totality of relationships', a term derived from the period of the first major Anglo-Irish summit in Dublin in November 1980. Of the so-called East–West institutions, the BIIC was the most significant. In recognition of the Republic of Ireland's special interest in Northern Ireland, the Conference met regularly to discuss non-devolved matters and was co-chaired by the Irish Minister for Foreign Affairs and the Secretary of State for Northern Ireland. The relevant members of the Northern Ireland Executive were also involved in meetings of the Conference. Following the suspension of the Assembly in October 2003, the BIIC met more regularly and took more direct involvement in the direction of Northern Ireland politics. For pro-Agreement unionists, the Intergovernmental Council represented the replacement of the hated Anglo-Irish Agreement of 1985 (Trimble 2001: 7). For anti-Agreement unionists this was a big lie and the changes to the Anglo-Irish Agreement were purely cosmetic. The Anglo-Irish Agreement had been merely 'renamed and recreated' (DUP 1998b). As O'Leary had predicted, the Agreement committed unionists to two Irish dimensions and for anti-Agreement unionists this was a double humiliation. For nationalists, on the other hand, the replacement of the Anglo-Irish Agreement by a new British-Irish Agreement was interpreted as a 'more comprehensive and far-reaching successor' (Farren 2000: 60). On this point, as one academic study noted, 'the silence of the British Government concerning the meaning of key phrases is as significant as the articulated opinions of others' (Hadfield 1998: 601). Perhaps the greatest change since 1985 was 'not institutional at all but psychological'. The new arrangement protected nationalist interests by preserving a role for the Irish government but protected unionist interests by healing the rift with the British polity and potentially opening up the intergovernmental process to greater accountability (Bew 2000: 47).

The Anglo-Irishry of the Agreement was made more palatable for unionists by amendment to Articles 2 and 3 of the Irish Republic's 1937 Constitution (the claim to the territory of Northern Ireland). The collapse of Sunningdale in 1974 had been partly a consequence of uncertainty about the Irish Government's intentions because the retention of Articles 2 and 3 contradicted the consent principle. That was also one of the problems with the Anglo-Irish Agreement. An Irish Supreme Court ruling on the McGimpsey case, taken against the constitutionality of the 1985 Agreement, declared that the 'reintegration of the national territory' remained 'a constitutional imperative'. Furthermore, the Supreme Court held that the Anglo-Irish Agreement did not derogate 'from the claim as a legal right to the entire national territory' (Power 1990: 35–7). In the 1998 Agreement the irredentist claim of de Valera's era was now replaced by new articles that put the principle of consent at the heart of the aspiration to Irish unity. It is quite correct to argue that the Irish people did not abandon the desire for unity but it is also correct to argue that the desire no longer resembles 'a programme of assimilation'. Nor is Northern Ireland's 'elimination as a political unit' a programmatic feature of the Irish Constitution (O'Leary 2001a: 64–5). There is a further point that has not been so fully remarked upon and of which unionists have made surprisingly little. The Downing Street Declaration of 1993 made Irish unity 'explicitly dependent on endorsement by referendum not only in the North *but also in the South*' and this potential Southern veto on unity was written into the Agreement of 1998 (Coakley 2001: 231; emphasis in original). These commitments implied that, irrespective of the question of sovereignty, the intention was that Northern Ireland should remain relatively autonomous as a form of regional government. As Hadden suggested, the purpose had been 'to provide stability in a communally divided society by guaranteeing proportional participation in government regardless of the precise population balance'. The implications of that, he thought, had not been properly absorbed by nationalists who saw the Agreement as a stepping stone to a united, sovereign Irish state (Hadden 2000: 25). That is another of those delicious paradoxes in which a 25-year campaign of violence by Northern republicans against a British 'veto' on unity ended with the erection of a further potential Irish veto on unity. In all the complexity and novelty of the Agreement's provisions that is quite a remarkable fact that, rather like the emperor's lack of clothing, is unremarked because it is so blindingly obvious. The repeal of the 1920 Government of Ireland Act could be a footnote in history compared with the explicit change in the disposition of the Irish polity towards unification.

The Agreement made provision for further institutions. A consultative Civic Forum of 60 members was established comprising representatives of the business, trade union, voluntary and cultural sectors. The Civic Forum was an institutionalization of the ideal of deliberative democracy, in principle to broaden and deepen participation in politics, promoting 'communication across social difference' alongside traditional party debate (Young 2002: 194–5). It has been claimed that implicit in the Civic Forum concept was the 'fact of offering more opportunities for women to play a fuller role in public life' (Fearon 2000: 156). The Women's Coalition strongly pushed this idea during the talks for the further reason of providing an alternative official platform for those who were neither unionist nor nationalist but 'other' (Meehan 1999: 28–9). Incorporated within the strong top-down consociationalism of the Agreement, then, was this concession to the bottom-up, civil society approach. To use one of Bagehot's constitutional expressions, the Civic Forum was designed to be a dignified rather than an efficient institution. Its purpose was to consult on social, cultural and economic matters. The principle of incorporating civic elements, however symbolically represented, was a shrewd political calculation on the part of some that if the Agreement was to embed itself, then more than the pro-Agreement parties would need to mobilize in its support (see Chapter 5). This calculation was demonstrated during the referendum in May 1998 when civic activism promoted by the voluntary sector did much to secure a favourable vote. Nevertheless, the Civic Forum has been characterized 'by a remarkable degree of inactivity' and it has made little or no impact upon the public consciousness (Wolff 2002: 226).

A Northern Ireland Human Rights Commission (NIHRC) was established to advise on the scope for defining, through Westminster legislation, rights additional to the European Convention that would reflect the particular circumstances of Northern Ireland. Those rights had to do with respect for the identity and ethos of both communities and with parity of esteem. The NIHRC was also to be responsible for promoting awareness of human rights, to consider draft legislation referred to it by the Assembly and, where appropriate, to bring court proceedings. The Irish Government was required to take comparable steps. The idea of a Bill of Rights had been for long common ground amongst the Northern Ireland parties and the NIHRC's role should have been relatively uncontroversial. Unsurprisingly, this has not been the case. The reason was that the agency charged with defining and monitoring human rights became part of the contested terrain of politics. The unfortunate controversies around the NIHRC confirmed Ignatief's maxim that good causes are not made better by confusing needs with rights (Ignatief 1999: 60). Striking a proper balance between communal claims and public needs proved impossible for the Commission's chairman, Brice Dickson. Not only had he to contend with unionist suspicion of the NIHRC's agenda but he also had to cope with nationalist criticism of the Commission's interpretation of human rights. Unionists claimed that the original appointments to the Commission did not fairly reflect the communal balance in Northern Ireland and were therefore suspicious, often without good cause, of its objectives and intentions. Human rights, it has been said, tread a delicate path between conceding a potential thugs' charter and pursuing a utopian form of justice (Freeman 1995: 37). For many unionists, the NIHRC unfortunately erred on the side of utopianism without properly addressing public concern about the thuggish abuse of human rights by loyalist and republican paramilitaries. The subtext of such criticisms was that the NIHRC continued to pursue the old nationalist struggle against the institutions of the state (J. McCartney 2003). Nationalists, on the other hand, accused the NIHRC of threatening to undermine the bi-communal basis of the Agreement itself by not giving sufficient priority to collective rights. The substance of their position was that most of the gains made by the Catholic minority, for example under fair employment legislation, depended on the monitoring of communal identities. Any weakening of group rights by an appeal to individual rights challenged the security of historic achievements. It has been argued that collective human rights are sometimes necessary to achieve justice and peace but that the desire for justice and peace may foster demands that are unjust and confrontational. There appeared to be no 'third space' for the reconciliation of claims of rights between demands and needs (Freeman 1995: 40). Habermas, for example, had criticized 'selective readings, tendentious interpretations, and narrow-minded applications of human rights' and the 'instrumentalization of human rights that conceals particular interests behind a universalistic mask'. He had warned that people may come to the conclusion that 'the meaning of human rights is exhausted by their misuse' (Pensky 2001: 129). The Northern Ireland experience confirmed his criticism and his warning and in many ways, the dispute about human rights encapsulated the central difficulty of the Agreement. There appeared to be no political 'third space' either.

The Agreement made further provision for an Equality Commission and a Victims Commission. Economic, social and cultural issues were also addressed, in particular issues relating to employment opportunities and language. The objective was to foster a new civic order in Northern Ireland based on parity of esteem for different traditions in the hope that all sections of the community would feel that they had a stake in the future of Northern Ireland. A Commission on Policing was established under Chris Patten and it reported in September 1999. The main recommendations were a new Policing Board, including political representatives and independents, with powers of oversight, and increased recruitment of Catholic police officers to achieve a 50/50 balance with Protestants. Patten also advised changing the name of the Royal Ulster Constabulary and changing the symbols of the force to achieve 'neutrality' (which meant erasing its 'Britishness'). Most serious of all not only for unionist backing for police reform but also for the Agreement itself was the Patten Report's failure to acknowledge the sacrifice of police officers and the contribution of the RUC to the containment of terrorism both in Northern Ireland and in the rest of the United Kingdom. These proposals provoked strong opposition within all sections of unionism, especially the changes to the name of the force and its symbols, and were to have an effect on electoral support for Trimble and the UUP. However, the new Policing Board is now functioning, though without Sinn Fein's participation, the renamed Police Service for Northern Ireland (PSNI), is operative and its agreed symbols represent one remarkable example of successful political compromise. A section of the Agreement was also devoted to the early release of paramilitary prisoners. Those who were members of groups that maintained a complete and unequivocal ceasefire were eligible for release within two years of the Agreement. It was both astonishing and yet quite predictable that the British Government proceeded with prisoner releases without requiring the disbandment of paramilitary organizations. It was astonishing in that it denied the Government a significant card to play in negotiations with Sinn Fein (see

Neumann 2003). It was unsurprising in that the Government always appeared willing to indulge the culture of equivalent victimhood (Godson 2004: 374–5). Another section was devoted to the decommissioning of illegally held republican and loyalist weapons and that issue will be addressed more fully in later chapters.

Conclusion

On 22 May 1998, the Agreement was approved in a referendum in Northern Ireland and the Republic of Ireland. The vote in favour in Northern Ireland was 71.1 per cent and in the Republic of Ireland it was 94.4 per cent. The turn out in Northern Ireland of 81 per cent (951,845) was exceptionally high. Of this number 676,930 voted yes and 274,892 voted no. The overwhelming majority of nationalists voted yes but only a small majority of unionists did likewise. Despite the extent of unionist opposition to the Agreement, the referendum result created a solid and positive platform for the Assembly elections. The result of those elections, held on 25 June 1998, showed how finely poised was support within unionism. Overall the pro-Agreement parties won 75 per cent of the vote and therefore slightly up on the referendum result. However, there was again a differential vote between the unionist and nationalist electorates. On an analysis of the first preference votes, pro-Agreement unionists gained 25 per cent of the vote and anti-Agreement unionists 25.5 per cent. The UUP secured 21.3 per cent of first preference votes. In terms of seats in the Assembly, pro-Agreement unionists were able to benefit from transfers from other pro-Agreement parties, in particular from the SDLP (Mitchell 2001). The 28 pro-Agreement UUP members were ranged against 28 anti-Agreement unionists (20 DUP, 5 UK Unionists and 3 United Unionists). The DUP, with 18.1 per cent of the first preference vote, had run the UUP a close second. The two members of the pro-Agreement PUP, a party linked to the paramilitary Ulster Volunteer Force, held the balance. On the nationalist side there was a high turn out and the SDLP, with 22 per cent of the vote, successfully outpolled the UUP. Sinn Fein's support continued to rise, the party polled 17.6 per cent of the votes and it closed the gap between itself and its nationalist rival. Sinn Fein became the largest party west of the Bann and it subsequently made much of the 'greening of the west'. In the Assembly the SDLP had 24 seats and Sinn Fein 18. The remaining Assembly seats were filled by six members of the Alliance Party and two members of the Women's Coalition (Norris 2000). Following a rather fractious session of the Assembly, in which anti-Agreement unionists did their best to discomfort the leader of the UUP, David Trimble was elected First Minister and Seamus Mallon, Deputy First Minister. In this vote Sinn Fein deliberately abstained 'to avoid the First and Deputy First Ministers being chosen by more nationalists than by unionists'. O'Leary took this to be a sign of growing republican political maturity (1999: 69).

Tactically this may have been so but there remained large doubts about the commitment of republicans to acknowledging in practice what they had dedicated themselves to in principle.

It has been argued that a peculiar characteristic of Irish politics is that issues are addressed in what is 'almost a laboratory atmosphere' (Boyce, Eccleshall and Geoghegan 1993: 5). Here was another laboratory condition. It did appear that the people of Northern Ireland were substituting one form of community of fate, distinguished by violence, for another form of community of fate, this time distinguished by compulsory cooperation. The historic promise contained in the text of the Agreement was about to be tested, perhaps to destruction. The new political architecture was undoubtedly a triumph of ingenuity and artifice. It was certainly clever. Yet large questions remained. Was the formula for the experiment based on reasonable expectations of success? Or was the experiment more political alchemy than political science? Unusually for Northern Ireland where formerly, it was thought, instability thrived on uncertainty one of the supposed virtues of the Agreement was its 'constructive ambiguity'. The legislation was not ambiguous about the constitutional status of Northern Ireland, so the ambiguity lay elsewhere. If that ambiguity were indeed to prove constructive, then it would require a degree of mutual understanding about how the Agreement was to be implemented and the shape Northern Ireland's society would take. In that sense, post-Agreement politics would indeed provide a laboratory atmosphere and it is examined further in the next chapter.

7 New beginning and modification of circumstances

A few months before the Belfast Agreement, the journalist Suzanne Breen identified the key presentational issue. Most people knew, she claimed, that the dialogue between the parties was mostly 'illusory' and that there was no sign that local politicians by themselves would ever reach 'a historic compromise'. London and Dublin would set the pattern as they always had and most people by now also knew in broad outline what the deal would involve. Nationalists would have to live with partition, a Northern Ireland Assembly and a local police service. Unionists would have to accept power-sharing, North/South institutions and the release of terrorist prisoners. The problem was that nationalists, especially Sinn Fein, would have to present any deal as transitional and argue that there existed a dynamic towards Irish unity. The UUP would have to sell the deal as one that made the Union safe for the future. Breen concluded that the challenge for the two Governments was 'to come up with something either so detailed and complex, or else so vague and ambiguous, that both sides can claim victory' (Breen 1998: 7). Arguably, that was the challenge the two governments met on both counts. The legislative outworking of the Agreement's provisions would be detailed and complex and they would require a period of years to be fully implemented. The meaning of the Agreement was open to interpretation and allowed the parties to identify favoured aspects of it as *the* significant ones. If the major political constituencies could accept the deal as satisfying honour without looking too closely at the terms, then perhaps it was possible to get beyond the politics of winning and losing. In doing so they might shift their respective visions from the ultimate ends of politics suggested by Breen's formulation of the problem and refocus them on the means to secure the well-being of everyone within Northern Ireland. Former Irish Prime Minister John Bruton certainly thought that this was possible. Politics, he thought, had persuaded 'both communities to realize that any total victory for their own ideology would be unstable, uncomfortable and unsustainable' (Bruton 2000).

The formula of the Agreement appeared to be neatly balanced. Northern Ireland would remain part of the United Kingdom because in that part of Ireland there was no consent for Irish unity. At least there was no ambiguity about that. On the other hand, Northern Ireland's place within the United Kingdom would depend on sufficient change to secure for it the consent of nationalists. That was also clear. As Mansergh pointed out, 'consent clearly means the consent of both traditions or substantial cross-community agreement, not just the consent of a unionist majority' (Mansergh 1996: 13). This was a subtle, perhaps sophistical, reformulation of the Ulster Question in which the logical opposites, the *either/or* of unionism and nationalism, might possibly become the *both/and* of a mutually satisfactory, widely agreed compromise. The whole structure of the Agreement was built on the assumption that the institutionalization of that formula of continuity and change could deliver cooperative government instead of intractable conflict. Post-Agreement, nationalism in all its forms would retain its aspiration to Irish unity and unionism in all its forms would remain committed to the Union. But there was intimated a third option that would be neither exclusively unionist nor exclusively nationalist but both in which Northern Ireland (implying the territory's Britishness) *and* the North of Ireland (implying the territory's Irishness) would become a focus of common loyalty.

Academic commentaries that set about clarifying this new condition have been only partially successful. An attempt to address ambiguity at one level often permitted ambiguity to survive at another. From a legal perspective, Hadfield accepted that politicians had legitimate reasons for drawing different conclusions about and giving different interpretations of the Agreement. On the strict issue of sovereignty, however, the repeal of the remaining section of the Government of Ireland Act of 1920 was of 'no significance' to the 'substance of the continuation of the Union'. This clarity on the constitutional issue notwithstanding, Hadfield admitted that other elements of the Agreement, such as the North/South Ministerial Council, 'must – and do – have a direct bearing on the nature of the Union' (Hadfield 1998: 615–16, 601). How that 'bearing' might affect the 'substance' of the Union remained open to question. From a political science perspective, Tonge argued that rival interpretations over the 'ultimate direction' of the Agreement were important to its survival for it permitted leaders to sell the deal to their respective parties. He believed that the problem appeared to be one 'less concerned with its overall constitutional direction (although this is important to members) than over how the accord forms part of the process of conflict management' (Tonge 2002: 62–3). From the perspective of political theory, Burke argued that the ability to interpret the Agreement in such divergent ways was not, as many people thought, a source of weakness but rather its essential strength (Burke 1999: 21). In all three cases there was a temptation to separate mechanisms and principles in a manner that intellectuals are trained to do. British sovereignty is in principle unaffected by cross-border cooperation. The difficulties of implementing the Agreement lay in arguments about the mechanisms and not about the principles. Contradictory thinking about the mechanisms of the Agreement did not necessarily mean incompatible views about the principles of their operation. Such distinctions were essential for academic debate but they are often irrelevant to voters. The merit of Harvey's critical legal perspective has been the acknowledgement of the intimate relationship between principles and mechanisms for if 'some mechanisms are not in place then the principles are not being complied with'. Talk of ambiguity, he thought, is often self-serving politics (Harvey 2003a). This was how most people, albeit in their different ways, thought of the Agreement and Harvey identified the real political battleground after 10 April 1998. The battle within and between unionism and nationalism was over how the mechanisms or institutions should embody principle and how principle should transform or sustain the institutions. The reality of politics meant that rival interpretations were not hermetically sealed. The fact that unionists could hear and read what nationalists were saying and vice versa was not without its effect.

For pro-Agreement unionists the selling point was that the British dimension would count in the long run. In the final plenary of the talks the UUP leader argued that unionists 'rise from the table with the Union stronger than when we first sat here' (Trimble 2001: 37). In a speech to the Northern Ireland Forum on 17 April 1998, Trimble claimed that the Agreement had achieved the unionist goal 'proposed separately by the UUP and the DUP in the 1992 Talks of placing Northern Ireland's future within a wider British-Irish context than the Anglo-Irish Agreement of 1985. One key objective had been now achieved. 'We have sought and secured a permanent settlement, not agreed to a temporary transitional arrangement.' He cited in evidence of this claim the Irish Government's modification of Articles 2 and 3 of its Constitution (Trimble 1998). North/South cooperation was no longer a threat because all the important constitutional issues had been successfully negotiated. A further enticement for unionists after 1997 was the prospect of devolution as part of a general British strategy of constitutional reform. This would make self-government in Belfast part of the United Kingdom norm rather than the exception. Certainly there appeared to be a superficial commonality between the Northern Ireland case and the other devolved institutions in the United Kingdom that also sought to address apparently contradictory objectives. New Labour's constitutional reforms in Great Britain were designed to reconcile two views of devolution. In the words of former Welsh Secretary Ron Davies, devolution was a process and not an event (though he did not intend separatism). In the view of former Labour leader John Smith, devolution represented a 'settled will' to stabilize a modified Union. Labour's programme of constitutional reform had been defined by the promise that greater autonomy could be ceded to the nations without threatening the United Kingdom's integrity. Those unionists who supported Trimble wanted to secure their part in that larger integral process.

For nationalists the expectation was that North/South cooperation would establish linkages the growing quantity of which would ultimately transform the quality of relationships on the island. In these circumstances

Irish unity would become not only necessary but also desirable, even for unionists. It was the Irish dimension that counted *in the long run* (Murray 2002: 51–2). Even so, some nationalist commentators found it difficult to restrain their anticipation of the changes to come. A former SDLP councillor argued that nationalists were 'no longer trapped by a unionist regime' and would 'work in the short term to strengthen ties to the south through the all-Ireland bodies'. The direction was clear. Nationalists 'know where they're going. They set the agenda now' (Feeney 2003a). In less triumphalist and more conciliatory terms, Mark Durkan confirmed that he remained '100% for a united Ireland, just as I am 100% for the Agreement'. The two were intimately linked for the 'united Ireland the SDLP believes in will be built upon the rock solid foundations of the Good Friday Agreement'. In that precise sense the 'SDLP is proud to call itself a party of true republicanism' (Durkan 2003). One implication of the rhetoric was that the Agreement had now secured for nationalists the appropriate means to achieve the desired end. For Sinn Fein, Adams argued that the Agreement was 'not a peace settlement' but was 'a transitional stage towards reunification' (cited in English 2003: 300). If there was to be an appeal to unionists it was an appeal for them to accept the hopelessness of their position.

> Those unionists who think there is going to be a united Ireland anyway, why don't they endorse what we are doing in terms of the work that is being done across a range of issues – the seismic shifts, the quantum leaps, the imaginative initiatives which have come from republicans?
>
> (Graham 2003)

This was a new gloss on an old argument and unity was to be achieved by 2016, on the anniversary of the 1916 rebellion.

For the two governments, however, the important characteristic of the Agreement was neither its unionist nor its nationalist inflections. If any 'ism' defined the disposition of London and Dublin it was 'stabilism' and they looked to the new institutions to provide continuity. The important thing was to secure order in the short and the medium run. Nor was it inconsistent to seek stability and to seek change for ideally the two were interrelated. Change was only deliverable through stable institutions (the unionist view) and the stability of the institutions was only achievable through change (the nationalist view). Indeed, the objective of the Brooke/Mayhew Talks of 1991/2 had been to get agreement on institutions that were stable but capable of development and the arrangements provided for in the Agreement were no different. At that time, it just did not seem possible to get those perspectives to fit together easily. In 1996 Fergus Finlay, one of the key Irish advisers in the early days of the peace process, argued that the British and Irish view was simple: 'if Sinn Fein want to see it (the settlement) as a transition and loyalists as permanent – we want to see it as durable' (cited in Schulze 1997: 103). Finlay's understanding implied a difficult and perhaps dangerous strategy of managing perceptions. It assumed that unionists and nationalists would keep their attention fixed exclusively on their own positive interpretation of the Agreement. And while attention was fixed there, political institutions would be able to take root and a common allegiance to those institutions would grow into a stable settlement. However, he assumed that sufficient majorities within each constituency would continue to see things that way. That was a very large assumption and the history of Northern Ireland provided no expectation for such continuity of perception. How, then, do we explain the fact that a majority of unionists and nationalists, supposedly so acutely alive to the politics of manipulation, voted in the May 1998 referendum for this strategically ambiguous Agreement?

Agreement: duck or rabbit?

One straightforward answer would be that the public was manipulated and hoodwinked by intensively funded government propaganda, political choreography, bad faith and a compliant media (Moloney 1998b). This was a widespread belief, especially amongst unionists, and its political effect will be considered more fully in Chapter 8. One other possible answer can be found in Kenneth Minogue's essay on the character of political disagreement. His concern was to explore a form of ambiguity that resulted neither from subjective ways of looking at the world (the sorts of ambiguity deliberative democracy believes can be resolved through discussion) nor from objective realities (the realities that an historic compromise seeks to accommodate). What interested Minogue was that element in politics, a split in perception, that often made problems immune to resolution or compromise. He thought that Wittgenstein's use of the famous perceptual puzzle pioneered by Jastrow – an image which can be seen as the head of a duck but also as the head of a rabbit – provided an insight into the intractability of some problems. Wittgenstein had been keen to examine the logical grammar of understanding such ambiguous objects. He proposed that the duck/rabbit image had different 'aspects' and to see the same image as a duck or to see it as a rabbit was to attend to only one of these aspects and to exclude the other. In this perceptual puzzle, the aspect is half visual experience and half thought. But our perception in this simple case is unstable for it 'might switch from one thing to another, from duck to rabbit, or back, without *either* any significant change in the object, the facts, or any thought, judgement or in any real sense, an act of interpretation on our part' (Minogue 1996a: 219). In politics, argued Minogue, the likelihood is that our perceptions are more stable. People usually become committed to one perception of reality. Leadership in politics was the exercise of will, 'a fixed determination to see things one way rather than another', and the capacity to persuade others to see things that way as well. The duck/rabbit puzzle illustrated how differences in politics may not be attributed to different values nor to a rational misunderstanding of the nature of things. Differences could not be put down to mere illusions, false consciousness nor to collective brainwashing. There is a great deal of illusion and deception in politics 'but an illusion is an idea which depends for its meaning on the contrast with reality'. Some things, however, '*are* nothing else but what they seem'. Accordingly, the problem in politics 'is that they can *seem* to be two, or even more things' (1996a: 220). That problem, of course, can be also an opportunity, the sort of opportunity that politicians like Finlay clearly recognize. Albeit highly abstract, Minogue's conclusions are appropriate to understanding the shape of the Agreement.

It is possible to argue that politics from at least the time of the Downing Street Declaration onwards was about convincing the IRA that their militaristic duck should really be a political rabbit. The peace process may have required republican initiative as the Sinn Fein leadership constantly claims but that was only a part of it. The larger part was the political equivalent of rehabilitation therapy, retraining republican eyes to see the rabbit and not the duck. To achieve this, the republican leadership required the resources of the British, Irish and American Governments, as well as the patience of others. It was also about convincing unionists that the peace process rabbit was not a republican duck. This was all the more difficult to do since the Sinn Fein rabbit claimed to be separate from the IRA duck. For Moloney, the republican ideological u-turn was so enormous and so obvious that anti-Agreement unionism could only be attributed to those 'who either cannot or will not see it' (Moloney 2001a). The problem with the Sinn Fein/IRA distinction was that unionists saw double. The new language they heard had older echoes. Like Orwell's interpretation of Soviet sophistry, the republican newspeak about the delicacy of 'transition' and 'process' sounded remarkably like 'I believe in killing your opponents when you can get good results by doing so' (cited in Thody 1993: 29). This made unionist rehabilitation therapy all the harder to effect. As Minogue was well aware, our ability to cope with the duck/rabbit problem is limited. We all face 'an indeterminacy so intractable that it can neither be attributed to the complexity of the world nor to the partisanship of our points of view' (Minogue 1996a: 226). So, depending on how you looked at the Agreement, it could be a duck, the shape of which revealed the emerging features of a united Ireland; or it could be a rabbit, the shape of which revealed the continuing strength of the Union. What is more, it could be both things at once.

At the time of the referendum even normally fatalistic unionist voters willed themselves to see the *principled* rabbit in the Agreement and turned out in just sufficient numbers to vote 'yes'. Subsequent experience of the *mechanisms* of the Agreement made many of them look again to see a republican duck and there were plenty of unionist politicians to say 'I told you so, that's the shape it always had'. The crisis in unionist politics can be attributed to this instability of perception, depending on mood, depending on circumstance and depending on the level of irritation caused by their opponents. Unionists in the main did not recognize a fundamental distinction between 'overall constitutional direction' and 'the process of conflict management'. The apparent appeasement of republicans on the management of decommissioning and on the reform of policing fed their concern about the direction of policy. The complex arrangements, argued unionist critics, were designed to conceal the betrayal of principle that had taken place. The betrayal was the willingness of the British and Irish Governments to accept an equivalence between the unionist position and that of the IRA. On the issue of guns and government, unionists thought that equivalence actually meant prejudice in favour of the bargaining strength of Sinn Fein. Thus critics of the emerging dynamic of the peace process challenged the claim that it was about securing a balanced accommodation between unionism and nationalism in Northern Ireland. On the contrary, they argued, it was a dispensation that would erode Northern Ireland's position within the United Kingdom. And nationalists enjoyed exploiting such concerns. One commentator described Trimble as unionism's very own Bishop Muzorewa, 'a unionist leader carrying out a nationalist project for a British Government' (Feeney 2003b).

Nationalist or republican opinion was less volatile but it was not immune from the duck/rabbit problem either. In the opinion of Sinn Fein's critics, the Agreement was being sold as a duck (the struggle continues by other means) in order to divide unionists but in the shape of a rabbit (the war really is over) in order to win over public opinion. The truth was that the Sinn Fein leadership had abandoned their principles and had accepted the mechanisms of partition (McIntyre 2001: 216–17). To conceal the gap between principle and practice entailed a tight management of republican opinion, what one observer called 'a type of censortainment, a means of distracting attention and thus avoiding debate' about the duck/rabbit problem (McDonald 2002). The hesitations within the broad nationalist constituency can also be attributed to an instability of perception, depending on circumstance and on the level of irritation caused by unionists. It can be traced in the columns of the *Irish News*. Feeney, for example, argued (here inverting neatly the unionist criticism of nationalism) that all the problems had been the result of the British and Irish Governments making concessions to unionist intransigence (Feeney 2003c). Nationalists too made the link between principle and mechanism and thought that the implementation of the Agreement should embody their view of what those principles meant. For the two governments, it was not the perceptual problem that was uppermost but ensuring stability of performance and delivery of reform. Nevertheless, the duck/rabbit puzzle *was* their problem for it threatened not only the delivery of the Agreement but the very survival of the Agreement. In short, perceptual disagreement about the Agreement itself became the major source of instability. People may see only part of the picture and not the whole; they may see only what they choose to see; or they may wish the whole to be something other than what it is. Whatever the reason, the devolved institutions in Northern Ireland have had a fitful existence and the alternation between operation and suspension seemed to match the perceptual alternation of duck and rabbit in Jastrow's puzzle.

One substantial academic reflection on these matters can be found in Ruane's readings of the Agreement. He was in no doubt that the situation in Northern Ireland had changed but the key question was: 'into what?' He thought three readings were possible. The first was an optimistic reading that located the changes of the 1990s in the familiar landscape of globalization and postmodernity. The former was shorthand for the transformation of political and economic relationships that had been symbolized by the fall of communism. This had changed how people perceived the reality of Northern Ireland. The latter was shorthand for a triumph of historical and cultural revisionism that undermined the old ideological certainties upon which unionism and nationalism had been grounded. Together these developments suggested that it was possible for everyone in Northern Ireland to achieve a common perception of their political status such that conflict and 'the conditions of its reproduction' would be eroded. The Agreement was a confirmation of that achievement. The rival interpretations of its ultimate direction represented the last vestiges of the old way of thinking as the 'virtuous circle of conflict reduction and resolution' spiralled to success. The second reading was less optimistic and located recent events 'within the unfolding dynamics of the traditional conflict'. The old struggle may have become less intense and definitely less violent but the wider changes presupposed by the first reading were more apparent than real. Globalization and postmodernization were having an effect but their modification of deeper cultural and political differences had been limited. The Agreement was an institutionalized holding operation whilst the forces of unionism and nationalism regrouped and repositioned themselves. This did not mean that violence was merely on sabbatical. What it did mean was that a return to conflict could not be ruled out. The third reading gave an even more pessimistic inflection to the second one. Despite the positive assessment some commentators made of the diametrically opposed communal understandings of the Agreement, these interpretations have had practical effect. Leaders are expected to deliver and the consequence of trying to deliver will continue to be communal tension, mistrust and low-level violence. Unionists and nationalists, albeit in different circumstances, remain compelled to do what they have done for the last 30 years: 'monitor change, anticipate threats and dangers, build up its resources, and struggle to defend or advance its position' (Ruane 1999: 151–65).

Ruane's concern was to examine the suggestion that some 'end of Irish history' had been reached. This had indeed been a particular hope invested in the Agreement. And since every end is also a beginning, the further hope had been that Northern Ireland would achieve a new foundation in democracy, equality and non-violence. It was, as we noted in Chapter 1, the ideal of those who imagined that changing the context of the Ulster Question would change also the nature of the problem, restructuring relationships in a positive manner in order to overcome the 'fatalistic sense of continuous conflict that undermines trust between communities' (Walker 2000: 121). Ruane's other two readings corresponded to the view that those efforts envisaging political harmony are futile and that assumptions of some rational end to Irish history are a distortion (Stewart 2001: 182–5). Although Ruane suggested that it was the first reading, emphasizing change, that took the long historical view, the opposite may be argued with equal vigour. One is reminded of Oakeshott's rather mischievous remark that the Bolshevik revolution of 1917 was really a modification of Russian circumstances, a judgement that appears to us today to be more judicious than it did when he originally made it. What he proposed was an historical rule of thumb to the effect that the further one gets from a major event the more one is likely to notice continuities. This raises important questions about the way in which a significant event (like the Agreement) does indeed modify circumstances or the way in which circumstances come to modify our understanding of the significance of an event. The emphasis will be either on radical disruption (a break in continuity) or on circumstantial adaptation (continuity by other means). Ruane's three readings may be conveniently compressed into two: one that reads the Agreement as a new beginning or a refoundation and one that reads it as a modification of circumstances. And, in the light of the duck/rabbit puzzle, we can also understand how it could sometimes be read in both ways.

A new beginning

To see the Agreement as a new beginning is to perceive Northern Ireland in its Sunday best, to awake from the dream of alliance and find it real. It is to expect that participation in the democratic process will encourage antagonists to change their minds and their preferences 'as a result of the reflection induced by deliberation' (Dryzek 2000: 31). It is to encounter a Northern Ireland that is born again, a Northern Ireland in which a new identity has emerged 'out of the very process of conflict resolution' (Delanty 1996: 30). It is an acutely moral vision and the use of quasi-religious language is often appropriate. Hannah Arendt has explored this approach to politics in *The Human Condition*, where she identified its radical anticipation. It is in 'the nature of beginning', she thought, 'that something new is started which cannot be expected from whatever may have happened before'. This 'startling unexpectedness' is the promise of a 'second birth', an idea that gives a moral underpinning of freedom and responsibility to the cynical political argument: that was then and this is now. In a passage replete with religious imagery, Arendt wrote that the 'miracle that saves the world, the realm of human affairs from its normal, "natural" ruin is ultimately the fact of natality'. This is the power of the 'new beginning' and it bestows on human affairs those two essential characteristics of faith and hope. She concluded by arguing that it

> is this faith in and hope for the world that found perhaps its most glorious and most succinct expression in the few words with which the Gospels announced their 'glad tidings': 'A child has been born unto us'.
> (Arendt 1958: 178, 274)

The Belfast Agreement had that glad tidings quality.

One insightful unionist commentator, long an advocate of political accommodation, observed that the 'days leading up to and immediately following the agreement were hopeful ones reminiscent of people in other times and places devising new structures bringing their respective conflicts to an end'. The birth of new institutions, like all new births, would be painful, slow and messy but the process itself ought to be one of hope in which people should have faith (Garland 2003a). It would mean the bringing forth of a commonality where before there had been only division. The new world that had been in people's hearts would now find embodiment and expression in the procedures of government. As Oakeshott once argued, the authority of political institutions is not so much a question of consent, as unionists and nationalists would believe, but rather the acknowledgement by citizens of their obligation to observe the conditions of political association. It is the authority of these obligations rather than the principle of consent that sustains a community (Oakeshott 1975: 152–8). Accepting the provisions of the Agreement and acting according to their spirit, as well as their letter, fully reconciled the form of the new beginning (sharing power) with its substance (sharing responsibility). The Agreement would become the foundation myth that told the story of how this new Northern Ireland had come about and explained the authoritative moral consensus in which its institutions were grounded. That myth would justify not only the political architecture of power-sharing but also its single passionate thought: that everyone was absolutely committed to democracy and the peaceful resolution of differences. Yet was it *really* possible, as the editor of *Fortnight* asked, to think that the drama of Easter 1998 will 'be communally remembered as the story we can all tell our grandchildren of how we got to where we are'? It was not myth but hard fact that would be critical and he thought that the Agreement was quite prosaic. Not only was no other deal imaginable but also no other deal was allowable (O'Farrell 2000: 5). None the less, polling evidence did suggest that a substantial proportion of the electorate at the time of the referendum did indeed think that the Agreement represented a 'new beginning' and that this was a more important consideration for Protestants than for Catholics (Hayes and McAllister 2001: 82). Both could buy into their respective mythologies of that 'new beginning' and so long as these mythologies emphasized expressions of goodwill and rather than long-term political intent then it was possible to conceive of a reconciled space and a common belonging.

Something like this reconciled space had been suggested by the publishing collective Field Day. Its concept of the fifth province could, at one level, describe that place, as Hederman put it, 'where all oppositions were resolved', that neutral space 'where all things can detach themselves from all partisan and prejudiced connection'. For Tom Paulin it provided an 'invisible challenge to the nationalistic image of the four green fields' (cited in Richards 1991: 140). That Field Day's reading of the Northern Ireland problem remained a nationalist one, that its ultimate objective was Irish unity and that its postcolonial framework of analysis was inappropriate, is not the issue here (see Ellis 1996). Never mind that *The Field Day Anthology of Irish Writing* was accused of perpetuating unreconstructed Irish nationalism, of trying to camouflage an old agenda under trendy and radical language (Ruane 1994b: 114–16). Though the 'fifth province' was indeed mythological, it did at least acknowledge the possibility of something other than the eternal replay of Orange versus Green. It was an intimation of an ideal third option that awaited circumstances to give it political reality and as Richards judiciously commented perhaps 'the exclusivist, unitary nature of some fifth-province thinking would seem to be a stage of development, a necessary prelude to a recognition of possibilities inherent in the 1990s' (Richards 1991: 148). Perhaps the Agreement was that recognition and had now changed the question. There was also another and earlier Protestant version of such a transcendent political and cultural space and it can be found in the work of the Ulster poet John Hewitt. In his view Ulster was a 'valid region with the inalienable right to choose its place within a smaller or larger federation' (Richards 1991: 146). It was this idea of a regional loyalty, rather than the claims of Irish or British nationalism, that would permit the reconciliation of Planter and Gael. For Hewitt, Ulster considered 'as a region and not as the symbol of any particular creed' could command the loyalty of all its inhabitants. It could do so because a region did not preclude, rather it required, membership of a larger association. Hewitt thought that out of a 'loyalty to our own place, rooted in honest history, in familiar folkways and knowledge, phrased in our own dialect' there could develop a vibrant culture with much to offer Europe and the rest of the world (cited in Longley 1994b: 126). Here was a fraught version of the argument for hybridity but one struggling to be realized as the twentieth century drew to its close (Longley 2000a: 65). To discuss a 'reconciled space' in terms of such contrary projects of reconciliation identifies the problem

Was it possible to reconcile the projects within a new Northern Ireland? John Wilson Foster examined the proposition that Catholic and Protestant could feel 'equally *of* Ulster'. What real reason did we have, apart from wishing away division, that a regional focus would promote a common identity? If Ulster's recent history had been distinguished by 'its inability to decide whether it is primarily a region of Ireland or a region of Britain' its cultural history had been distinguished by its inability to assume a unique cultural form that represented both. There could never be, so Foster thought, 'a synthetic non-sectarian Ulster culture'. The only hope lay in dropping the 'veils of outside causes and dogmas' – that Ulster is as British as Finchley or that Ireland is one cultural community – and concentrating on sharing the region as best one could (Foster 1991: 278–95; emphasis in original). Even if the inflection of Ulster regionalism remained unionist, the important thing was the acknowledgement of an imaginative space beyond that particular interest. Indeed, one could argue that the Agreement spelled out that condition in cold print. It was up to the people of Northern Ireland to determine their own future and it was precisely this condition that Akenson thought now required a new set of 'scriptures'. Protestant and Catholic needed to forget the savage truths about one another and substitute agreeable lies. They also needed to surrender their respective 'tribal unconscious' and substitute reasoned discourse. These 'new and pacific scriptures' might lead eventually in Northern Ireland to the emergence of an 'awkward and prickly' entity: a nation (Akenson 2000: 58–61). Perhaps, as one of the sharpest cultural critics argued, 'the concept of "Northern Ireland", and how it might evolve, is where the really interesting prospects lie' (Longley 2000b: 21). That was a hopeful view but it still required an amazing leap of faith.

That leap of faith was systematically theorized in Porter's *The Elusive Quest* (2003), a theorization where politics had indeed become a secular religion announcing Akenson's new scriptures. The fatedness of the old ugly conflict, argued Porter, needed to be moralized into the new beauty of 'strong reconciliation'. The objective should be a 'Northern politics of belonging' where the instrumental machinations of politicians gave way to 'fair interactions between citizens' and where civic virtues would become crucial and dialogue indispensable. 'It is when we conceive of a reconciled society as a goal that is possible through fair interactions and through pursuit of commonality that respects our non-sectarian differences' that we then have good reason to condemn undemocratic and militaristic challenges to the Belfast Agreement (Porter 2003: 264). At great length, Porter set out the principles of a new beginning in and a democratic transformation of Northern Ireland. As a prophetic vision, the book had a certain merit, mapping the terrain of a Jerusalem to be built on Ulster's green and pleasant land. On the other hand, it appeared to be a map of a Jerusalem without actual people. Of course, 'anti-Agreement unionists and republicans offer no hope of a reconciled society'. Unfortunately, 'pro-Agreement unionists and republicans offer limited hope of it too' (2003: 255). This conclusion rendered the argument politically irrelevant. Reviewing the book, Trimble grasped its critical intent but also pointed to the void at its core. He suggested that Porter had treated the Agreement 'as a foundational event allowing the radical reconstruction of a new politics in Northern Ireland' rather than 'an honourable historic compromise' between unionism and nationalism. Moreover, Porter provided no clue as to how the radical transformation he required could be brought about. No thought appeared to have been given to agency and as a consequence its 'highly moralistic approach to politics' made 'high, not to say impossible, demands on a population which is emerging from thirty years of polarising terrorist violence' (Trimble 2003a). For all its sophistication of argument, Porter's approach was yet another example of a beautiful vision of Northern Ireland corrupted only by the inconvenient fact that unionists continued to be unionists and nationalists to be nationalists. This is the banality of goodness. However, it did provide a useful digest of those principles that were implied in the ideal of a 'new beginning' as a well as a measure of how distant from reality that ideal really was. Porter clearly found distasteful the moral equivocation and ethical slipperiness involved in the business of practical politics. He shared this distaste with many of those who were *opposed* to the Agreement and this illustrates the irony, as well as the contrariness, of such a moralizing approach to politics. Despite the lack of substance in the refoundation theoretically explored by Porter it was a rhetorical theme that constantly recurred in pro-Agreement unionism and nationalism. To the traditional and one-sided, messages of securing the Union or paving the way to Irish unity was another that chose ethics rather than ethnics.

For example, and despite his criticisms of Porter, the idea of a new Northern Ireland formed a key part of Trimble's speeches and interviews. Since, he argued, the principle of consent had been accepted and since there was not going to be constitutional change as far as anyone could see, the incentive was there for unionists to say: 'There is not going to be a united Ireland. How can we make Northern Ireland work for all its citizens?' (Trimble 2003b). Changes required in Northern Ireland demanded much of unionism but ultimately it was worth it. There were two dimensions, the first external and the second internal. The vision, first, was one in which practical cooperation between North and South could end what Trimble once called the 'cold war' between the traditions on the island. In a reflective address to the Irish Association in November 1998, Trimble implied that the Agreement had created a new situation in which old antagonistic strategies could be overcome.

> Economic co-operation, we trust, is no longer advanced as a strategy for creeping unification. After the Agreement there is no longer any need to engage in such tactical manoeuvres and a growth in co-operation is consequently possible.

A more fruitful approach was proposed.

Is it not better to say: 'This area has proven potential, let us see how we can build upon it', rather than, 'This was on the agenda in 1965 and 1975 and the situation now demands more'?

(Trimble 1999)

It was a pragmatic understanding to which Southern nationalists could also respond. As Mansergh argued, there was nothing inevitable about cross-border cooperation leading to Irish unity (cited in Moloney 2000a). This view of North/South matters complemented Trimble's vision for Northern Ireland set out in a speech to business and community leaders in Belfast a few months earlier. 'We can now', he proposed, 'get down to the historic and honourable task of this generation: to raise up a new Northern Ireland in which pluralist unionism and constitutional nationalism can speak to each other with the civility which is the foundation of freedom' (Trimble 2001: 79). As he had put it earlier, with conscious reference to Lord Craigavon's famous assertion about a Protestant parliament and a Protestant state, 'new unionism' aspired to 'a pluralist Parliament for a pluralist people' and a government by its people for its people. Indeed, he argued that there was only one political ethic and agreed with Seamus Mallon's proposition that unionists and nationalists had to underpin one another. Only politics conducted in this spirit could save the Agreement from destruction (Trimble 2001: 137). Or as one pro-Agreement spokesman for the loyalist paramilitaries put it, only thus could Northern Ireland become (as Hewitt would have wanted) a 'rational region' (D. Adams 1995: 16).

That spirit was obvious enough to nationalists, North and South. For Fergus Finlay the peace process was an endeavour to replace zero-sum politics, the politics of winning and losing, with an alternative, what he called 'the principle of mutuality'. It was a principle that 'tacitly asserts that the principles of both sides must be respected, while the interests of both sides must be reconciled' (Finlay 2003). Finlay's interpretation was the practical thinker's version of Porter who, by contrast, wanted to achieve the more difficult task of reconciling principles and respecting interests. It was a more astute reading of possibilities and though Finlay acknowledged the hesitant and fitful achievements of its application he did think that it held out some possibility of success. Equally, Sean Farren of the SDLP proclaimed a major conceptual change ushered in by the peace process in which the principle of self-determination was being replaced by the principle of co-determination. This was an intellectualized version of a longstanding claim of Hume's and identified the SDLP's purpose to be that of shifting the focus of politics from territory to people (a real fifth province). Irish unity now required 'the assent of significant sections of both communities in the North as well as the assent of the people in the South'. As a result, the people of Northern Ireland would have to take responsibility for their own future, albeit within a framework set by cooperation between London and Dublin (Farren and Mulvihill 1996). Reluctantly and ambiguously, it also appeared that republicans had tacitly come to accept that framework. If Irish unity was still thought to be inevitable, the political task now appeared to be that of creating 'equality' within Northern Ireland, which was a rather new objective. Sinn Fein, it has been argued, was responding to a 'psychological watershed for many Catholics' in which the old identity of victimhood had become redundant. Catholics were at last comfortable enough 'to feel at home in Northern Ireland' and this was a key factor in the politics of the new beginning (Mitchell 2003: 66).

Therefore it was possible to interpret traditional notions of saving the Union or promoting Irish unity as rhetorical flourishes that served to ease the foundations of a new Northern Ireland. For example, Durkan's recommitment of the SDLP to a united Ireland could also be read as taking the Agreement to represent an enduring settlement between unionism and nationalism. It was one that really did permit the parties to underwrite, as Mallon had hoped, 'each other's legitimacy and underwrite shared institutions instead of undermining each other's legitimacy and cherished aspirations' (Durkan 2003). That sort of enduring arrangement was the one to which Trimble aspired in his requirement of republicans to acknowledge the Agreement as a full and final settlement of the conflict. And it was such an enduring arrangement that Adams appeared to accept in his statement of 21 October 2003: 'Implementation of the agreement provides the context in which Irish republicans and Unionists will, as equals, pursue their objectives peacefully, thus providing full and final closure of the conflict' (Godson 2004: 788–90). Unfortunately, things were not that clear cut as subsequent events proved. The solidity of the refoundation and the mutuality of the new beginning were open to question, not only in terms of the practice but also in terms of the theory. This suggested that the new rabbit pulled out of the Agreement hat could look to unionists and nationalists suspiciously like a duck by other means.

Modification of circumstances

Harvey provided an interesting case study of the ambivalence in nationalist perspectives. The legal theory suggested something determinate, the emergence of a 'new constitutional order'. The political theory suggested something indeterminate in which everything remained 'up for grabs'. The first implied that there was now a fixed shape to public expectations. The second implied that everything was in a state of transition. The new constitutional order, predicated on institutional stability, appeared to clash with the further claim that this stability, a stability based on the principle of consent, was only temporary. The consent principle was 'the deliberative basis for productive instability from a nationalist/republican perspective'. There may be some truth, Harvey claimed, in the term 'constitutional settlement' but 'by the nature of the system it may only be for now' (Harvey 2001a: 10). If the virtue of the Agreement lay in the twin values of transformation and transition, Harvey did not believe that everything had been transformed. Nor did he think that the transition had been completed. Northern Ireland realities were not so immediately tractable. Nevertheless, he believed that 'the normative basis for a new beginning is clearly established'. The normative basis was explicit in the Agreement's commitment to human rights, equality and democratic governance and the progressive task was to set about reconstructing constitutional law and democracy in Northern Ireland accordingly. Importantly, it was the idea of a constitution that was in greatest need of reconstruction and that involved not so much a new beginning as going over old ground. 'Northern Ireland', Harvey proposed, 'was born from violence and it has proved difficult to bury the memory of this.' Historically 'the partition of Ireland seems more an exercise in avoidance than polity formation' and this led him to the observation that one could argue 'that Northern Ireland never "constituted" itself legitimately as a political entity' (Harvey 2001a: 14). One could – but one would be wrong historically, legally and politically. If in the interests of an historic compromise unionists accepted the need to address nationalist alienation in the manner prescribed by Harvey, his subsequent ambivalence threatened to undermine the very compromise entered into.

For Harvey a constitution is 'both a constitutive act and the basis for continuing dialogue' (Harvey 2001b: 51). There were two interpretations of the relationship between constitutive act and continuing dialogue. The first suggested that, reconstituted under the Agreement, Northern Ireland had now been legitimately refounded and that all reform should be designed to confirm that legitimacy. The principles of the deal here really do inform the mechanisms and under a stable constitution the nature of the old political divisions would be radically transformed. It would require a period of transition but the end and the means would be fully acceptable to everyone. This would conform to the sort of new Northern Ireland that Trimble sought to raise up. The second implied that Northern Ireland could never be legitimately constituted in that manner because the transformation necessarily involved the removal of British sovereignty and the transition also necessarily involved steady progress towards Irish unity. In this sense, the reconstitution of Northern Ireland had become the deconstruction of Northern Ireland. Of course, the Agreement did not rule out this second meaning. Harvey was justified in referring to it as an ultimate goal. Unfortunately, the emphasis upon this goal's parallel life cast a shadow over the integrity of the institutions. The benefit for unionists appeared to be that republicans had stopped trying to blast them out of the United Kingdom and that was hardly something they would appreciate as a great concession. The 'constitutional status of Northern Ireland remains open to contestation, but this is a conflict confined in the future to something approaching the force of the better argument'. Nevertheless, 'the contest over the status of Northern Ireland has not ended'. The constant repetition of status *contestation* suggested that the new beginning had become a modification of nationalist circumstances in which it is only 'the way that the contest will be conducted that has fundamentally altered' and not the nature of the contest itself (Harvey 2001b: 29).

Unfortunately, the very premises of Harvey's nationalist argument (like Porter's) came close to conceding the position of those unionists who remained anti-Agreement. If it was indeed true that 'contrary to what is often said, the status of Northern Ireland remains contested by the nature of the normative principles upon which it is based' the same could be said of the status of the Agreement. Its unionist critics argued that it was born out of the threat of IRA violence, was sold on a deceitful basis, was morally insupportable and, given the growing disillusion of unionist voters, lacked democratic legitimacy. Harvey's position implied that it was illegitimate to permit continuing dialogue on the value of nationalist gains for these were the 'constituted' elements of the Agreement. 'Continuing dialogue' was appropriate to those aspects of the Agreement that were unionist gains. That was an astute political manoeuvre and conceived to secure partisan advantage. As an intelligent nationalist reading of the new circumstances, it was a position readily adopted, implicitly and explicitly, by the leaders of Sinn Fein and the SDLP. However, it struck unionists as a case of having your constitution and eating it – or constituting an advantage in order to deconstruct Northern Ireland. It appeared another example of 'the slippery slope syndrome' (Guelke 1997: 13). One unionist whose reconciliatory credentials could not be doubted thought that this approach was against the notion of a new beginning. He accepted that the SDLP and Sinn Fein were within their rights to promote unity but this was at odds with the spirit of the Agreement. Of course, such a settlement 'must be open to change but that is not the same as saying it was only a means to a specific end that subverted the central aspirations of one of the partners'. This represented no 'change of heart' on the part of nationalists and so did not free 'unionists from the terrors of obliteration' (Garland 2003b; see also A. Foster 2003). For republicans, the 'historic compromise' may have been no compromise at all, just a modification of positional logic in which 'what was agreed in 1998 would ultimately prove to be a far more effective way of ending partition than armed struggle' (Patterson 2002: 26). Some unionists with a longer historical and literary perspective might have recalled Patrick Pearse's comment on Douglas Hyde's dove of peace: 'his peace is necessary to my war' (cited in Stewart 2000: 43). After the Agreement, this republican peace appeared to many unionists to be war by other means. This may have been a misreading of a more subtle reality but if so it was an understandable one.

A nationalist reading of unionist behaviour frequently made as little acknowledgement of a new beginning as unionists did of theirs. Indeed, there was a strong consensus amongst nationalist commentators that there was nothing new at all, just a modified and more divided dance around traditional sectarian totems. The unionist argument that the IRA needed to disarm and disband in order to set the seal on a new settlement in Northern

Ireland often met the response that since nothing would ever satisfy unionists such gestures were irrelevant. The demand for IRA decommissioning became, therefore, just one more example of unionists resisting the need for change and all problems of implementation were the result of this irredeemable attitude. Unionists, it was claimed, were still trying to revise 'traditional methods of containing Catholics' (McGurk 2003). They had seen the future the Agreement unfolded before them and 'naturally they are agin it'. Since the whole purpose of Northern Ireland was to maintain unionist domination the prospect of equality destroyed its reason for existing. The 'inevitable outworkings' of the Agreement 'are too much for unionists to stomach'. Despite the fine language, the strategy of Trimble since 1998 had been to frustrate the rights of nationalists and to demand constant revisions to suit the most reactionary elements within his community. 'His own intemperate language and his rejection of any radical change the agreement requires have confirmed for many middle-class unionists that their suspicions about the agreement were well founded.' That is what unionism is for and within it 'nothing has changed, nor will it'. What is worse, the British and Irish Governments have continued to give in to it (Feeney 2003d). If unionists could never accept anything, then the message appeared to be that they should be given nothing. Was it imaginable, asked one literary republican (echoing the Schmittian notion), that the UUP could ever become

> a party that would not confuse the meanings of 'opponent' and 'enemy', would not feel itself doomed to be at permanent odds with almost half the population, and would not go into self-destructive paroxysms every time it failed to get its own way?

Could unionists ever contribute to an enduring settlement that would command the support of both communities? The short answer was: 'Almost certainly not' (Bennett 1998). Those sorts of comment captured a mood within nationalism that was increasingly dismissive of any unionist objections to events. That response hardly measured up to the rhetoric of underwriting each other's cherished aspirations. If, as Harvey claimed, the principle of consent created instability from a nationalist and republican perspective, then the principle of nationalist contempt created instability from a unionist perspective (this will be discussed more fully in Chapter 8).

There was a deeper problem. If the Agreement simply modified the way that the contest was to be conducted, then republicans, having lost their war, appeared determined still to win the argument. If this were so what incentive was there for unionists to operate on the assumption of a new beginning? It was easy to criticize unionists for not acknowledging the great steps republicans had taken except that the IRA had not signed up to anything. The duck/rabbit distinction that republicans made between Sinn Fein and the IRA meant that there was unionist uncertainty about the bargain entered into. If Harvey's reflections on legitimacy return us to 1920, then there was a more immediate anxiety for unionists. That the outcome of nearly 30 years of struggle against armed republicanism should issue in Sinn Fein in government and a fully armed and equipped IRA still in place was an obvious 'deliberative basis for productive instability' from a unionist perspective. The obvious difficulties this created were shrugged off as not being Sinn Fein's responsibility (O'Doherty 2003a: 3). Moreover, even moderate nationalists fell into the habit of a politics of equivalence in which the real and open deliberative democracy of the Ulster Unionist Council was put on a par with the secret deliberations of the IRA Army Council (Durkan 2003). These attitudes can also be found in the debate over the policing reform. For republicans, winning the argument about the abolition of the Royal Ulster Constabulary (RUC) was not only about better policing but also about the nature of the IRA's campaign of violence. There was slippage between the legitimate proposition that policing must become more acceptable to Catholics and the illegitimate proposition that there was moral equivalence between the acts of the IRA and those of the RUC. The claim that unionists should have accepted the need for generosity on policing ignores the role of the SDLP in this matter. It has been argued that the SDLP placed a literal interpretation of the policing reform above the spirit of maintaining broad-base support. The result of their 'absolutist position stood in contrast to their demand that others compromise on other outstanding areas of the Agreement'. In this Alliance Party view, few of the issues that have caused disruption between unionists and nationalists have been peculiarly intractable. The problem has been an absence of mutual responsibility and an inability of the major parties 'to abandon exclusivist demands and interpretations in order to facilitate progress' (Farry 2002: 38–41). The lament was for a real commitment to refounding the basis of politics and for the absence of what Porter called strong reconciliation.

The core of the difficulty is easy to state. It is a question of will rather than ingenuity. Consociational arrangements of the sort found in the Agreement are political rather than legal or constitutional constructs. The constitutional procedures must be willed for procedures alone are unlikely to call forth a genuinely supportive popular culture. If that willingness was absent, then it was unclear 'how a grand exercise in constitution-writing can bring it into existence' (Noel 2001: 223–4). Here, perhaps, was another example of an error of intelligence, an intellectual aspiration to get beyond the frustrating limits of the past that left undisturbed the passionate intensity that set those limits in the first place. It was not impossible to channel those passions constructively but that only begged the unresolved duck/rabbit question: what *was* being constructed?

Conclusion

The Spanish American philosopher George Santayana once observed that between 'two nothings there is eternal peace; but between two somethings if they come within range of each other, there is always danger of war' (Santayana 1951: 449). Even in peace there remained the possibility of a contest of non-negotiable demands, a modification of the circumstances of conflict into the politics of communal self-assertion. The way to avoid this consequence, Santayana believed, was through what he called 'chivalry'. As O'Sullivan interpreted it, chivalry resembled the idea of a historic compromise, one that 'does not require any abandonment of one's own interests; it does not aim, as liberalism aims, at the elimination of power from the world; what it does is reject man's tendency to attach absolute significance to those interests' (O'Sullivan 1992: 88). The duck/rabbit puzzle of the Agreement meant that most people could appreciate its chivalrous potential (the desire for a new beginning) but found it hard to accept that others no longer attached absolute significance to their own interests (a modification of circumstances). Whether the modification in conduct was sufficient to sustain the new beginning of the Agreement remained open to question. Northern Ireland politics had been brought as far as the institutions of the Agreement. Unfortunately, the uncertainty about the nature of the deal revealed a profound tension between the traditional vocabulary of politics, albeit in modified circumstances, and the half-formed one of a new beginning. The desire for a new beginning was palpable but in the 'absence of widespread agreement on fundamental political principles, such a desire represents an insecure basis for a permanent settlement' (Hayes and McAllister 2001: 87). The political dynamic was hardly conducive to stability and the institutions of the Agreement were far from stable. Disagreement on principles – duck or rabbit? – meant differential expectations and anxieties not only about the direction of the Agreement but also about the equity of its implementation. These expectations and anxieties, in their many forms, are examined in Part III.

Part III

Consequences

8 Anxiety and expectation

On the basis of a detailed analysis of public opinion in the period immediately following the Belfast Agreement, Evans and O'Leary identified a differential reception of the Agreement's terms. The polling evidence suggested that nationalists were more ready to compromise and therefore more likely to put pressure on their representatives to deliver stability. Unionists, on the other hand, were less committed to compromise and more politically alienated but the possibility did exist that, given time, they would come to reconcile themselves to the Agreement. The 'major bone of contention' for them was the linkage (or lack of proper linkage) between Executive formation and the decommissioning of paramilitary weapons. If that impasse could be resolved then there was a good possibility that the new institutions would securely bed themselves down. In short, the greatest difficulty appeared to be the stabilization of pro-Agreement unionism and the difficulty they recognized was that this process 'cannot be obtained by unwinding those features of the settlement, both procedural and substantive, that have made it acceptable to Republicans' (Evans and O'Leary 2000: 98–9). What they had discovered was the distinction between, on the one hand, unionist anxiety and, on the other, nationalist expectation.

This distinction is a useful rule of thumb but has its limitations. Expectations were also encouraged amongst unionists about what politics could deliver in terms of peace, security and stability and not only anxiety about the price to be paid for these objectives. Nationalist expectations also involved anxiety about delivery in terms of rights, equality and justice. Most sensible observers thought that any workable settlement in Northern Ireland depended not only on an intelligent management of anxiety and expectation *between* political communities but also on a subtle management of anxiety and expectation *within* communities. Nationalist expectations on employment, policing and symbols were more likely to be achieved once unrealistic 'hopes have been removed and unnecessary unionist fears have been assuaged' (English 1997: 25). And if the Agreement were to take proper hold, republicans would have to uproot their culture of denial and protest and unionists would have to overcome their suspicion of political ecumenism (Moloney 1999). For the political historian it was nothing new:

In the late-1960s Ulster stumbled into conflict against a background of rising Irish nationalist expectation, of unionist anxiety in the face of changing times, and of a London government which took too long to recognize the gravity and nuance of the local situation.

(English 2002a: 30)

Unionist expectation

There were two key reference points within which unionist expectations were set. The first was the joint unionist manifesto for the General Election of 1987, agreed by James Molyneaux of the UUP and Ian Paisley of the DUP. That manifesto had committed unionists to seek 'an alternative to and a replacement of' the Anglo-Irish Agreement of 1985. The second reference point was the rejection by all unionist parties of the Framework Document of February 1995. If the Framework Document had set the outer limits of nationalist expectation, the minimalist unionist proposals of 1991/92 set the outer limits of unionist expectation. It was within these political limits that the parties were required to manoeuvre. If an agreement were reached, then the criteria of judgement were well established. To what extent did agreement attain the objectives laid down in the joint unionist manifesto of 1987? Were the institutions to be stable within the Union or were they designed to be transitional to an all-Ireland state? Was the influence of Dublin in the affairs of Northern Ireland diminished or significantly increased? Given these constraints of negotiating expectation, could something be delivered and sold to the unionist electorate?

The UKUP and the DUP had thought it impossible. For McCartney, the only outcome would be getting stuck fast to a process designed to destroy the Union:

Without doubt the whole purpose of these talks is to wring further concessions from the majority that would both undermine the strength of the Union and the quality and nature of their British citizenship and identity.

(McCartney 1995: xiv)

This was a view also held strongly by the DUP. Ulster Unionists were not negotiating a satisfactory alternative to the Anglo-Irish Agreement and the outcome of the talks would be a reformulation that only made matters worse. That claim, of course, was rebutted by Ulster Unionist negotiators and their engagement in the process involved a profound change from 'a low risk strategy' that had only brought a high penalty of marginalization to a 'high risk strategy' that at least held out a promise of success (McGimpsey 1995: 18–19). When agreement was finally reached in April 1998, that high risk strategy was to be severely tested and unionists had to swallow some deeply unpalatable concessions. In an oblique reference to the emotionally charged issues of prisoner releases, police reform and, above all, the prospect of republicans in government without disbandment of the IRA, a senior Ulster Unionist argued that, from the political point of view, 'when the essentials are attained, other elements fall into place'. The proper expectation that the Union was now safe should still the anxiety about accommodating the practical needs of terrorists looking for a way out (Maginnis 1998). From an academic point of view, Bew conceded that the Agreement did demand much of unionists and their anxiety was entirely understandable. It asked them 'to go a long way to meet the concerns of the nationalist minority'. However, in his assessment it was the right thing to do. As a consequence of meeting those concerns unionists could expect to see Northern Ireland's place within the United Kingdom properly secured (Bew 1998). From a journalistic point of view, it was the ambivalence of the unionist position that struck John Lloyd. The Agreement, he reported, 'looks like a huge triumph for David Trimble'. He appeared to have achieved everything on the constitution unionists could reasonably have expected. Why, then, were unionists 'so full of doubt and foreboding'? He reasoned that it was because the 'sweeteners' in the Agreement were republican and the unionist electorate could not bring themselves, after 30 years of violence, 'to see republicans being sweetened' (Lloyd 1998: 12–13). This profound distaste notwithstanding, some veteran political commentators thought that only a dramatic breakdown in the paramilitary ceasefires could restore the fortunes of anti-Agreement unionism. That breakdown seemed highly unlikely and the future appeared (relatively) congenial to unionist expectations (Moloney 2000b).

Certainly Trimble calculated that the anxieties for unionists would be short-term ones and he expected that the long term could now look after itself on the basis of consent. He had certainly taken a risk but that risk had delivered the right structures of governance (Trimble 2003c). Defending his strategy against unionist critics, Trimble argued that the anti-Agreement camp had no alternative and refused to acknowledge the real constraints of negotiation. He further argued that the Belfast Agreement had achieved the unionist goal 'proposed separately by the UUP and the DUP in the 1992 Talks' of placing Northern Ireland's future within a wider British-Irish context than the Agreement of 1985. In order to reach a settlement nationalists had been compelled to lower their expectations from the heights of the Framework Document. It had been the UUP that secured the key aims and this should still unionists' fears, giving them confidence about the future (Trimble 1999). He argued that the parties could

> now get down to the historic and honourable task of this generation: to raise up a new Northern Ireland in which pluralist unionism and constitutional nationalism can speak to each other with the civility which is the foundation of freedom.
>
> (Trimble 2001: 79)

In the referendum in May 1998 a slight majority of the Unionist electorate suppressed their anxieties in favour of this wager on the future. The stilling of anxiety may be associated with an expectation of constitutional security and this was one of the crucial factors that swung the balance in Trimble's favour.

Amid this fragile optimism, however, one can detect two anxieties that actually deepened in the years after the Agreement. For unionists, what was on offer appeared to be a *passive* acknowledgement of the constitutional status of Northern Ireland. For nationalists, by contrast, what was on offer appeared to be an *active* programme of government to address their grievances. This relationship between a static condition of principle – accepting the fact of Northern Ireland's status – and a dynamic set of policies – accepting claims about the historic inequity bound up in that status – did act to destabilize pro-Agreement unionism. This anxiety was the *anxiety of process*. The second and related anxiety concerned the logic of implementation. One of the demoralizing aspects of unionist politics since the Anglo-Irish Agreement had been the sense of political marginalization. With a new deal unionists could be once again at the heart of devolved institutions and could ensure that their voice was not ignored. This positive expectation was matched by a negative anxiety. There was an apprehension that in return for being on the 'inside track' unionists could get trapped in a political logic inimical to their long-term interests. Under pressure from the British, Irish and United States Governments, it might prove very difficult for a leader to resist compromising the unionist position in order to preserve the peace. This was the *anxiety of influence*. In both cases, unionist anxiety can be located in the gap between expectation and, as they saw it, the practice of the Agreement's implementation.

Anxiety of process

The realization of unionist expectations was not entirely in Trimble's gift. It depended on what had been impossible so far in Northern Ireland's history, a sense of mutual responsibility rather than a strategy of sectarian manoeuvre. Unionist disaffection can be attributed in large part to a lack of responsibility on the republican side. The objectionable elements of the Agreement, even if they did not outweigh the considerable constitutional gains, significantly diminished them. Even these objectionable elements like police reform would have been made more palatable if there had been a clear indication that the IRA was in the process of disbandment and that decommissioning of illegal weapons was seriously in progress. Unfortunately, the reverse appeared to be true as incident after incident confirmed the IRA's disregard for exclusively peaceful methods. Sinn Fein appeared to have committed itself only to an 'abstract' version of the Agreement and had refused to accept the real 'responsibilities of making it work in practice' (Trimble 2002a). Five years on Trimble was still appealing to republicans to commit clearly to exclusively peaceful methods, arguing that this was not just a unionist demand but everyone's expectation (Trimble 2003c). The republican response was inadequate to his needs. Moreover, the political cost to unionism of that inadequate response provoked widespread anxiety.

A substantial part of unionist disaffection can be attributed to the outworking of this anxiety of process. The Conservative Party thinker Ian (Lord) Gilmour once argued that ideas and symbols are important weapons in political argument but that a party, rather like an army, marches on its stomach (cited in Norton and Aughey 1981: 9). One could extend that analogy from a party to a political community. In other words, rational conviction can only take you so far. To be popularly persuasive reason needs to have an emotional underpinning. On the eve of the referendum, the editor of the *News Letter* suggested that unionist anxiety was a result of people 'trying to weigh up the obvious benefits that would materialize from a long period of stability' against 'a gut instinct that tells them that what the agreement amounts to is rather more than a tampering with the edges of their society' (Martin 1998). In this light, the story of the years between May 1998 and October 2002 has a rather straightforward narrative. The edifice of rational expectation that Trimble constructed around the constitutional principles and institutions of the Agreement was not so much denied as discounted by a mode of policy implementation that his own party and the wider unionist electorate found alarming and increasingly difficult to accept.

The divide within unionism was thought to be between those 'who take a rational view of the centrality of the consent principle' and those who are not only sceptical of the vitality of that principle in public policy but who also detect 'a micro-agenda alleged to undermine symbols of Britishness'. In short, for this latter group 'the peace dividends are unsatisfactory or non-existent' (Tonge and Evans 2001: 127–8). That did indeed appear to be the key to understanding the anxiety of process. There was a sense of public inequity that contributed to growing unionist disaffection and this position was at first sight rather difficult to explain since republican critics of the peace process claimed that the Agreement showed little or no gain for Sinn Fein after nearly 30 years of violence. However, for unionists the Union was anyway a fact and not an aspiration. To argue that acceptance of the principle of consent was a major achievement that permitted concessions elsewhere was a rational proposition but not an emotionally persuasive one. To have won the battle on the big constitutional issues was a battle that unionists thought should never have had to be fought in the first place. Here was one of the deep ironies of unionist politics after 1998. Historically dominated by the constitutional issue, unionism felt vulnerable to an apparent trade-off between the form of the constitution and the substance of being British. 'If the peace process was aimed at resolving the problem in Ulster, and if fashionable opinion saw that problem as one of Catholic disadvantage, then change would be change hostile to unionist interests'

(English 2002a: 29). If the real politics of the situation required compensation for the impossibility of republican objectives the extent of the compensation could be judged by unionists as nothing other than morally suspect.

This politics of compensation, it has been argued, was directly related to the 'vacuousness at the core of Sinn Fein's reunification project'. Once that had been exposed, republicans required an alternative reform agenda based on ethnic grievance and the British Government's 'indulgence of this agenda became the single most important cause of Unionist disenchantment with the Agreement' (Bew, Gibbon and Patterson 2002: 246). What was required by the politics of compensation provided anti-Agreement unionists with an easily enumerated negative balance sheet. The list included the release of terrorist prisoners whilst paramilitary groups remained active; the 'destruction of the RUC'; a 50/50 recruitment system for the new police service that 'discriminates against Protestant applicants'; and perhaps most systematically threatening of all, the 'erosion of British culture with an equality agenda which discriminates against the unionist community' (Robinson 2003a). The association of an erosion of Britishness with a discriminatory social, economic and security agenda was a potent political mix that the DUP and Trimble's critics within his own party had no difficulty in developing. For example, assessing the merits of the 'human rights agenda', McCartney noted that victims of the republican terror campaign had no real redress against those who had committed crimes against them. This left the unionist community 'with an understandable feeling of resentment at what they see as a denial of justice and their human rights'. On the other hand, they viewed with dismay inquiries like the Bloody Sunday Tribunal that appeared 'biased in favour of nationalists' (McCartney 2003a; see also Foster 2003).

Moreover, New Labour often appeared insensitive to this unionist anxiety. Tony Blair explicitly linked resolving the constitutional issues with the unspecific notion of nationalist 'inequality'. He declared that there 'can no longer be a Northern Ireland based on other than the principles of justice, fairness and equality and recognition that sectarianism is a thing of the past' (Blair 1999). Unfortunately, the Prime Minister associated the obstacle to achieving this universally acceptable vision of the future with a unionist unwillingness to form a power-sharing executive with Sinn Fein. The implication was not only that injustice, unfairness, inequality and sectarianism were features of Northern Ireland life exclusively associated with unionist politics (even though unionists had not been in office for 30 years) but also that there was a moral equivalence between the IRA's refusal to disarm and the unionist refusal to share power. In a brilliant response to a speech on unionist alienation by former Secretary of State for Northern Ireland John Reid, Foster observed that to call 'growing unionist estrangement from the State a "conundrum", as though a mysterious thing, is utterly, indeed insultingly disingenuous'. Unionists had expected agreement to mean settlement but they now understood it to mean 'merely a staging-post for republicanism'. This was not as blatant as the British Government being a persuader for Irish unity. It was a more subtle strategy of morphing Ulster Britons into Ulster ex-Britons by removing the symbolism of state from public display. For Foster it was not the rightness or wrongness of each particular change that was troublesome but rather the rapid accumulation of change and the disorientation this had unnecessarily promoted (Foster 2002: 22).

So within unionism different aspects of post-Agreement politics were emphasized. Pro-Agreement unionism stressed the process of delivery. While it could not, of course, ignore the negative impact on unionist opinion of the way change was being implemented it was compelled to highlight the positive. The term that emerged to describe this approach was Empeyism (after Sir Reg Empey, one of Trimble's closest colleagues). Empeyism was all about how the institutions of the Agreement had delivered for the common good on economic development, job creation, peace and prosperity. Indeed, the UUP campaign for the 2001 General Election was coordinated under the comprehensive slogan 'Unionism: Delivering'. Anti-Agreement unionism emphasized the process of biased concession and while it could not, of course, ignore the positive impact of Trimble's approach on unionist opinion (he was consistently identified as the most effective leader of unionism) it was compelled to highlight the negative.

An incisive explication of the unionist anxiety of process was provided by the DUP MP, Gregory Campbell. He asserted that the programme of reform pre-supposed 'unionist contentment' (passivity) and 'nationalist dissatisfaction' (activity). This, according to Campbell, had been the fundamental mistake. 'If there is no acceptance of a template that gives recognition to legitimate unionist concerns and grievances, and only begins by recognising a single set of grievances, then every attempt [at political accommodation] will fail.' Campbell articulated a profound sense of unionist dissatisfaction with the tendency of the policy agenda to assume that inequality, disadvantage and discrimination only worked one way. Moreover, he captured a growing mood of resistance to the notion that each and every nationalist demand was justified because of unionist majority-rule at Stormont between 1921 and 1972. Campbell rejected the proposition that unionist hostility represented a refusal to countenance the equality agenda. 'This is not the case at all. It is because unionists are convinced that the current process disadvantages them and assists nationalists/republicanism that they so strongly resist.' This was, of course, a tendentious interpretation of the facts and, interestingly, as unspecific in its details as the claim of nationalist inequality. However, it was a relatively accurate interpretation of the state of unionist feeling and academic research showed that anxiety for the future was not entirely without foundation (Osborne 2004). Campbell posed the question: Is unionism ready to deal? He recognized that, from a 'mainland' point of view, the demise of Trimble might appear to presage 'unionism retreating back into the trenches'. There was no need to worry. Those 'who fear that the unionism they see beginning to assert itself and think that it only does so to maintain the status quo completely misunderstand the unionist perspective on present day Northern Ireland'. What unionists wanted was a better deal not an end to dealing. They wanted, claimed Campbell, to see a better 'delivery mechanism' to address their anxieties (Campbell 2002). By the time of the delayed election to the Assembly in November 2003 the DUP's slogan 'Time for a fair deal' captured best the anxiety of process but also a modification of the DUP's opposition to the Agreement.

Anxiety of influence

One of the crucial battles in politics is who decides what is and what is not 'realistic'. The definition of realism in politics is logically prior to what Rab Butler once called 'the art of the possible'. And the subsequent cultivation of the art of the possible may involve a logical unfolding of certain political objectives or the denial of others. The definition and cultivation of a particular idea of what is reasonable allows a powerful group to rationalize its view of the world (Hampton 1995: 309). Unionists were anxious that a situation could develop in which improvement, such as a cessation of the IRA's military campaign, might be bought at a price they felt to be unfair and unconscionable. After 1998 there did indeed develop the view that, as crunch issues emerged during the implementation of the Agreement, too often did the British Government concede the definition of what was realistic politics to republicans. The result, unionists thought, was the skewing of political expectations in favour of nationalism. The reason for this was simple. It was the IRA that possessed the determining card – its weaponry. Not only did that materially affect the balance of persuasion between unionism and nationalism, it also affected the balance of power within nationalism between Sinn Fein and the SDLP. It has been claimed that Tony Blair told the leader of the SDLP in December 2000, 'You guys – your problem is, you don't have guns' (Godson 2003). That was a stark truth and all the starker since it was thought not to be in the 'interests of peace' to say it so candidly.

That the guns were now (mainly) silent did not affect the role they played in politics. As one commentator perceptively noted they were the same guns. Only the use was different. 'If the guns were smuggled into Ireland to gain political power, what better opportunity to use them – especially since no one actually gets hurt?' Republicans were trading military threat for political influence, thus complementing their electoral mandate (Murphy 2003). To propose that unionists need not be anxious because the guns were silent was rather disingenuous. Their anxiety remained that the political eloquence of the guns had been actually enhanced. In a new dispensation that made much of the idea of parity, then the only party on the level of parity-plus was

Sinn Fein. It was politically impossible for unionists to ignore this disparity even though the process of removing it continued to be costly. The anxiety of influence comprised a simple conundrum. Implementing the Agreement without decommissioning was unsustainable. Achieving decommissioning required implementing the Agreement in a manner that compromised unionist expectation. This was a critical engagement about the realities of politics. For example, one apologist for the republican position claimed that since no one was being killed there was no need for urgency in the decommissioning process. If the issue were to be pushed too hard and republicans were expected to concede, then it would be a disaster. It would mean 'an almost certain split in the movement and the replacement of the current leadership'. Unionists, it was claimed, only pushed the issue because they needed to feel that they were in charge (O'Dowd 2000). Of course, it was just as easy to argue the opposite case. If unionists were being asked to respect the slow adaptation to democracy in republican culture, then why could not republicans acknowledge unionist anxiety about making allowances for terrorists? (Lloyd 1999: 27).

O'Dowd's argument was not entirely unpersuasive. For example, the continued intimate relationship between Sinn Fein and the IRA could be rationalized as a necessary one. Only if the republican movement held together under Adams's leadership could the smooth transition be made to exclusively democratic politics. It was possible to argue that this was very much in the interests of unionists themselves. In return for the *de facto* acknowledgement of Northern Ireland's position within the United Kingdom it was necessary to allow republicans a 'soft landing' (Bew and Gillespie 1999: 360). One consequence of that rationalization was to arrange the implementation of the Agreement to the convenience of republicans and to shift the political costs of transition onto the shoulders of the UUP. It was Trimble, rather than Adams, who had such constant and exhausting problems of party management. It was Trimble, and not Adams, who had to take the very *public* risks. It may have been the case that the Sinn Fein leadership was also taking risks but the secrecy of its deliberations meant that it was impossible for unionists to understand even if they wished to. This simply opened up a wider space within which unionist discontent could grow. Jeffrey Donaldson, for example, asked the appropriate question. 'Why should unionism be divided when the pressure ought to be on the paramilitaries and their political surrogates? They are the ones in default.' There really should be no need, he argued, for further divisive meetings of the Ulster Unionist Council if only the Government would do its job and hold republicans to their commitments (Donaldson 2001).

Trimble also alluded to the anxiety of influence when he noted that unionist opinion was becoming increasingly hostile to the assumption that the 'logic' of the Agreement meant accepting whatever interpretation their opponents cared to put on it (Trimble 2000a). His party had been carrying the weight of implementing the Agreement too long and he criticized other parties 'for not carrying their share of the burden' (Trimble 2000b). Trimble's solution to the problem was that republicans and unionists should set aside the objective of winning the argument about whose 'reality' should prevail and should instead concentrate on sharing the political risks of managing change. 'Jumping together' (as it was called in 1999) or the principle of 'simultaneity' were different ways of avoiding the politics of blame and securing both leaderships from their respective critics. If republicans saw unionist fixation with decommissioning as 'a destabilizing fetish' was not their own opposition to decommissioning equally so? The obvious conclusion was surely that 'the ballast can be shared' (Gilchrist 2002). For the IRA it wasn't obvious at all. It became much easier for unionist critics of the Trimble strategy to play to the anxiety of influence and to interpret the process of the Agreement as a republican one.

This involved a textual analysis of Sinn Fein and IRA statements to reveal their inner logic. Republican understanding that the context for IRA disbandment was the 'full implementation of the Agreement' equated 'full implementation with the achievement of their united Ireland goal through the Agreement's transitional mechanisms' (McCartney 2003b). The political agenda of republicanism reserved the right of the IRA to decide when full implementation had taken place. That was 'not a recipe for the end of the IRA but for more and more negotiations down the road extracting further concessions' (Robinson 2003a). In both cases, the assumption was that the British and Irish Governments were complicit in that process and that Trimble's claim that unionism could expect to be on the inside track was the greatest illusion of all. In response, the UUP leader claimed that while the Anglo-Irish Agreement revealed that unionist views did not count, the Belfast Agreement showed that unionists were 'no longer marginalized'. To vote for the anti-Agreement line of the DUP would ensure that they returned to the ineffective margins (Trimble 2003d). Unfortunately, the benefits that his supporters claimed for the inside track – suspension of the Assembly in February 2000 and postponement of the Assembly elections in May 2003 – were not seen as strategic victories but as merely tactical exercises in 'Saving Private Trimble'. A unionist leader might be flattered by such concern on the part of the powerful but personal flattery did not necessarily signify collective political success. That the logic of the institutions favoured the 'simply British' slogan of the UUP was a difficult expectation to sustain.

Following the IRA spying allegations at the Assembly in October 2002, the conditions appeared to exist for a mode of implementation that might still unionist anxieties. Blair's speech on 17 October of that year seemed to make it plain that a republican definition of what was and was not 'realistic' to expect of the IRA was no longer acceptable and that Sinn Fein was required to deliver on its responsibilities (Blair 2002). Trimble's most consistent supporter, Esmond Birnie, argued that the UUP's flexibility in the face of republican resistance proved that unionism could accept change, was open to sharing power and had strengthened the influence of unionism with British and world leaders (Birnie 2003). However, Trimble's most consistent critic within the party accepted that while he did enjoy 'popularity amongst the great and the good in high places' in Northern Ireland, the electoral record had been a disaster. If Trimble continued to be in a position where he could not claim to speak for a majority of unionists 'then who will want to do business with a minority stakeholder?' (Donaldson 2003). That was a good question. It had become the campaigning question of the DUP which now presented itself as the one that could deliver anxious unionists to a new Agreement that better met their expectations. In the contest within unionism, the significance of the fiasco on 21 October 2003 cannot be underestimated. In the choreographed sequencing of events, Trimble appeared to have been fooled yet again by the IRA on the 'transparency' of decommissioning, thus confirming all the old anxieties about his leadership. The credibility of the Agreement amongst unionists had taken another serious blow and the consequence was the DUP victory in the Assembly elections of November 2003. This result was quite ironic. Five years after the Agreement it was possible for well-informed commentators to argue the terms of *militaristic* 'realism' had now moved against republicans. Unfortunately, that shift was to the advantage of Paisley rather than Trimble unionism (Moloney 2004).

Nationalist expectation

Bew argued that the nationalist project had shown little in the way of a positive vision. There was not even a slim volume, despite a voluminous literature on contemporary Irish politics, setting out the case for unity. Rather, one found 'many volumes occasioned by the Troubles in which a great deal of effort has gone into outmanoeuvring, either militarily or politically, the unionists'. In the place of a positive vision 'there is a notion of expiating some kind of original historical sin' for which history will be the redeemer (cited in Lynch 1994: 12). That argument was meant to be provocative but it did provide an important clue to the nationalist response to the Agreement. A political settlement had to address not only specific grievances but also had to expiate a sin against the 'nationalist people'. The traditional expression 'unionist supremacy' was the code for identifying both the grievance and the sin. The significance of this notion was its unchanging constancy. After 25 years of direct rule, the idea that unionists still constituted a privileged political caste or dominated public life did not bear close examination. The grievance and the sin can be understood as the interpenetration of the democratic and the national questions. The former concerned questions of comparative Catholic social and economic disadvantage, the latter concerned the question of whether Northern Ireland should remain part of the United Kingdom (Bew and Patterson 1987: 45). This complicated Trimble's expectation that the Agreement would assist the raising up of a new Northern Ireland. That expectation assumed the emerging priority of the democratic over the national question whereas for nationalists the distinction could never be so simple.

Nationalists, it was claimed, remained alienated by reminders of the present arrangements that confirmed Northern Ireland's British identity. The constitutional status meant 'an important inequality between the two main national communities in Northern Ireland with regard to the political self-expression of their national identities' (O'Neill 1996: 94). The Irish border 'privileged' the unionist majority politically (though not necessarily economically or socially) and the interests of nationalists 'have not been and cannot be satisfied if the assumption is unquestionably made that Northern Ireland is legitimately British' (O'Neill 1994: 374). The Agreement had been designed to settle that issue on both counts first, by reforming the arrangements within Northern Ireland to accommodate nationalist self-expression and second, by confirming Northern Ireland's place within the United Kingdom on the basis of consent. Here would be a real seismic shift in political attitudes but the question remained whether it was possible to satisfy nationalist aspiration in a manner that delivered on the democratic question but did not also deliver on the national question.

Republicanism had always said no. The reason, as one study has shown, was a tension within provisional discourse between these democratic and national dimensions. The question of justice and rights within Northern Ireland, 'rather than being reducible to the national question, are actually constitutive of it, and it is in this specific sense that they can be seen as supplementing or giving form to that claim'. The strategy of republicanism had been to make 'an explicit link between the national question and a number of other phenomena such as reaction, sectarianism or discrimination' (Clohesy 2000: 80–1). Accepting the principles of the Agreement would be an implicit acknowledgement that it was indeed possible to distinguish these two things or at least to argue that reform could become the basis of a transition to national unity. Sinn Fein would then have transformed itself into the object previously scorned, a constitutional nationalist party. Rather than being an absolute transformation this would have confirmed the changing character of Northern republicanism. This shift of emphasis within republicanism was not new. Status resentment, as Garvin pointed out, had been one of the key motivations of Irish republicanism. Like the modern provisional leadership, older republicans had been obsessed by a sense of moral superiority and were angered that their obvious ability was politically unfulfilled. Like the modern provisional leadership that thinks itself more virile than constitutional nationalists, more sophisticated than unionists and more intelligent than everyone, older republicans desired their proper recognition. 'A curious inverted snobbery encouraged the embracing of a partly artificial counter-culture, constructed as a compensation for the discomfort generated by the existing status system' (Garvin 1987: 90–1). It was possible to trace the trajectory of contemporary republican politics as an outworking of that pattern, leaving behind the counter-culture of radical politics for the establishment culture of representative politics, from duffel coats to Armani suits. This has been the accusation of Sinn Fein's critics and it was sufficiently well targeted to bring a defensive response from Gerry Adams. When asked in 1999 what kind of Northern Ireland he would like to see emerge in five years' time, Adams replied 'I'm not interested in Northern Ireland as a polity at all' (Beggan and Indurthy 2002: 353). The notion that 'republicans grew up and got smart' he later dismissed with the reply that republicans 'are the same as they always were'. As the interviewer observed, that is 'what strikes fear into the heart of Northern Ireland's unionist population' (J. Johnston 2003).

In a perceptive anticipation of the republican manoeuvre, Breen noted how Sinn Fein was beginning to colonize respectable space. It was almost impossible, she argued, to get a job in the community sector in West Belfast unless one was a republican or republican sympathizer. Adams's denial notwithstanding, here was an emerging political elite, demanding recognition of its status and desiring the respect and security that came with it. These 'chuck lites' had 'outed themselves in the safer and gentler peace process climes' and seemed set 'to become the main beneficiaries of any post-settlement funding for deprived areas' (Breen 1997: 7). Individual, communal, party and ideological expectations neatly combined to create a new dispensation. The British Government, she thought, had no problem with Sinn Fein in office. 'Far better to have them strolling around Stormont than up to their old tricks.' Originally the British strategy had been to build up the Catholic middle class and to permit the SDLP and the Church to mediate between nationalist communities and the state as an alternative to Sinn Fein. The inclusiveness of the process in the 1990s meant bringing republicans within that fold and turning its leadership into part of the Catholic middle class. The expectation was that it would conform more closely to the hopes and ambitions of the broader nationalist constituency. In this view, unionist resistance to such 'sweeteners' was misconceived. The price of inclusion was the abandonment by republicans of their cherished objectives (Breen 2000: 18–19). Breen's analysis was sharp though it was never that clear that republican goals had been abandoned. Nevertheless, when Seamus Mallon of the SDLP spoke of postponing the question of unity to the next generation, he intimated a resolution that would involve concentration on the practical means of Catholic security and advancement rather than the (immediate) end of Irish unity. The implication some put on the Agreement was that republicanism had already accepted this condition.

One important academic study suggested that this process was well under way in the period after 1998. Mitchell understood the transition to be a movement from victims to equals. The old notion of Northern Ireland being a 'nationalist nightmare' had certainly not disappeared but she thought it made less sense in the contemporary era of social and political change.

Catholic support for the Agreement was an expectation that it represented 'the beginning of a long process of transformative change'. There was a widespread sense that economic conditions had improved, that there were greater opportunities for young people and that there had been political progress. She found that the expectation was now 'of equality as a right to be demanded'. Mitchell interpreted her evidence to mean that the shift in attitude removed 'the zero-sum nature of the traditional republican struggle for self-determination and may help lay to rest the idea that no justice is possible for Catholics in Northern Ireland'. Her interpretation was not without its qualifications and caveats but she did believe that it pointed to a political culture that signalled a new Catholic sense of 'ownership' and an expectation that a fair deal was possible within Northern Ireland (Mitchell 2003: 51–71). The principles of the Agreement would be instituted in the mechanisms of governance to deliver the equality nationalists expected but also the stability that unionists desired. That was one possible benign dynamic of post-Agreement politics. Unfortunately, it was not the only one for there were other currents at work that cut across it. They were the subtext of all the talk about nationalist self-confidence and were indeed the subtext of all the talk about unionist supremacy. They combined to conceive of unionism as a force in Irish politics whose day had gone. This conception actually intensified some of the old communal animosities and it became more difficult to tolerate what was understood as unionist resistance to change. This was the politics of winning and losing in a different guise and it was revealed in the reluctance to take seriously the political objections of opponents. This can be called the *anxiety of frustration*. The other side of frustration was irritation with obstruction. It revealed itself in an expectation of irresistible advance and an anticipation of rapid progress. This can be called the *anxiety of impatience*. Both anxieties had their effect in nationalist politics after the Belfast Agreement.

Anxiety of frustration

The substance of the anxiety of frustration lay in the scope of nationalist expectation. As Mitchell so perceptively grasped, the recognition of their economic and social weight in Northern Ireland could foster rather than ameliorate the nationalist sense of resentment. That they were not under the unionist thumb could be less relevant than not being fully 'self-determined'. After 1998 nationalists may 'no longer suffer the indignity of oppression as a dominated minority' but this did not mean that they believed the 'dominating tendencies that are partly constitutive' of unionist identity had been overcome (O'Neill 1994: 371–7). So there remained significant frustration when, even after the Agreement, nationalists discovered the annoying truth that unionists remained 'unionist'. It was easy to resort to old explanations, philosophically based or not, that unionists still had the same dominating tendency. Elliott expected the new dispensation to mean a new sense of Catholic belonging 'without the resentment' (Elliott 2001: 481–2). That was the positive future that Mitchell expected as well. However, it was possible to envisage a sense of belonging with intensified resentment. One critic thought that was precisely the emerging reality: material advancement amongst a solid block of nationalists combined with intensified chauvinism (O'Hagan 1998). Trimble observed that there was often unwillingness amongst nationalists to accept the implications that flow from accepting the unionist commitment to remaining within the United Kingdom. 'Too many people in nationalism', he concluded, 'see unionism as a problem to be got around rather than a noble tradition to be accommodated in a spirit of genuine engagement' (Trimble 2002b). The anxiety of frustration is the concern that unionism still has the ability to deny nationalists their due.

According to republican mantra, unionists at first having been 'afraid of peace' were now equally 'afraid of change'. Moreover, the unionist fear of change was defined as a 'deflated superiority complex'. Northern Ireland's problem in a nutshell was that such 'supremacist attitudes towards Catholics' had become 'out-of-line with reality, but many Protestants are unable or unwilling to come to terms with the changed circumstances and the resulting insecurities' (Anderson and Shuttleworth 1994: 87). The unionist anxiety of process in this reading represented a pathological outworking of a positional logic that could only interpret Catholic prosperity and advancement as a threat and could only understand equality as defeat. Unionist politics was defined by an ideological inability to trade supremacy for parity of esteem. Yet here was the rub. By a transposition of logic this culture of supremacy had also become a culture of defeat. The instability of the relationship between the culture of supremacy and the culture of defeat defined the crisis of unionist identity. While nationalists denounced the supposed culture of supremacy, the frustration of some lay in the fact that unionists would not come to acknowledge their defeat (and accept nationalist 'supremacy').

Summarizing the academic literature and media commentary, Finlay claimed to have detected a shift in the identification of Northern Protestants. Where formerly Protestants had defined themselves in terms of modernity and progress, increasingly they had become identified in terms of 'tradition, defeat and associated emotions such as confusion, alienation, fatalism, resentment, fear and cognates such as anxiety and paranoia' (Finlay 2001: 3). A substantial proportion of this was nationalist invention and wishful thinking but, as Finlay correctly pointed out, there was some material basis for that larger ideological invention. A self-pitying tendency in unionism also embraced fatalism like a comfort blanket in the way in which nationalists embraced victimhood (see Chapter 1). However, nationalist identification of unionist decline was bound up with an identification of nationalist advance and the consequence was a style of reflection that bordered on the patronizing. Indeed it replicated by inversion what nationalists had always denounced in unionism – a rather smug commentary on the failings of the 'Other'. Over the past decade or more, it was argued, the nationalist community had 'grown in confidence through political development and cultural revival'. It was now 'in the political and cultural ascendant'. On the other hand, 'British identity in the mold of Protestantism, empire, war and remembrance, that is central to the unionist identity' was in terminal decline (McCall 2002: 198). Unionist Britishness was not only in its death throws. It was actually vacuous because it was defined in terms of separation from nationalism rather than in terms of its British 'self'. This, it was argued, made it difficult if not impossible for unionists to accept a new Britishness 'that emphasises inclusivity, plurality and tolerance, because such a subscription, in the communally divided context of Northern Ireland, necessarily implies drawing closer to those from whom Ulster unionists wish to remain separate – Irish nationalists' (McCall 2001: 156). Most of this was actually wrong but the trajectory of the argument is politically significant. Unionists had to move closer to nationalists (now progressive and modern) rather than nationalists drawing closer to unionists (now reactionary and primitive). To make concessions to unionism or to accommodate its requirements was almost by definition a regressive political move. The anxiety of frustration became explicit whenever such concessions *were* made or whenever such requirements *were* expressed. Moreover, the fact that Trimble did not fit the reactionary and primitive template made him, ironically, the subject of Northern nationalist scorn. This was evident in the decommissioning debate where the difficulty unionists had with armed republicanism was dismissed as a frustrating impediment to progress.

One prominent journalist and former SDLP politician articulated that mood. He thought that the implementation of the Agreement had been determined by 'Trimble's supremacy reflex jerking'. Unionists had tried unilaterally to 'set the criteria Sinn Fein must meet in order to be in an executive'. If Sinn Fein 'don't perform to unionists' liking, unionists walk away and the executive collapses' (Feeney 2003c). Recent history showed that unionists could not 'elect a leader who is prepared to cooperate on equal terms with the rest of the people on the island. But then, isn't that what unionism's for?' (Feeney 2003a). The 'self-abasement' of Adams in his statement of 30 April 2003 on IRA activities showed that everything was irrelevant in Northern Ireland politics 'until the IRA make a statement which satisfies our proconsul, for whom read said D. Trimble' (Feeney 2003e). The tone was one of frustration and the anxiety lay in the expectation that not only the British Government but also the Irish Government were dancing to Trimble's tune. Repeated suspensions of the Assembly and the postponement of the elections in May 2003 aggravated nationalist resentment at the frustration of their expectations. For republicans, of course, the demand for decommissioning was typical unionist insistence on 'a final, excruciating act of humiliation' (McKearney

1999). Moreover, the call for the disbandment of the IRA represented the natural disposition of those 'who were raised in supremacist politics for 60 years or more'. The requirement showed that the unionists' war was not over. Anyway, it would not stop the onward march of Sinn Fein since nationalists voted for it no matter about unionist notions of what was moral or principled. Sinn Fein's vote had grown despite breaking its ceasefire, despite the Florida gun-running, despite persistent IRA activity. 'It will increase again because nationalists – despite the allegations of a republican spy-ring – recognize that Sinn Fein is working for peace, not war' (Morrison 2002). That assessment was correct and it was a substantial revelation of the disposition towards unionism of a majority of nationalists.

The Sinn Fein leader appeared to take a more diplomatic line but the message still fed the same anxiety of frustration. 'I don't blame the unionists if they refuse to move [on going back into the Executive with republicans], because they can pass the buck to the government and then try to influence the government.' But then 'it was the British government, it wasn't David Trimble who suspended the institutions. It was the British government, four times!' (Adams 2003a). Adams did not bring out the implicit connection between those two sentences but his supporters would. The message was that unionists had not embraced the politics of the new beginning, were frustrating the *final* objective of peace and still had the British on their side. When others consistently pointed out the self-serving nature of this world view they too were rejected as being part of the problem (see for example Myers 2002; O'Doherty 2003b). Trimble's dogged endurance in keeping alive the possibility of an inclusive form of power-sharing was dismissed by those who, in frustration, criticized him for not 'selling' the Agreement. Indeed, it was claimed that all unionists could do was to find new obstacles to 'productive change' (accepting a republican agenda) 'every time an old one has been flattened' (Collins 2004a). Resentment at the political and institutional obstacles to the proper recognition of nationalist rights flowed easily into the anxiety of impatience. The anxiety of impatience provided the best guide to the political success of Sinn Fein in its competition with the SDLP.

Anxiety of impatience

Impatience and its corresponding anxiety were illustrated in the debate leading up to and following the publication of the results of the 2001 Northern Ireland census. Anticipation that the result of that census would show a substantial growth in the Catholic population had undoubtedly encouraged the scope and confidence of nationalist demands. Moreover, the anxiety this demographic shift would provoke within unionism was confidently expected to create further demoralization and instability (Bourke 2003: 306–10). Republicans began to speak of Irish unity by 2016, coinciding with the hundredth anniversary of the Easter Rebellion.

Though this was mainly designed for the symbolic consumption of Sinn Fein's electorate and for the provocation of unionists it did raise expectations that other nationalists felt obliged to address. The SDLP did not respond by arguing that talk of Irish unity was not only premature but also irrelevant to stabilizing the institutions of the Agreement. Rather, it responded by condemning Adams for appearing to make unity dependent upon unionist consent (Rodgers 2002; McKeown 2003). When the census reported the religious balance to be 43.76 per cent Catholic and 53.13 per cent Protestant, it was much less than some journalistic predictions of 47 per cent Catholic and 49 per cent Protestant. Ultimately, the mathematics was less important than the anticipation. 'No matter what the figures say the perception has taken root that Catholics are outbreeding Protestants' (Moloney 1998a). Nationalist impatience with unionists based on that perception remained a factor in political relations. Even though, as Adams acknowledged, demography was not an argument, there was little by way of internally generated inducements either by Sinn Fein or the SDLP to persuade unionists of the merits of constitutional change. Sinn Fein was reduced to calling on the Irish Government to produce a Green Paper on unity in its manifesto for the 2003 Assembly elections. The ugly if possibly honest face of Ireland's culture wars remained trial by breeding (Longley 2000b: 20).

For Protestants, as one nationalist commentator argued, things were not getting better. Happily anticipating the 'tidal waves' of Catholic youth coming out of the schools, he thought they could only get worse (Collins 2002). Nationalist demographics assumed then, irrespective of when there would be a majority for Irish unity, Northern Ireland was going to get 'greener' and that unionists had to face up to that reality *on nationalist terms* (McIntyre 2002a). It was to be on nationalist terms since, as Bew had noted, there was a sin of historic grievance to be expiated. In this case nationalist expectation went beyond democratic politics and it came close to denying that unionists should have any part at all in debates about equality except in so far as they accepted their responsibility for past wrongs. This has been a constant in the nationalist position despite evidence that the trend towards equity in the share of jobs at all levels has been long established (Equality Commission for Northern Ireland 2003). Hence the impatience with or dismissal of those who cast doubt on the extent of discrimination against Catholics (see Cadogan Group 2003: 7–11). Casting doubt on discrimination was put into the same category as casting doubt on the growing power of politicized Catholicism.

Feeney made that connection and his argument captured succinctly the anxiety of impatience. The reason for Northern Ireland's existence was that it represented the largest space in which Catholics could be kept in order. Unionists in 1920 opted for six counties because the nine contained a Catholic population of 43 per cent. 'So', he asked, 'what does that make a six county entity with a 44 per cent Catholic population?' One inference of the question was that the 'reason for the entity goes', which is a traditional demand for Irish unity. What was the purpose of the north? Feeney thought unionists no longer had any ideas and were already half way into the dustbin of history. Nationalism, self-confident and vital, knew where it was going and the frustration of having to deal with the paranoid residue of defeated unionism was evident in his tone. The substance of the argument, however, was that in the interim Northern Ireland must be shared on equal terms with nationalists. 'The north of Ireland is still a unionist entity in its civil service, its security forces, its judiciary, its emblems, parts of its public broadcasting and business elite.' That would have to change as nationalist electoral strength made its impact. Feeney's argument was a strong one and he expressed Catholic impatience for these changes to happen. He also expressed the anxiety that the unwillingness of unionist leaders to spell out the consequences to their own voters was storing up trouble for the future. They 'have watched the *raison d'être* of their wee six vanishing' and this has left unionist voters 'bewildered and frightened for the future' (Feeney 2003f). Certainly there should be no modification of public policy that would restrict the achievement of nationalist rights just to accommodate unionist concerns. This was the issue that informed the crisis within the Northern Ireland Human Rights Commission. The philosophical dispute between commissioners over the relative merits of individual and group rights became a political struggle informed by the anxiety of impatience. Nationalists argued that to question group rights was to threaten present and future gains of the Catholic community. When they heard reference to multi-ethnic integration 'they naturally are concerned that their gains will be lost'. To reject group rights would undermine the conditions for equality (Harvey 2003a; see also O'Leary 2001c). Moreover, it sounded too much like liberal unionism.

The contemporary ascendancy of Sinn Fein in nationalist politics actually struck one commentator as rather anomalous. It was rising in support 'while promoting issues which the electorate appears to have very little interest in; the Irish language, Irish unity, the equality agenda – whatever that is'. Sinn Fein represented Catholics 'as a disadvantaged ethnic and national group which needs constitutional and statutory endorsement of its national rights' but actually appeared to be short on issues where Catholics really were disadvantaged. 'One suspects', he concluded, 'that the rise of Sinn Fein is predicated on its ability to annoy Unionists' rather than to represent group rights (O'Doherty 2002a). That apparent anomaly disappeared in the communal politics of Northern Ireland. As the debate over the definition of human rights revealed, the real question in nationalist politics had become which party could best secure and promote the group interest of Catholics/ nationalists *as* Catholics/nationalists. Voters looked increasingly to Sinn Fein because it seemed best placed to maximize the communal advantage whilst addressing most effectively the anxieties of impatience and frustration. Indeed, the nationalist frustration with the (apparent) last vestiges of unionist Ulster and the impatience to achieve what was theirs as of right were intelligently cultivated by republican leaders. Had republicans been weaker, argued Danny Morrison, the SDLP would have sunk back into its old compromising ways. The vote for Sinn Fein 'changed the political landscape and added real muscle to the negotiating position of the nationalist community'. Under republican leadership never again would Catholics have to settle for less (Morrison 2002). There was no need to feel ashamed about 'assertive Catholic tribalism' (even a tribalism connected to the IRA) for that was the only thing that delivered on expectations (Moloney 2001b). That was a seductive and an effective message. The cultivation of this new republicanism that now made a priority of equality, discrimination and injustice helped to fill the empty space at the core of Sinn Fein's reunification project left by the failure of the IRA.

So seductive and effective was it that the SDLP was drawn into competing with Sinn Fein on republican territory. So convinced did the SDLP leadership become that republicans had plotted correctly the expectations, the anxieties and the tolerance of the Catholic electorate that it would have taken a political risk of enormous proportions to challenge it. The SDLP did show courage in joining with unionists on the new Policing Board, but for very understandable reasons the SDLP calculated that taking a position other than moral equidistance from the UUP and Sinn Fein on decommissioning would have been electorally disastrous. Understandably, it also calculated that appearing to break communal ranks to form an alliance of the centre with the UUP would have been equally disastrous. Nationalist expectations as well as its anxieties seemed to preclude it. Unfortunately, *not* to do so was also electorally damaging, for Sinn Fein easily outmanoeuvred the SDLP in the contest for communal championship.

Conclusion

The situation, then, was rather more complex than the one suggested by Evans and O'Leary. The problem could not be defined exclusively in terms of unionist reluctance to compromise. Nor could the problems of the Agreement be addressed alone by attending to the proper arrangements for decommissioning of the IRA's weaponry. The destabilizing potential of unionist anxieties was directly related to their disappointed expectations of republican behaviour and the destabilizing potential of nationalist expectations were directly related to their continuing anxieties about unionist obstruction. The mutual suspicion remained that no party to the Agreement was willing to play by the rules and this was due in part to an experience of the ambiguity of those rules. Unionists and nationalists condemned exceptions to the rule when they seemed not to be in their interest and demanded exceptions when they did. Both felt that too many exceptions had been made that were inimical to their interests and that the 'principles' of the Agreement were only adhered to when demanded by their opponents. That hostile atmosphere continued to foster mistrust and a sense that no one was telling the truth, an atmosphere explored in the next chapter.

9   Lies noble and ignoble

A journalist observed that those who wondered why so many people had become disenchanted with the Belfast Agreement 'should consider what it is like to live in this, our parallel universe'. In this universe there appeared to be no firm principle upon which policy was grounded, nothing that's white that just can't as well be black, no truth that cannot just as well be a lie. In short, the peace process was promoting a radical disordering of political and moral values (McDowell 2002). There had been a transition of sorts in Northern Ireland but it was from a state of war (the Troubles) to a state of fraud (the Agreement). An academic provided a context for that journalistic observation by interpreting the Agreement as a stage-managed strategy, the purpose of which had been to 'spin' the people of Northern Ireland into an accommodation 'rather than to persuade supporters and public opinion to support the peace process'. For the Agreement to survive he thought 'the "credibility" gap between political spin at the front of the political stage and the back stage political "realities" should be and could be reduced and democratic debate and accountability enhanced'. If this were not done the consequence would be that 'the public is no longer able to make the distinction between truth and lies', a pathological state in which reasoned political communication simply became impossible (Dixon 2001: 16–17). Indeed, Dixon believed that a mood of disillusionment had already eaten 'into the culture of democracy, producing cynicism and resentment' and this was unlikely to promote the trust necessary to sustain the institutions (2001: 306–7). The history of the Agreement, especially the suspension of the institutions in October 2002 and the subsequent polarization of electoral politics, appeared to confirm the journalistic mood and to bear out the academic analysis.

The difficulty appeared to be cultural and historical as much as moral and institutional, as much to do with myth as with technique, with popular memory as with political practice. In an interesting if hyperbolic study of the way in which 'the labyrinthine character of social memory' formed political expectation in Northern Ireland, Allen Feldman asked what 'would political transparency and democratized public institutions look and function like' given the history of conspiratorial paramilitary organizations and given the necessarily secretive response of security intelligence. The Troubles had nurtured 'a political culture of deniability' that went from the top – government ministers and public officials – to the bottom – terrorists and agents – and as a consequence 'secrecy, just as much as exposure' had formed memory and imagination (Feldman 1997/98: 234). This hidden history of Northern Ireland had been always beyond the bounds of decency and morality and its influence was all the more pervasive because of its concealment. It was a world of manipulation, deceit, betrayal and bad faith so it is little wonder that people anticipated its continuing influence. The problem of contemporary democratic disillusion, of course, is not peculiar to the Agreement nor is it peculiar to Northern Ireland. However, the cultural intensity of the disillusion *is* distinctive as is the political effect since not only the practice of governmental institutions but their very existence is at issue. Suspicion of the inherent deceit of the peace process has been a powerful factor in public opinion and when journalists have written about 'lack of trust' this is often what they mean. This pessimistic interpretation of political opinion needs to be qualified somewhat. The public mood has been more complex and there is another dimension that warrants consideration. It is true that unionists were predisposed to be suspicious of the motives of republicans and republicans were predisposed to be sceptical of unionist good faith but it was not inconceivable that a virtuous circle of mutual trust could be slowly built up. In the expectation of a greater good it was not at all unthinkable that people would implicitly agree to pull the wool over their own eyes, to suspend disbelief for the best of reasons and to turn a blind eye to democratic indiscretions by paramilitaries as an act of trust in the integrity of the process. That disposition was also a part of the public mood, although it has been of diminishing effect since the referendum in 1998. To grasp this ambiguity of post-Agreement Northern Ireland requires further consideration of the notion of political lying.

There are at least three aspects that invite consideration. The first is the Platonic tradition of the 'noble lie' and its distinctively ambiguous relationship to the equally noble objectives of the Agreement. The second is the notion of the 'creative lie' associated with Hannah Arendt and its ambivalent relationship to the 'creative ambiguity' of the Agreement. The third is the gap between two forms of political discourse, the demonstrative and the circumstantial, and the effect this has had on the popular mood. Together these three aspects deliver important insights into the course of post-Agreement politics.

The noble lie

Political lying has been a traditional source of satire. Perhaps the most concise and yet penetrating of such satires is Arbuthnot's review of the never published *A Treatise of the Art of Political Lying*, and for our purposes it bears re-examination. This eighteenth-century spoof was a thought experiment in which the political system is 'less a state of war than a state of fraud', precisely the criticism of the Agreement made by McDowell (Condren 1997: 121). Simply stated, political lying is 'The art of convincing the People of Salutary Falsehoods for some good End'. Public susceptibility to lying as well as the necessity for political lying has to do with the two-sided nature of our soul or character. The first side is plain, which reflects objects as they are. The second side is cylindrical which renders true objects false and false objects true. It is upon this cylindrical side of human nature that the art of political lying depends. Political lying may be deduced from a principle that may be rendered thus: people have a right to truth from neighbours and family but they have no right at all to political truth. The people 'may as well all pretend to be Lords of Mannors and possess great Estates, as to have Truth told them in Matters of Government'. Political morality is quite different from private morality and in this contest of cylindrical slipperiness, the best way to contradict an existing political lie is to tell another one. The treatise also advocated the project of uniting all the smaller groups of liars into one large association, consisting of the heads of each political party. No lie would become common currency without their approval, political leaders 'being the best Judges of the present Exigencies, and what sort of Lyes are demanded'. The skill needed to sustain one's position in this association is the ability not to blush or to look out of countenance in telling the lies agreed upon (Condren 1997: 176–84). For many, even supporters of the Agreement, that would be a good description of the political 'pantomime' conducted for public consumption while the secretive 'scripting' by political leaders was very different (Dixon 2003).

The message of Arbuthnot's satire, like politics itself, is far from straightforward moralism. Indeed, Condren argues that *The Art of Political Lying* 'presupposes and requires forms of socialization, and so expresses a sense of civilization'. In a stable form of government politics will remain in part mendacious, but it is political lying within the bounds of institutional norms and limits. This is not all we should expect of politicians but at least there exists a code of what is acceptable and unacceptable. The question that *The Art of Political Lying* raises is 'whether total honesty and sincerity is as corrosive of political life' as total dishonesty (an implicit caveat for those in favour of a Truth Commission for Northern Ireland). The conclusion to which Condren thought Arbuthnot's satire points is that 'political discourse is never that simple, except perhaps for those be-limed in its prejudices and prearranged truths' (Condren 1997: 162). In other words, *The Art of Political Lying* is just as much a satire on the moral self-righteousness of the critic as it is on the deceit of the politician. Furthermore, there is the implication that those who proclaim the purity of their principle and the virtue of their behaviour may very well be the biggest liars of all. The politics of the 'plain' side (even of the 'honest' Ulsterman) is as one-sided a misrepresentation of political reality as the politics of the 'cylindrical' side. To take one example, the public statements by 'P. O'Neill' on behalf of the

IRA make much of republican moral integrity and a reputation for honesty. This is quite laughable, though one suspects it is a joke that would be lost on P. O'Neill.

The big question, though, is also the simple question: Is lying excusable when it is undertaken for the best of purposes, to make people, in Plato's words, more inclined to care for the state and for one another? This 'noble lie' distinguishes a myth necessary to stability and social harmony from venal deception. The nobility of the deceit is in its intent and in its consequence. The purpose is to deceive the people in their own interest and not in the interest (alone) of the deceiver. There are two levels of understanding here. The first is foundational. In this case, the noble lie seeks to persuade people that they have a common interest and, even though this may be mistaken, the objective can be politically admirable. It is to make people believe that 'each is bound to the other by important ties, shares an identity, and is assured that the others think similarly' (Archard 1995: 476). In Chapter 3 the Northern Ireland problem was in part explored by discussion of how the means of politics had confounded the ends of politics. The noble lie is intended to make means and ends commensurate because the procedure and the goal are one and the same, a just political order. Moreover, the functionality of the noble lie should hold an appeal to those who desire, as the Agreement intended, a 'new beginning' for Northern Ireland. One of the problems of politics that the noble lie addresses is a general one of 'refounding' a society in justice and it is the problem of what one scholar has labelled 'intergenerational tension'. In short, this is 'the problem of particular past generations for those who found new cities, begin new orders, or try to establish a new sense of justice – the inescapable (and tragic) hold of the past on the present' (and one of the pieties of the peace process has surely been 'overcoming the legacy of the past'). If the jargon term of the peace process has been 'ownership' then the noble lie rephrases this as 'parentage'. The difficulty for a new beginning is twofold. It means 'establishing a lasting parentage' and coping 'with the hold of the past on the present' (Carmola 2003: 41). For those wanting to 'draw a line under history' or to make the transition from terror to politics, the polite fictions of the Agreement provided both the appropriate parentage of a shared undertaking for the present and a risk-sharing strategy for dealing with the claims of the past.

The second level is circumstantial. As Newey has persuasively argued, not only are political lies sometimes justified, in certain circumstances 'citizens have a *right* to be lied to'. While this may appear to be an explicit insult to democratic self-regard, the truth may be that the lie is closer to the 'best' judgement of the people. It could be that to win popular support for the best option would incur such costs that would make it politically impossible. The people 'might explicitly condone the government's use of dissimulation from time to time where this secured, or was thought likely to secure, public benefits such as national security or economic stability'.

Dissimulation may be a necessary condition for achieving what the people *truly* want if they were being honest with themselves (Newey 1997: 108; emphasis in original). It is a question of circumstantial judgement. For example, the citizens of the Irish Republic have been 'publicly mad for Irish unity in the abstract but would run a mile from it – and Northern nationalists – in practice', especially if they had to pay for it (Harris 2004). The explicit recommendation here was that a mature political culture in the Republic should now replace the dishonest public conviction with the honest private disposition. Newey's insight permits a rather different understanding, namely that the popular demand upon Irish state policy has required it to trace a path between honouring the public conviction whilst *also* satisfying the private disposition. Not being honest has been a circumstantially effective means of balancing the demands of democracy and the requirement of good government. Irish Governments have done just that even if this has had serious consequences for instability in the north (see O'Halloran 1987). One benign interpretation of the Irish Republic's reformulation of Articles 2 and 3 of its Constitution is that it represents a belated attempt to make Southern nationalism a force for stability in the north.

These arguments for the noble utility of political deceit, the foundational and the circumstantial, are not without their merits and not without their relevance to post-Agreement politics. The telling of falsehoods in both cases would not really be lying in a morally despicable way but rather 'a mere image of lying'. The strength of this defence, however, assumes a moral and intellectual superiority on the part of those charged with leading their people (Dombrowski 1997: 575). Even if someone like Gerry Adams actually believed that of himself it still begs larger questions and the Platonic tradition may not look so benign from the perspective of those who have been deceived since they cannot take for granted 'either the altruism or the good judgement of those who lie to us, no matter how much they intend to benefit us'. The criticism that 'those who raise moral concerns are ignorant of political realities' should 'actually lead to a more articulate description of what those realities are' rather than a dismissal of such concerns as irrelevant (Bok 1978: 169–70). This touches on a significant point regarding any assumption that the Agreement embodied a noble lie and it is a political rather than a philosophical question.

Were all the participants to the Agreement agreed on the nature of the noble lie? Was there acceptance of a common objective? The evidence hardly delivers a positive response to either question and so generates a degree of doubt about Dixon's interpretation of the choreography of the Agreement. He assumed a type of knowledge to which insiders were exclusively privy (back-stage realities) while the electorate existed in a cloud of unknowing. But is that distinction a real one? For example, the confusion that attended the third act of IRA decommissioning on 21 October 2003 revealed either an unfortunate general cloud of unknowing that frustrated everyone's good intentions (the benign explanation) or it confirmed deceptive manoeuvring by one or more parties for partial aims (the malign explanation). Whichever explanation one chose it was unlikely to sustain confidence in either the competence of the choreography or the virtue of the noble lie. As one Irish official admitted, choreography had a habit of going wrong (McDonald 2003). The popular response has been to reverse La Rochefoucauld's maxim and to hold that deceit on their part fully justifies suspicion on our part (La Rochefoucauld 1959: 48). That suspicious state of affairs, what all commentators acknowledged was a profound lack of political trust, has been corrosive of the integrity of the Agreement. In short, it meant that the democratic option of pulling the wool over one's own eyes became rapidly discounted. As one exceptionally astute commentator observed, the desire for peace encouraged a grudging willingness amongst many to accept legalistic distortions.

> It wasn't that people couldn't see the anomalies themselves, it was that they didn't see any point in labouring them when there was a big project in hand – a peace process which would gradually end all violence if we could but keep our nerve.

Whether people blamed the IRA or intransigent unionism, by the fifth year of the Agreement few believed in the nobility of that grand project any longer (O'Doherty 2004). It just appeared deceitful.

The instability of the institutions has been a consequence of a widespread popular view that no one is really prepared to keep their covenants because there is no sovereign myth or noble lie that encourages them to do so. The inclusive and deliberative institutions of the Agreement required the effective containment of manipulative strategies and deception and their replacement with a sense of common responsibility (Young 2002: 77–80). That common responsibility for the fate of the Agreement has been noticeably absent and it is questionable if it were ever present. If the main players were performing according to some well-understood script they certainly had a strange way of acting it out and its incoherence could not be attributed to improvisation alone. Nor does it appear to have been a problem, as some have suggested, of playing to different audiences. Nor was it even the case of leaders temporarily losing the plot. They were following different plot lines. No amount of expertise on the part of those whom Arendt called the 'image-makers' in government could disguise that fact. Modern communications, she thought, had convinced intellectuals that half of politics is 'image making' and the other half making people believe in the imagery. Unfortunately, the imagery can displace the reality it seeks to control while media-managers, speech-writers and policy advisers become divorced from everyday experience, a criticism of government that is now all too familiar (Arendt 1972: 30). One 'imaginative' difficulty for the Agreement was the outworking of the 'constructive ambiguity' that some took to be key to its survival.

Political ambiguity occurs when two forms of moral concern generate paradoxical political intensity. On the one hand, there is 'the concern that granting exceptions to the rule would compromise the authority of principle'. On the other, there is the concern 'that without the possibility of such exceptions, without some court of moral equity, the rules would become absurd, irrelevant and lead to moral obscenity' (Condren 1997: 101). This is a paradox that nationalists and unionists both confronted. Both condemned exceptions to the rule when they seemed not to be in their interest and demanded exceptions when they did. The ambiguity they both denounced has attended the slippery transitions in government policy between the authority of principle and the necessity of exceptions. The 'moral obscenity' in this case was either the perceived appeasement of terrorism or capitulation to a unionist veto. It is important to explore this further.

Constructive ambiguity

Arendt's examination of political lying involved another and, at first sight, startling proposition that some forms of political lying are actually related to freedom. Deliberate 'denial of factual truth – the ability to lie – and the capacity to change facts – the ability to act – are interconnected; they owe their existence to the same source: imagination' (Arendt 1972: 11). Lying, she argued, did not creep into politics by accident or sinfulness and moral outage will not make it disappear. In politics, facts and opinion inhabit the same space and both appear contingent. Facts can be treated as mere opinions and mere opinions as facts. The incompleteness of politics leaves it open to constructive possibilities for the 'lie' may be more useful than the facts. Simple truth-telling in politics is difficult because the truth-teller's facts themselves are bound up in contingency and opinion. Political argument is always contextual argument and it requires a form of language that in other circumstances would appear slippery and evasive. This is no accident but a necessary part of the political art. 'Communication rests upon ambiguity' (Pocock 1984: 31). The very distinctive ambiguity of political language has prompted some notable comment.

For instance, Mario Vargas Llosa described the difficulty in making the transition from being a writer and critic to being a politician. The key transition, he suggested, was from one use of language to another. He did not claim that his difficulty lay in forsaking precision of the literary for imprecision of the political. Rather, it lay in moving from one sort of linguistic precision in the cause of clarity to another sort of linguistic precision in the cause of *calculated* ambiguity. He found that the art of politics involved its own linguistic discipline just as taxing in its demands as the art of the novel or of the learned essay. To formulate ideas and proposals in such a manner as to be both distinctive and ambiguous was an experience that Vargas Llosa found challenging and profoundly disturbing. But it was part and parcel of the political craft. Not to acknowledge its necessity and therefore to fail to become proficient in the lexicon of ambiguity was *not* to become a serious politician. To eschew it altogether would represent a dereliction of professional duty. When one engages in the craft of politics, in other words, one cannot indulge the honesty of the tender conscience. Ambiguity is often necessary not only to attain self-interested ends but also to avoid destructive – or self-destructive – political dogmatism (Vargas Llosa 1991). This, in short, is the art of 'constructive ambiguity'.

A more devious version of this condition has been explored with great subtlety by Czeslaw Milosz. This may be called the politics of Ketman. 'He who practices Ketman lies. But would he be less dishonest if he could speak the truth?' (Milosz 1981: 80). The word 'Ketman' Milosz found in a work by Gobineau called *Religions and Philosophies of Central Asia*. It is the philosophy (as described by Gobineau) of those in possession of a truth who must not sully that truth in the presence of those whom God has chosen to keep in error. It is important to hide one's true opinion and resort to all manner of deceptions in order to wrong-foot one's enemies. It is also necessary to go through the motions of conformity to rituals and practices of the existing order. 'One must, therefore, keep silent about one's true convictions if possible.' But this outer conformity is all a sham and all the more necessary to sustain the inner purity of fundamental belief. One dupes the power that thinks it has you under control. This bad faith in the service of the true faith brings with it feelings of superiority and its own pleasures of secret knowledge. There will certainly come the day when it is possible to throw off the veils of deceit. Then the truth will be revealed and the final objective will be attained. That mentality, not unusual, one might think, in the long and secretive tradition of Irish republicanism, can provide an insight into the ambivalent character of Sinn Fein politics.

The politics of Ketman goes some way to explain the course of Sinn Fein's peace strategy. Its first meaning entailed a collective engagement in 'pulling the wool over its own eyes'. Ketman begins with the acknowledgement that all human behaviour involves a significant amount of acting and in politics it means assuming a role or, to use contemporary terminology, it means accepting a 'line'. Once this substitution of the collective line for independent thought becomes habitual, a politician may 'no longer differentiate his true self from the self he simulates, so that even the most intimate of individuals speak to each other in Party slogans' (Milosz 1981: 55). The party fools itself because it is necessary for it to be fooled. For Sinn Fein, fooling itself was the condition of making sense of its own position. As Gibney succinctly put it: 'Give me the language of ambiguity. It has served the people of this country well over the last ten years. It has oiled the engine of the peace process' (cited in McIntyre 2003a). In this case, the language of ambiguity meant adjusting every previous belief to coincide with the requirements of current policy such that republicans 'are prepared to collude in their own forgetfulness of the poisoned roots out of which Sinn Fein grew and in which they still thrive' (O'Hanlon 2003). This involved, as it always does, an energetic process of rewriting history exemplified best in the work of Gerry Adams (2003b and interview with Billen 2003). As one critical historian pithily put it, republicans now argued that IRA activity was really 'a struggle for justice and equality, a kind of civil rights movement with teeth, not a terror campaign to coerce unionists (Gerry Adams's "Protestant brothers and sisters") into a united Ireland' (Murphy 2003). If the historian found that disturbing, it was also possible to identify a positive aspect. The IRA had lost the terror campaign to coerce unionists and, as one former member wrote, its leaders had been compelled to 'rescue something, anything, from a complete mess which was largely of their own making' (O'Callaghan 2003). The rewriting of history could be read as an implicit admission of that mess and as an attempt to soften the loss of the ideal through the retrospective construction of another purpose. That purpose was now the electoral eclipse of the SDLP.

In the new dispensation, the SDLP felt itself compelled to connive at its own undoing. According to Mark Durkan, then chairman of the SDLP, 'The politics of the last ambiguity is preferable to the politics of the last atrocity' (cited in Breen 1995: 7). Of course it was, but this tolerant attitude served Sinn Fein so well that it boosted its credibility at the expense of the SDLP. Indeed, the very thing that had been the SDLP's distinguishing attribute throughout the Troubles, its moral dignity in the context of republican violence, was compromised by accepting such ambiguity. The nobility of its intention was clear but the consequence was to weaken the party's very foundations. It was too late in the process of political equivocation for Durkan, now as SDLP leader, to argue that people 'should not be in a position where language and logic are turned inside out', that people 'should not have to live off euphemisms' (cited in O'Doherty 2002b: 5). The SDLP's strategy of political equivalence between Sinn Fein and Ulster Unionists and moral equidistance between the IRA Army Council and the Ulster Unionist Council actually left it in political and moral no man's land.

The second meaning of Ketman was equally ambiguous. On the one hand, an absolute distinction between the inner truth of purpose and the external lie of conformity was one option for the Sinn Fein leadership to sell the peace process to its own constituency. The followers were brought comfort, permitted to keep their dream of what will be. The humiliation of sitting at Stormont and helping to administer Northern Ireland, of having to distance Sinn Fein from the IRA's armed struggle, these things and more became palatable in so far as republicans remained assured that their leaders were practising Ketman. The Agreement could not be a 'sell-out' for really the humiliation was the British Government's and, more importantly, the betrayal was the unionists'. In the early days of the peace process the spirit of Ketman was revealed in the TUAS strategy. To those in Washington, London and Dublin whom Sinn Fein needed to impress 'TUAS stood for Totally Unarmed Strategy and it implied that Republicans really were committed to peaceful ways and implicitly suggested that eventually they would get rid of their weapons'. To their own followers TUAS meant Tactical Use of Armed Struggle, implicitly suggesting that peace was a tactic and arms would never be decommissioned. 'The ability of each constituency to accept the explanation given to them and their conviction that it was really the other that was being misled gave the peace process its real momentum' (Moloney 2000b; for a fuller account see Moloney 2002: 423–501).

Here was the cleverness of Ketmanesque distinctions: it appeared to secure the privileged knowledge of the few while making fools of the many. Significantly, it allowed the republican leadership to make its peace strategy serve whatever purpose it thought fit. Republicans flattered themselves that their political awareness was more sophisticated than anyone else's and this hubris – rather like those willing to see the emperor's new clothes – actually made them more susceptible to manipulation (McIntyre 2003b). The only compromise, it seemed, was that unionism would be compromised and that assumption alone brought enormous psychic gratification to Sinn Fein supporters. Since this sort of Ketman was consolidated by the appropriate external responses, the outrage of unionists was actually functional to its general success (Patterson 2002: 26). Republican cleverness was confirmed, the terminal political ignorance of Sinn Fein's opponents revealed, the certainty of final victory and the success of the deceit made obvious as Sinn Fein marched through the institutions of governance. A united Ireland, then, surely could be only a matter of time. In the meantime, however, republicans would be bound in to an institutional framework that bore no relationship to their historic demands. As another historian observed, if ten years previously someone had argued that the IRA's war with the British state would be over and that Sinn Fein would occupy ministerial office in a devolved Northern Ireland administration, few would have believed it (English 2002b: 5). It had indeed happened albeit in the politically unstable manner of Ketman.

That the British Government well understood the utility of constructive ambiguity was conceded by the British Ambassador to Ireland. 'The ambiguity with which the Republican movement handled the relationship between Sinn Fein and the Provisional IRA', he admitted, 'may have helped to oil the wheels of the peace process in the past.' The British Government understood it because it was also playing that game and a substantial proportion of the electorate in Northern Ireland, mainly but not exclusively unionist, thought that Tony Blair's failure to honour his pledges about decommissioning made during the referendum campaign was a case in point. That ambiguity about paramilitarism and politics had become, after the suspension of the Assembly in October 2002, destructive and it was 'the grit which has brought its machinery to a grinding halt' (Roberts 2003). The demand was now for clarity of intention. Even so, the call for clarification before the postponed Assembly elections in May 2003 did not receive an adequate response.

Adams had announced on the IRA's behalf that it would engage in 'no activities which will undermine in any way the peace process'. This did not satisfy unionists. Trimble responded by noting that it would have been easy for Adams to answer 'yes' to the question 'Is there going to be an end to all paramilitary activity?' His failure to do so, he thought, was 'fairly illustrative' of Sinn Fein's addiction to self-serving ambiguity. It did not satisfy the British Government either because, as Blair's official spokesman confirmed, the Prime Minister was sending the message 'that the transition has to be over' (Harding 2003). In short, republicans could not any longer be 'half in and half out' of the democratic process. In the run up to the November date for elections, Trimble and Adams appeared committed to resolving the problem in a way that would satisfy their respective electorates. For the first time it appeared that the Agreement was delivering on the promise of sharing risks rather than seeking advantage. Unfortunately, ambiguity again succeeded in destroying the promise. When the IRA vetoed a 'transparent' decommissioning of arms on 21 October 2003 it rendered the whole process so opaque that Trimble 'realized at the last moment that he had bought a pig in a poke' (Johnston 2003). This was a betrayal of the UUP leader but a Ketmanesque coup for the leader of Sinn Fein who knew that the discomfiture of a unionist would play well with his electorate. The irony was that Trimble remained one of the few unionists who understood the delicacy of the republican position for he too had his own politics of ambiguity to deal with (for an excellent account see Godson 2004).

It took a very sophisticated unionist to see an opportunity in republican ambiguity. Trimble saw it and tried to construct his own policy around it. The policy stated that unionists would not share power with '*un*reconstructed terrorists' but that expression involved its own constructive ambiguity. In so far as republicans were in the process of *re*constructing themselves then, however nauseating for unionists, it was always possible to keep open the door to compromise (for evidence of Trimble's capacity for constructive ambiguity see Moloney 1999). If the revelations of Adams's role in the peace process revealed him to be a 'dishonest adversary' they also appeared to confirm Trimble's assessment of him 'as the republican leader who realized a very long time ago that the traditional republican project in Ireland was unattainable and had to be quietly buried' (Bew 2002). Furthermore, Trimble's own assessment was not far removed from that of one former IRA prisoner. 'As a movement that began its life vowing to remain in existence until it secured British withdrawal' the IRA had been 'pushed into a position from which it can only pursue the effective disbanding of the IRA and the reform of the RUC' (McIntyre 2002b). Trimble got little credit from nationalist commentators whose traditional contempt for the ability of unionist politicians made them incapable of acknowledging the subtlety (and difficulty) of his position. Indeed, Trimble's approach appeared so to disorder their expectations that they could respond only in the meanest of ways (O'Connor 2002).

There were great dangers in this understanding of how the process was to be managed. If the IRA was to be given the opportunity for a soft landing there needed to be clear evidence for unionists that it was indeed on its way down. For it not to be engaged in 'offensive military action' was inadequate reassurance since that implied the IRA was merely holding its position. A full commitment to exclusively peaceful methods required it to demonstrate a measured programme of disbandment corresponding with the progressive functioning of devolved institutions. And the most effective way to achieve that was by agreeing a schedule for decommissioning. Even when this was not properly delivered, Trimble continued to hold to his analysis with a doggedness that passed the understanding of those in his party who could see only republican bad faith. Not only unionists saw things that way. A leader in the *Spectator* argued:

> Sinn Fein is a minority group dedicated to dissimulation, conspiracy and infiltration according to the true and trusted principles first laid down by Lenin, with a definite and non-negotiable goal: the unification of Ireland, whether Ireland wants it or not.
>
> (*Spectator* 2002)

Not only did unionists see republican bad faith they also felt that the Trimble strategy was delivering neither republican responsibility nor electoral benefit.

This neatly dramatized the paradox of the UUP position. On the one hand, its constituency was told that republicans had signed up to a partitionist settlement and could not circumvent the principle of consent. On the other hand, the party worried that the Agreement's implementation required of them a heavier sacrifice. For Trimble's critics the ambiguity was a political disaster. One consequence of accepting the need for an IRA soft landing was actually to be complicit in arranging the implementation of the Agreement to the convenience of republicanism. Republicans, as one journalist claimed, came quickly to realize that there would never be any effective sanction for breaching the principles of the Agreement. 'Sinn Fein can confidently expect no serious rebuke from either the Dublin or London governments, or from their fellow nationalists' over the continuing actions of the IRA. However, the UUP 'cannot tolerate this farce, without being historically extinguished by the forces of Paisleyism' (Myers 2002). There was also a cultural difference in the way republicans and unionists used political language. As one former IRA activist argued, 'for many in unionism everything must be spelt out in bold capital letters and underlined with an indelible marker'. The only problem was that the authors of the republican script had its own constituency for whom everything must always be 'written in invisible ink' (McIntyre 2000: 8). In the contest for unionist hearts and minds, the significance of 21 October 2003 cannot be underestimated, for Trimble's objective of historic compromise had been compromised in historic fashion by the secretive cult of militant republicanism and its use of invisible ink. That provided an open opportunity for the forces of Paisleyism.

Though the DUP claimed to have remained true to principle and virtue it confirmed a political rule of thumb that the most ideological of parties can also be the most pragmatic of parties. The public face of honest dealing concealed a more ambiguous strategy. Since the referendum the DUP's policy had changed from fundamental rejection of the Agreement to arguing for its renegotiation. For some this meant that the DUP was seeking a way to accommodate itself, with slight modifications, to the Agreement. For others, the logic of the Agreement meant that the DUP had no choice but to work within the new dispensation. Indeed, the DUP might even be the preferred vehicle to deliver the unionist electorate to a stable settlement. This was the 'Nixon in China' syndrome as one commentator put it, a syndrome that the DUP quietly helped to propagate (O'Doherty 2003c). This involved a delicate political manoeuvre of continuing to condemn the UUP leadership for negotiating weakness, political misjudgement and blind commitment to a failed Agreement while at the same time moderating the party's tone about inclusive government and the need for accommodation with nationalism. By 2003, even Sinn Fein was prepared to acknowledge a more 'pragmatic approach' on the part of the DUP. As Trimble's credibility appeared to wane, the DUP presented itself as the party that could deliver the majority of unionists to a renegotiated Agreement. Could a hegemonic DUP really be ready to deal? If Paisley denounced the UUP as the party of 'the big lie and half truth' that denunciation was reciprocated. For Trimble, the DUP were really only looking for a 'fig leaf' of renegotiation before accepting 'the places and power the Agreement gives' and the party's 'bombastic claims cannot cover up the hollowness of their position'. He was equally convinced that the DUP was incapable of delivering any sort of workable deal (*News Letter* 2003). Had not the DUP already taken all the advantages of the Agreement like assembly salaries and ministerial posts but shouldered none of the responsibilities and taken none of the pressure? Had not the DUP pursued an entirely self-interested course that required of the UUP admission of guilt or (political) self-annihilation? The DUP defence – that it constituted an opposition *within* the Executive – was logically incoherent but politically convenient (Aughey 2000: 69–70).

Selling the DUP to London and Dublin as the party of effective leadership ignored one big problem. Its own support base had been so convinced by the party's rhetoric of betrayal that there was little support amongst its core vote for power-sharing, not only with Sinn Fein but also with the SDLP. In supporting the DUP, unionists were actually 'voting for an end to ambiguity, and what it has brought them' (McCartney 2003). Unfortunately, only opposition can be unambiguous because it is mainly impotent. The DUP would have to manoeuvre into its own position of ambiguity if it were serious about achieving devolved government but that ran the risk of alienating its own supporters without satisfying its potential partners in devolution. For British and Irish officials seeking some way to engineer an accord between the DUP and Sinn Fein the main hope was that, despite the very different public use of language, the respective private desires of these parties were both written in 'invisible ink'.

Axioms and maxims

In Chapter 4 we noted Rorty's observation that it is possible for politics to become trapped between two vocabularies, one that is a nuisance and one that vaguely promised better things. The deceits of post-Agreement politics can in part be traced to this condition and a useful guide to unravelling its complexity can be found in Oakeshott's essay *Political Discourse*. For Oakeshott, all political discourse 'may be said to be the recognition of a political situation and the defence or recommendation of a response to it in terms of a special vocabulary' (Oakeshott 1991: 74). These vocabularies are distinguished one from another not only by different vocabularies of belief but also by different logical designs. There is one sort of discourse with its own logical design that attempts to overcome the uncertainties of politics. Oakeshott calls this 'demonstrative political discourse'. Demonstrative political discourse is one in which beliefs are accorded the status of *axioms* and while Oakeshott clearly disapproved of both the form and the consequences of that axiomatic design, he admitted that it is not mere political error. It is not error because it can be persuasive and persuasiveness is a measure of political success. Indeed, it is the sort of political discourse that people often *do* find persuasive. The craving for certainty may, Oakeshott believed, corrupt us 'by suggesting that we can pass off the responsibility for making these choices upon some axiom or "law" for which, in turn, we have no responsibility' (1991: 81). This is the vocabulary of positional logic. The second political vocabulary is 'concerned with contingencies, not necessities; with probabilities and expectations, not with demonstrable certainties; with conjectures, not proofs; with surmises and guesses, not with calculations'. It involves argument premised on *maxims*, that is general statements about desirability and ethical rules of thumb. In politics, Oakeshott argued, we should try to make the effort 'to understand our "principles" and our "admitted goods" in such a way as to recognize each as a choice we have made for ourselves on our own moral responsibility' (1991: 95). Those for whom absolute fidelity to principle is the only measure of politics, this recommendation is not only inadequate but also treacherous because adjusting principles according to their due allows casuistry to poison the well of ideological truth.

Sinn Fein's strategy, for example, has been bound up with the ideological meaning of 'process'. The original republican definition of process – encompassed by the phrase 'the peace process' – came under the category of a law, a law of historical development moving inexorably towards the achievement of nationalist destiny. The peace process in this sense projected a predetermined course that no party should frustrate. It was not the *active* consent of unionists to this process that was required but unionist acquiescence in political arrangements that promoted that end. The task was to 'manage the transition' in order to secure that objective. In other words, the legitimacy of abandoning the 'war' was based on the expectation that negotiations about delivering peace would achieve republican objectives. The means were defined by the logic of the end and it was an end that reflected the direction of world history (English 2003: 344). For those republican critics of Sinn Fein's strategy writing in the journal *The Blanket,* there was no axiomatic process in the Agreement towards Irish unity. Indeed, the idea that the Agreement would deliver Irish unity inevitably (by 2016) was a lie. That lie was 'the pinnacle of falsehood, perched atop a pyramid of untruths and deceptions'. In this case, the truth of the 'process' was not the attainment of a united Ireland 'as the IRA's base was constantly assured was the goal'. Rather, its purpose was the consolidation of power by the Adams leadership (Luby 2003). The most systematic critique was that of McIntyre, who argued the peace process 'witnessed republicanism describing its strategic failures as either "new phases of struggle" or as "staging posts"'. The Agreement was transitional, certainly, but transitional from political honesty to 'a strategy of deception' (McIntyre 2001: 206). In its course, the meaning of process had been transformed from movement towards a predetermined end to limited progress, circumscribed by facts and realities. Process now involved normalization within Northern Ireland as a part of the United Kingdom and all-Ireland arrangements had been made consistent with that status. McIntyre recalled that the politics of 'interim arrangements' was not new in republicanism and had been accepted in 1973 (McIntyre 1995: 108). Under the terms of the Agreement, however, arrangements had been achieved but they were not interim and there would be no transition (McIntyre 1999). The Sinn Fein leadership had thereby decreed a 'regime of deceit which has become the lifeblood of the peace process' (McIntyre 2003c). The force of McIntyre's criticism was not directed against the end of violence but against Sinn Fein's continued reliance on demonstrative political discourse to justify it. It was a criticism that disliked the peace process because of its remorseless organized lying but did not dislike the peace. It was an invitation to the Sinn Fein leadership to accept their moral responsibility for the choices made, to end, in other words, the ambiguity of their 'organised forgetting' (McIntyre 2003d). However consistent critics like McIntyre would wish Sinn Fein to be, the truth was that through 'organised forgetting' it had now become the largest party within the nationalist camp. In the Assembly elections of November 2003 it confirmed the 2001 Westminster General Election success. With 24 per cent of the vote, up almost 6 per cent on 1998, Sinn Fein was drawing further ahead of their demoralized rivals the SDLP, which had slumped to 17 per cent, down 5 per cent on 1998.

These were the circumstances that permitted the DUP to argue that the assumed grand historic compromise, IRA decommissioning and inclusive executive power, was actually irrelevant to the conditions of Northern Ireland. It required too great a level of trust in a society in which bad faith and political lying (by others) were assumed to be pervasive. It argued persuasively that there was a 'need to find a form of administration which can actually survive the result of any election or the bad behaviour of any political party'. Any new agreement would have to be based on what the DUP determined were the 'political realities' and 'not those which are based on a level of trust which is utterly unrealistic in the current environment'. Indeed, the DUP's electoral success in the November 2003 Assembly election was declared a vote for 'clarity and certainty', an end to a process of 'cryptic words and hidden gestures' (Robinson 2003a). It topped the poll with 26 per cent of the vote, nearly 8 per cent up on the 1998 result and with 30 seats became the largest party in the Assembly. Even though Trimble saw his party's vote go up marginally as well there was no doubt who had won the current battle within unionism. The result confirmed that a majority of unionists had become disillusioned with the Agreement and even the rise in support for the UUP could be attributed to the strong performance of anti-Agreement candidates like Jeffrey Donaldson. The DUP had profited with an uncomplicated message that appealed to alienated unionists and successfully attracted the votes of the other smaller anti-Agreement unionist parties.

There would be, it claimed, 'no room for ambiguity' any longer (Campbell 2004). Nevertheless, the real challenge for the DUP was to leave the secure, axiomatic world of principled opposition and to move into the messy world of compromise, from a party of protest to a potential party of power. This was not inconceivable but it would involve the calling of another significant bluff. It would require the leadership gradually to play down its fundamental opposition to dealing with Sinn Fein/IRA and gradually to play up the prospect of an historic compromise. The public position of the DUP appeared to be, as ever, forthright and unwavering. Speaking at the party conference in May 2004, deputy leader Peter Robinson proposed that there was a world of difference between the DUP approach and that of the UUP. 'The UUP sought as its strategic goal to seek peace with terrorists. The DUP wants an end to their existence.' This was not the DUP's idea of an historic compromise since 'if your strategy is to seek peace with the terrorists then you will inevitably be sucked into paying for the silence of their guns'. That, according to Robinson, was the rationale of the Belfast Agreement and the legacy of Trimble unionism (Robinson 2004). However, proclaiming that the party had 'not deviated one iota from our principles', Nigel Dodds MP also argued that the DUP's proposals in the policy document *Devolution Now* demonstrated 'our determination to bring devolution back to Northern Ireland on a democratic basis'. The DUP approach would be sufficiently flexible 'to allow the most appropriate arrangements to be put in place. Parties therefore have a place in "Executive

Government" if they are willing to act to meet the tests of democracy' (Dodds 2004). He meant Sinn Fein. So the potential was there – on conditions – for republicans to enter into government with the DUP, something that would have been thought unimaginable a few years before.

Conclusion

Oakeshott observed the distinction between people keeping 'troth' with one another, the sort of fidelity demanded by common observance of the law, and people united in recognition of a 'truth', the sort of fidelity demanded by a common purpose (1975: 233). The parties to the Agreement did not deliver the first. The IRA's continued activities meant that unionists could not trust the word of Sinn Fein. In Burkean terms Sinn Fein wanted to maximize the benefits of civil and uncivil society together. So long as republicans felt this was a realistic option then it was rational for them to pursue a politics of compensation for the failure of the IRA's project of Irish unification and incrementally raise its value as a condition of moving exclusively into civil society. It was remarkable the extent to which this ambiguity was indulged (even for the best of reasons) and for how long. As a philosopher said of a similar intellectual indulgence, making 'sense of cannibalism relative to the sum of the practices which constitute the life of cannibals is one thing; abandoning all further judgement is another' (Hollis 1998: 120). Unfortunately, all further judgement was abandoned too frequently. It was the sort of intellectual indulgence that could allow Adams to continue to argue that the 'question of armed struggle therefore for those who espouse armed struggle can only be dealt with if we make politics work' and that this required 'all parties to the agreement to use their influence to try and bring about disarmament by all the armed groups' (cited in Beggan and Indurthy 2002: 351). The reluctance of the UUP to commit itself unequivocally to power sharing with Sinn Fein without the disbandment of the IRA (which is what Adams's formulation required) made it easy for republicans to convince the Catholic electorate of unionist bad faith. This, of course, ignored the enormous risk Trimble had taken by 'jumping first' in 1999 and waiving the UUP's policy of 'no guns, no government'. Indeed, that very initiative revealed the insufficiency of trust. As Hobbes had warned, he that performed first had no assurance that the other would perform after because words were not enough. Nor did the Agreement deliver on the second notion of trust for the major parties remained committed to their separate truths. The idea of a community of fate – of the kind suggested in Chapter 2, one that could bind these different truths within a common institutional framework – was lacking still. The distinctive unionist sensibility was related to this gap between what they felt – the unnecessary evils of paramilitary irresponsibility, political manipulation and government appeasement – and what they heard being proclaimed – the Agreement is the best of all possible worlds and everything in it is a necessary good.

On 3 February 2004 the Agreement entered what was felicitously called a period of 'review'. This review involved the DUP (and the UUP) demanding changes to the Agreement because that represented the wish of a majority of unionists and Sinn Fein (and the SDLP) resisting change because that represented the wish of a majority of nationalists. If one had a measure of the progress made in the last 30 years it was that no one now expected there to be, as in 1974, a Workers' Council strike to enforce the former demand nor, as in 1972, a Bloody Friday to enforce the latter. Assessing the quality of those changes is the subject of the next chapter.

10 For better and for worse

In a book published in 1994, two academic lawyers tried to map the options for a stable political settlement in Northern Ireland. The stark choice they identified was between sharing and separation, and it is appropriate to revisit their arguments since this book has also followed the pattern of examining present circumstances through the exploration of opposed conceptions of them. *Northern Ireland: The Choice* began by asking a simple question: 'How can the ordinary people in Northern Ireland be given a democratic choice between conflict and compromise, between separation and sharing?' In one major respect, they thought, the choice had already been made in that 'the forces of communal separation', especially residential segregation, had been at work throughout the Troubles. Nevertheless, official policy remained dedicated to 'the objective of greater integration and sharing between members of the two communities', not least in the sharing of governmental authority (Boyle and Hadden 1994: 1–3). As they observed, no commentator ever had difficulty suggesting structures for sharing power in Northern Ireland. Unfortunately, none of those structures had yet been established. The problem seemed to lie not in the range of imaginative suggestions for sharing but 'in achieving sufficient agreement among unionists and nationalists on a set of structures to make them work'. At this point, Boyle and Hadden were prepared to think the unthinkable. If sharing were to prove impossible then perhaps separation was inevitable. They did not regard this as either a welcome or a satisfactory outcome but were prepared to admit the possibility that it might be better 'to recognize that those involved cannot realistically be expected to go on living together in a state of perpetual conflict, but must make sensible and practical arrangements to live apart' (Boyle and Hadden 1994: 192). To a large degree that simple choice appeared to be overtaken by events after 1994, events that Boyle and Hadden, like most people, had not anticipated. If the process of negotiating the Agreement temporarily displaced the significance of sharing versus separation, then the implementation of the Agreement returned that question to the centre of politics as the practicalities of devolved power-sharing were tested to destruction. If the Boyle and Hadden analysis, for the sake of academic clarity, exaggerated the distinctiveness of the two options it did not misrepresent the tendencies present in politics although, as they later admitted, it was much more likely that 'a confusing mixture of elements from both will materialize' in the unfolding of the peace process (Boyle and Hadden 1995: 281).

It can be argued that there developed two alternative narratives of post-Agreement Northern Ireland. The first narrative was a narrative of progress that emphasized the extent to which things had improved. Its centre of gravity remained the idea of sharing and it was concerned to trace the present opportunities that made that idea a realizable one. The second narrative was a narrative of regress that emphasized the extent to which things had worsened. Its centre of gravity remained the idea of separation and it was concerned to illustrate the intensification of communal hostility. This chapter argues, as Boyle and Hadden also conceded, that there was a third, and more comprehensive, narrative that combined elements of both improvement and worsening. Its centre of gravity was the continuing ambivalence of post-Agreement politics and it acknowledged that things were not so progressive as the first narrative suggested nor so regressive as the second implied. Since the English language is not very inventive of paradoxical terms, the expression used here is a German one. *Verschlimmbesserung*, the rough translation of which is 'as things get better they also get worse', conveys that paradoxical condition of contemporary Northern Ireland. It attempts to capture a complexity that had already been detected by subtle academic analysis. For example, at the very time of the publication of *Northern Ireland: The Choice* this complex condition was prophetically defined as one in which aspects of communalism would be challenged while others would be strengthened. 'As in so much that concerns Northern Ireland, it is hard to hold both sides of the story in one's head at the same time' (Todd 1995: 165). This chapter attempts to hold both sides of the story together.

Narrative of progress

There are a number of dimensions to the narrative of progress and they can be grouped together under the heading of the 'peace dividend'. The first of these is economic. The changing skyline of commercial Belfast, the mood of general prosperity and the buoyant property market throughout Northern Ireland have been attributed at least in part to the outworking of the peace process. These changes are often quite striking to those familiar with the Northern Ireland of the Troubles and who have returned to visit after 1998. However questionable the coincidence may be between economic improvement and political change, there is little doubt that there is *some* connection and it is one that continues to inform public opinion. Moreover, the peace process has been significant not only for what has happened but also for what has *not* happened and this provided a second dimension to the narrative of progress. Though security force intelligence had been increasingly successful in saving the loss of life, it could not prevent limited terrorist successes and if the IRA and loyalist paramilitary campaigns had continued, even in their circumscribed form of the early 1990s, then the Troubles would have claimed a significantly higher death toll. This is a figure that is almost impossible to calculate accurately but is likely to be substantial. To public opinion outside Northern Ireland the narrative of progress has been the dominant story and unionist and nationalist engagement with that opinion has attempted to show which side has been responsible for holding up progress or failing to deliver. Defending the record of his party since 1998, for example, Trimble argued that republicans could 'no longer hide behind the myth of unionist intransigence' because the UUP had been 'prepared to allow time and space for a transition to a totally peaceful and democratic future' and had been willing to share power (Trimble 2004). By contrast republicans tried to present their own fidelity to the narrative of progress by denouncing the incorrigible forces of 'rejectionist unionism' that were impeding the implementation of the Agreement, aided and abetted by 'securocrats' (Adams 2004). With regard not only to economic and security matters but also to the cultivation of an optimistic mood, the British Government has continued to stress the advantages that have accompanied the Agreement. In doing so it has been trying to bring to bear upon the resistant conditions of Northern Ireland politics a very British expectation and a paradigmatic illustration was Blair's keynote speech at Stranmillis College, Belfast in 1999. The Prime Minister began his address by relating a proposition he had encountered on both sides. It was the claim that after 1998 nothing had changed. He disagreed and, like all government ministers, was obliged to acknowledge the negative but was determined to emphasize the positive. The Agreement, he claimed, was 'a million miles further than we've ever been' and he enumerated the progress that had taken place: 'the ceasefires are in place; fewer soldiers on the streets; fewer roadblocks; ordinary life returning to our streets and homes; new investment and economic development all around us'. For those who believed that nothing had really changed for the better, the Prime Minister's reply was blunt: 'it's all rubbish' and he stated the central premise of the narrative of progress. The Agreement had succeeded in making Northern Ireland 'a symbol of hope around the world', the complete opposite of its image only a few years before (Blair 1999). Like the ancient Roman, Blair's argument required people only to open their eyes and to see the cranes over Belfast: *si monumentum requiris, circumspice*. And do not let fatalism spoil it.

Of course, the British Government had an interest in promoting the positive virtues of the Agreement and one suspects that the narrative of progress echoed that longstanding and popular objective of policy to conjure the Irish Question out of existence. The appeal of a narrative that suggested 'problem solved' was a powerful one to a wider British (and Irish) public that desired nothing better than that Northern Ireland return to that state of provincial languor prior to 1969. This represented the condition of indifference. As one official at the Northern Ireland Office remarked, 'the British government cared only that the parties agreed; for the most part, it did not care what they agreed to' (Horowitz 2002: 200). However much wishful thinking it contained, it is important to stress that the narrative of progress was *not just* wishful thinking. Not only, as Blair pointed out, had there been manifest improvements but also there really was a certain potential in the situation that intelligent observers could extrapolate to benign conclusions. According to this interpretation, the Agreement had created a new, if at first sight rather contradictory, dynamic in which apparent electoral polarization complemented a substantial political moderation. The logic, in other words, revealed a sort of Hegelian cunning of reason, all the more cunning in its profound historical irony. The moderate parties that had done so much to give life to the negotiations, the UUP and the SDLP, would find their utility and their significance exhausted in the process. The rose at the centre of this cross of electoral suffering would be the moderation of the politics of Sinn Fein and the DUP, both of which would be compelled to make their accommodation with the new, post-1998 reality. In this manner, the 'extremes' would become the 'centre' and the centre would be immeasurably strengthened. Sinn Fein and the DUP would become the preferred vehicles to deliver at last the nationalist and unionist electorates to a stable settlement. With no enemies to the right and none to the left, the way would now be clear for a final compromise. There was a reductionist rationality in that perspective and it assumed that when the extremes surpass the moderates then they really do have nowhere else to go but to return to the middle ground.

This proposition was advanced in a persuasive explication of its electoral logic in an article by Mitchell, O'Leary and Evans. Their argument was that politics helps to transform identities as well as promoting their expression and they detected a distinct metamorphosis of Sinn Fein and the DUP in the course of the 2001 Westminster General Election. In sum, despite 'misleading rhetoric to the contrary, both "extreme" parties moderated their platforms, and may continue to do so, and this softening of their positions partly explains their electoral success'. The logic of the consociational framework of the Agreement had now made both Sinn Fein and the DUP 'stakeholders' in the institutions and thus provided both of them with incentives to be participative rather than anti-system. This interpretation was intelligent enough to insert caveats and qualifications but it did suggest 'a fascinating if dangerous spectacle' when both parties secured clear majorities in their respective electoral blocs. Here was the emerging choice. The DUP and Sinn Fein 'would have to choose between stealing their opponents' clothes and wearing them, or showing that they remain wolves in sheep's clothing' (Mitchell, O'Leary and Evans 2001: 725–42). In so far as politics is rational, then, the rationality of the Agreement's institutions would impose itself upon party politics and the dynamic of the process would be towards a softening rather than a hardening of positions, misleading rhetoric to the contrary being discounted. This academic perspective is not that far removed from the commentary of those who were critical, for reasons of party or principle, of the trajectory of DUP and Sinn Fein politics.

On the unionist side, Trimble's withdrawal of the UUP from the Review of the Agreement in March 2004 led him to criticize the DUP for offering 'to share the power of a devolved Assembly right now with Sinn Fein if only there appears to be no Executive'. Their *Devolution Now* (DUP 2004) submission to that Review, proposing a 'corporate Assembly', was, he thought, a mere fig-leaf and pretence. 'This is the DUP today, so anxious for power that they are ready to give up on the big moral and political issue – the need for an end to paramilitarism' (Trimble 2004). That criticism repeated a simmering anger within the UUP leadership that their unionist opponents had taken all the advantages of the Agreement, like Assembly salaries and ministerial posts, but had shouldered none of the responsibilities and had taken none of the risks. On the other hand, it could be argued that such behaviour, while hardly honourable, was far from a threat to the larger goal of political stability in the search for which Trimble and the UUP were expendable commodities. Since 1998 the DUP's policy had indeed changed from one of rejecting the Agreement outright to one of arguing for its renegotiation. In the script of the narrative of progress this meant that the DUP was seeking a way to accommodate itself, with some slight modifications, to a new dispensation that required cooperation with nationalists. Welcoming this development, one unionist commentator thought that by 2004 the DUP was the party courageously breathing 'new life into the stalled process'. Ian Paisley, he claimed, 'is, in effect, setting out his party's ideas on saving the agreement'. Power-sharing was now acceptable with even Sinn Fein and this showed that the DUP leadership was facing up to the single truth about Northern Ireland, 'the existence of another tradition that will not go away' (Garland 2004a). Here was a startling disordering of expectations but one that the narrative of progress prescribed as fully necessary.

On the republican side, there was also an assumption that neither the DUP nor Sinn Fein would any longer have 'to fight debilitating rearguard actions because there were no parties more "extreme" than the DUP and Sinn Fein to cry "sell out"'. Like Trimble's argument, it was thought that the DUP leadership longed for ministerial office and recognized that the only way to achieve this was to do a deal with republicans. It was also thought that the DUP would find no absolute resistance on Sinn Fein's part on its call for the disbandment of the IRA. From this perspective, the republican duck had already become a political rabbit the moment Adams had conceded in practice the principle of unionist consent. Since the whole purpose of the IRA's military campaign had been to force the British to withdraw and to compel unionists into a united Ireland, compulsion and consent were contradictory. The substitute for armed struggle was supposed to be the republicanization of politics that would achieve military ends by other means. 'A decade on from the first ceasefire and with a united Ireland no nearer, the most significant outcome of the peace process has in fact been the "constitutionalisation" of the Provisionals' (Morley 2004). As one former IRA activist also observed, Sinn Fein (like the DUP) had demonstrated the ability to contort itself ideologically and 'is rapidly acquiring all the appearances of a fairly mellow social democratic grouping' which will make it 'indistinguishable from a host of other "somewhere in the centre" parties' (McKearney 2004). For the purposes of the narrative of progress, of course, that judgement could be nothing other than glad tidings. Sinn Fein becoming constitutional and the DUP becoming compromising intimated the consolidation of political stability. One can venture a little deeper into the substance of this narrative of progress by suggesting the following interpretation.

In an examination of Hegel's philosophy of history, McCarney argues that its appeal is to be found in its profoundly reconciling power. He suggests that we are brought to understand the paradox that 'the good is already fulfilled just in virtue of the fact that it is in the process of being fulfilled'. Moreover, this is so because 'all will be well' and in so far as the all 'is presupposed, or implied, by the achievement of freedom, all is already well here and now'. In short, things 'are as they ought to be because they are on the way to being what they ought to be.' *Becoming* can be read as *being* and this is the condition for radicalism to transform itself into conservatism (McCarney 2000: 215–16). That may seem an esoteric way of addressing the specific circumstances of Northern Ireland after the Agreement but it is not totally outlandish. On the one hand, there is, as critics like McIntyre have long argued, a deeply conservative implication in a so-called radical party like Sinn Fein selling the Agreement as the transitional mechanism to Irish unity. In this case, the Agreement really is as it ought to be because it is on the way to becoming what it ought to be. Except in the meantime the 'ought' (Irish unity) takes on the shape of the 'is' (a partitionist settlement) and republicanism becomes complicit in making things work rather than being dedicated to wrecking the place. Here the narrative of progress (which really concerns itself with procedures and not with ultimate objectives) elaborates the traditional 'poacher turned gamekeeper' trajectory of radicalism where the experience and enjoyment of power encourage it to suppress dissent and challenge. That trajectory was yet another aspect of the critique of Sinn Fein's 'constitutionalism' found in the running commentary of *The Blanket*. On the other hand, the narrative of progress believed the secret of the Agreement to be its capacity to reconcile republican supporters to the 'is' of Northern Ireland by encouraging them to believe that it is in the process of becoming other than what it is. This was also the condition for Sinn Fein to replace the SDLP as the dominant party of nationalism. Reconciling the 'is' and 'ought' of nationalism would appeal to the largest constituency of voters.

For republicans to find that paradox persuasive was not simply a case of 'pulling the wool over their own eyes' for they are not without hope or evidence that the 'is' (working the Agreement) would deliver the 'ought' (Irish unity). Furthermore, this was also the basis for the willingness of the narrative of progress to make allowances for certain forms of political violence since that violence already has become other than what it was (no bombing campaign) and already is in the process of becoming what it ought to be (gone for good). If that sort of theodicy would appeal to republicans seeking solace for their military defeat and making the best of all possible cases in a necessarily evil world what relevance could it have for the DUP? Had not its leadership denounced the Agreement and all its works as the foulest betrayal? Fortunately, the Hegelian formula is nothing if not accommodating and inclusive and the following construction can be put on the DUP's own trajectory. Agreement, if not exactly *The* Agreement, the DUP could argue after its electoral successes in 2003, is in the process of becoming what it ought to be through renegotiation and yet already is what it ought to be, because the DUP leadership had signalled its willingness to do a deal. As Peter Robinson stated the case to a nationalist readership in the *Irish News*, the DUP 'is not a threat to you nor is it a threat to progress' since an 'agreement that embraces the DUP is the only one that will bring stability and will last' (Robinson 2003b). For those who read things positively, this was rather like the history of Harold Wilson's renegotiation of Britain's terms of entry into the European Common Market in 1974 – not a renegotiation at all but an accommodation. And that was precisely how some unionists and also the two Governments read the logic of the DUP's position (Garland 2004b).

However, even if one acknowledged the truth that on the major indicators of political violence and material prosperity things had improved since 1998; even if one were to accept that there was a detectable moderation in the public positions of Sinn Fein and the DUP; and even if one were to accept that the narrative of progress was not without its attractive optimism, it was also possible, on a range of other indicators, to argue that things had worsened. Indeed, one could argue that as the peace dividend came to be accepted as the norm, concern about these other matters became as, if not more, influential in the judgement of public life after the Agreement. When these matters were expressed in whole or in part they can be said to constitute a narrative of regress.

Narrative of regress

In the narrative of regress the positive and optimistic reading of the politics of 'becoming as being' was neatly reversed. Far from contributing to stability and mutual accommodation the elision of 'ought' and 'is' had become another source of instability and communal assertion. On the nationalist side, the regressive truth of the Agreement was that, far from reconciling nationalists to the 'is' of Northern Ireland it had encouraged them to believe that Northern Ireland should already be *other* than what it is. In this case the 'ought' (nationalist advance) encountered the 'is' (Garland's other tradition that will not go away) as a mere obstacle and this encouraged the promotion of non-negotiable demands. It helped to explain the impatience, exasperation and contempt with unionism so often found in nationalist discourse and so obvious to unionists (King 2003). As one nationalist commentator proposed, the idea that support for the Agreement implied nationalist accommodation with Northern Ireland's Britishness was a profound mistake. 'People in Ireland no longer equate criticism of Britain with bigotry, or commitment to national unity with extremism and far from abandoning their goal of national unity, increasing numbers of nationalists, north and south, have begun taking practical steps to see that it is realised' (Collins 2004b).

Though the polling statistics were more ambivalent on that point, Collins certainly conveyed a distinctive mood within nationalism (a *Belfast Telegraph* poll of 14 November 2003 put Northern Catholic support for Irish unity at 57 per cent). Moreover, according to the narrative of regress, the electoral advance of Sinn Fein had little to do with moderation and everything to do with effectively antagonizing unionists. In this view, the public rhetoric was not misleading at all and the dramatic truth remained that 'Sinn Fein has a mandate to reject the police and continue to support the IRA on behalf of the majority of nationalists'. This was not a mandate for reconciliation but an indication 'that a nationalist leader who gives unionists a hard time will be rewarded' (O'Doherty 2003d).

Equally, on the unionist side, far from reconciling the majority of unionists to the 'is' of the Agreement, the growth of support for the DUP was an encouragement to believe that the Agreement must become *other* than what it is. Immediately after the DUP's success in the 2003 Assembly election, the party began talking of the 'new realities' that now obtained and these new realities also represented a heightened sense of communal requirement. As Gregory Campbell argued, for 30 years unionists had been compelled to respond to nationalist demands but, with a DUP victory, unionism's day had come. Unionists would now be making the demands (Campbell 2003). Nor did a prominent nationalist journalist think the DUP's proposals for devolution 'courageous'. They were yet another attempt to establish a unionist-controlled Assembly like those proposed in the 1970s and this just went to show that 'unionism hasn't changed a bit since then' (Feeney 2004a). Here was regress for sure since it implied that not only had unionists learnt nothing but now they had forgotten everything as well. In short, the political cultures of Sinn Fein and the DUP did not appear to constitute a hopeful basis for political progress. The 'rational core' of the narrative of progress – that the leaderships of both parties would quite like to exercise executive power – ignored the deeply antagonistic political cultures of republicanism and democratic unionism that informed the narrative of regress (Patterson 2003). The dynamic was not towards sharing but towards separation, now re-labelled 'polarization', and there have been a number of dimensions to the polarization thesis.

A major aspect of this sense of regress has been, first, the experience of the polarization of party support. As Guelke observed, the Agreement had been followed by an intensification of divisions during its implementation. While violence remained well below levels prior to the paramilitary ceasefires of the mid-1990s, 'fears of a resumption of lethal paramilitary violence and ongoing inter-communal clashes at sectarian interfaces have undermined confidence in the peace' (Guelke 2002). Indeed, in a perceptive article that anticipated the problems attending the Agreement in the following year, Guelke admitted the attraction of the 'moderation of the extremes' argument but also noted its central difficulties. In the first place, there was as yet little evidence that the DUP and Sinn Fein were willing to play the roles allotted to them. In the second place, there appeared to be little public support for such an alliance of the extremes. Here was the central paradox of contradictory public expectations and anticipations. On the one hand, the benign *expectation* of unionists had been that nationalists would vote SDLP in the interests of conciliation and the benign *expectation* of nationalists had been that unionists would, for similar reasons, continue to vote UUP. On the other hand, the malign *anticipation* of unionists had been that nationalists would continue to vote in ever larger numbers for Sinn Fein in order to maximize communal advantage and their hostile reaction to that very development actually encouraged further polarization on the nationalist side. Guelke held out little hope for an 'alliance of the extremes' delivering stability despite the 'hypnotic influence on some policymakers' that it continued to exert (Guelke 2003: 6). The outcome of the November 2003 Assembly election merely confirmed a trend that had been detectable for some time. Furthermore, the polarization within unionism and nationalism did not extend the opportunity to mobilize in the middle ground of politics; on the contrary, it marginalized further the 'one community' tradition in Northern Ireland politics (Evans and Tonge 2003: 26). The logic of electoral polarization was clearly explicated for nationalists in the *Irish News*. They would never give 'their second preferences to unionists if a fellow-nationalist is on the ticket' even if that fellow-nationalist was a party enemy. 'Nationalists sense that profound political change is on the way on this island, and in their guts they believe that supporting nationalist candidates all the way down the ticket will hasten that change' (Collins 2003). If this anticipated change was thought to be driven more effectively by republicans then Sinn Fein would get the vote. And a similar logic applied within unionism.

This polarization had an effect, second, on the conduct of government. Those who had long been critical of the 'institutionalization of sectarianism' implicit in an historic compromise between ethnic blocs argued that the Agreement had served to perpetuate rather than to dissipate traditional antagonisms. The problem was easy to identify. The Agreement had resolved a 'short-term problem of sustaining paramilitary ceasefires' and of keeping the main communal parties around the same negotiating table. 'But it did so at the expense of shoring up longer-run difficulties by entrenching the divisions that these sectarian and paramilitary forces lived (and in some cases killed) by.' The Agreement had, ironically, sponsored the cult of separation and neglected the need for sharing (Wilson 2002: 6). The consequence was a vicious circle of crisis, institutional suspension and recrimination when what was needed was a 'virtuous circle of reconciliation, normalisation and stability' (Wilson 2003). Unfortunately, each proposal for reforming public procedures to deliver the virtue of sharing over the vices of separation – changing the voting system, abandoning the registration of Assembly parties as unionist or nationalist or modifying the process of government formation – presupposed the very culture of responsibility that was absent in the first place. This was the 'tragedy of the commons', the sort of self-interested competition that delivers short-term gain but longer-term ruin, self-interest played out not in terms of rational choice but in terms of sectional competition (Fealty 2003: 8). That was an interesting way of looking at the problem except an original commonality of interest was precisely what Northern Ireland lacked.

Academic research, third, pointed to the extent and intensification of social polarization, as well as to its political manipulation. This was a very different perspective on the political condition of Belfast (and by extension of Northern Ireland) than that provided by the Prime Minister in his Stranmillis speech. Here was a world in which 'politicians and community leaders constantly promote the language of opposition where the imperatives of communal difference, segregation and exclusion predominate over the politics of shared interests, integration, assimilation and consensus'. This world was fed by a sectarian rage very much at odds with a Belfast seeking to promote 'the illusion of renewed civic pride' (Shirlow 2000). The Agreement did not even come close 'to deconstructing the atavism and antagonisms that exist between communities'. In short, people in Northern Ireland did not live in 'Liberalville'; they lived in or not far from 'Sectarianopolis' and there was no party aspiring to Executive office committed to an anti-sectarian discourse (Shirlow 2001: 12–13). The conclusion of this research programme was that despite the cessation of large-scale paramilitary violence, Northern Ireland continued to exhibit 'a situation within which the creation of territorial division and rigidified ethno-sectarian communities means that fear and mistrust are still framed by a desire to create communal separation' (Shirlow 2003: 91). Hence the uncomfortable reality that 15 new 'peace walls' had been erected in Belfast since the Agreement to protect one community or the other from continued sectarian harassment (Harding 2004). This was not a purely Belfast phenomenon since the *Life and Times Surveys* also showed a widespread preference amongst Catholics and Protestants throughout Northern Ireland to live and work apart and this indicated a deterioration in community relations and a retreat towards 'single-identity environments' (McGonagle 2003). Moreover, the polls revealed that younger people were more likely to hold sectarian attitudes than their elders and only a minority of them believed that community relations would improve in the near future (Devine and Schubotz 2004). The Agreement, then, appeared to strengthen the very tendencies it was designed to weaken. How can one account for that? One suggestive interpretation proposed that as the constitutional question became less prominent 'so cultural and purely sectarian conflicts have risen to the fore'. In this view, the disabling, if logical, irony of the community relations understanding has been that its elevation of cultural difference has fostered a new divisiveness, 'driven not by equality and discrimination but by the idea that Northern Ireland has two distinct communities whose culture and interests are different, and who must be constantly policed and kept apart'. In the post-Agreement world cultural diversity had become the new sectarianism (O'Neill 2002). There was a measure of truth in that reading though the contrast the author made with the more 'political', and therefore less base and atavistic, condition of the Troubles was insupportable. It expressed the last remnant of paramilitary virtue. The form of the Agreement had displaced antagonisms, certainly, but it was incapable of ameliorating them without a significant investment by the parties in responsible engagement and this seemed just as absent as before.

Perhaps the central problem remained, despite the contrary thesis found in *The Blanket*, that Sinn Fein still considered itself a revolutionary organization and continued to endorse an IRA that continued to steal, kill and intimidate (Clarke 2004). The Provisionals, moreover, continued to use violence as a political bargaining counter. 'No one', argued one journalist, 'should doubt that the kneecappings are political', a way to exert community control and to define the course of the peace process (O'Doherty 2004: 3). Loyalist violence was directed less at defining the course of the peace process and more at defining the course of criminal profiteering. For the narrative of regress, the transition that was currently taking place represented a coarsening of public life in which the boundaries between the civil and the uncivil were being slowly eroded. Again, this is not a problem that is exclusive to Northern Ireland and the popular sense of the state losing effective control of some areas of society is common not only in parts of Eastern Europe but also in parts of Western Europe and North America. Political scientists have directed their attention recently to those conditions where communities 'have few resources to escape mafia-type networks of political co-option and control' (Whitehead 1997: 96). However, Northern Ireland is relatively distinctive in the European Union in the way the civil (democratic) and the uncivil (paramilitarism) overlap.

The extent to which it does or is assumed to do so has encouraged a cynical response to politics, one often provoked by a personal sense of betrayal. The Agreement has been accused of 'institutionalising gangsterism' and permitting those with terrorist connections to sit 'on the board, the committee, the steering group, the advisory panel in every area of our society' (McDowell 2003). That analysis found its politicized version in the review by McCartney of the experience since 1998. Expressing a unionist anxiety about the corruption of public life, McCartney argued that the Agreement had only succeeded in encouraging sectarianism at every level of government. 'Far from providing democratic institutions affording equal rights and protection to every individual citizen, and provision for their enforcement subject to the rule of law, the Agreement gave rights to political parties sevicing the sectarian and sectional interests of the communities they purported to represent, including parties patently linked to terrorist organizations.' For McCartney, the consequence had been the worst community violence for 25 years and a growth in organized crime with which a depleted and demoralized police force could not properly cope (McCartney 2002). Nor, he predicted, would this be confined to the marginalized and the deprived as Shirlow's research asserted. The intimidation and threats would soon be visited on the affluent middle classes, the comfortable and complacent who had voted 'yes' for the Agreement in order to secure a quiet life. Soon they would not have to enquire 'for whom the bell tolls in the ghettos, for by then it may be tolling for both them and their children' (McCartney 1999). The temptation has been to dismiss this as that familiar pedigree of unionist alienation out of political fatalism or as tales to scare the Protestant electorate. However, the revelation of the high suicide rate in Catholic North Belfast linked to paramilitary violence encouraged a widespread feeling, substantiated by academic findings, that things had indeed got worse since 1998 (Oliver 2004; McDonald 2004).

The extent of the problem was revealed by the International Monitoring Commission (IMC) that had been established to observe the conduct of the paramilitary ceasefires. The Commission's First Report noted that the IRA maintained a capacity to undertake acts of terrorist violence. Indeed, the Commission went so far as to argue that 'serious violence' was under the control of the most senior leadership in the republican movement 'whose members must therefore bear responsibility for it' (IMC 2004: 14). The loyalist paramilitaries were also considered to present a continued threat, with the Ulster Volunteer Force (UVF) tightly organized and ruthless and the UDA mainly engaged in crime and drugs but also engaging in 'serious, if crude, attacks' upon Catholics (2004: 15–16). The conclusion of the IMC was that:

> while the number of murders, attacks on the security forces and bombings by paramilitaries has strongly decreased, the level of other

paramilitary violence has been and continues to be considerably higher than before the Belfast Agreement.

(IMC 2004: 25)

Moreover, the shift of primary activity from terrorism to an intensification of criminal activity – extortion, smuggling, protection rackets, fraud – 'may present the biggest long-term threat to the rule of law in Northern Ireland' (2004: 33). The 'peace dividend' for republican and loyalist paramilitaries appeared to be a less dangerous environment in which to line their own pockets but only at the expense of the communities in which they operated and to the detriment of a common public life in Northern Ireland.

By 2004 the promise of sharing, elaborated in the provisions of the Agreement, appeared to be retreating rather than advancing. Those who had done much to sustain that promise accepted that things looked less than bright. The building blocks of the Agreement were being knocked down one by one. The SDLP was in decline, the UUP was seriously divided and the centre ground was contracting. 'Agreements that cannot preserve the core constituencies that brought them into being do not usually survive' and the official policy that was emerging seemed to be one 'not just of inclusion of the extremes but exclusion of the moderates'. An arrangement based on the principle of conciliation or sharing required the cultivation of those genuinely committed to that principle rather than the accommodation of 'those who have been happier with the politics of ethnic rage' (Bew 2003). Whether the starting point of analysis was support for or opposition to the spirit of the Agreement, the narrative of regress argued that this politics of ethnic rage was the flourishing weed choking the emergence of a healthy politics in Northern Ireland.

Verschlimmbesserung: for better and for worse

It is perhaps to be expected that these two narratives developed as a response to changing circumstances for it is not at all unusual to find optimistic and pessimistic readings of political events. Of course, optimism and pessimism are not neutral analytical categories. Reasons to be cheerful for some are the very reasons for others to be miserable and it is understandable that the intellectual drive is to go beyond optimism and pessimism in order to achieve a perspective undistorted by such subjective moods. It is tempting to call this a narrative of realism but that would be to claim too much, for realism *of this sort* implies objective certainty and has a habit of being unrealistic precisely because it ignores the subjective. What is needed is a perspective conscious of a contradictory reality. For example, Ruane and Todd thought that the inherent difficulty of the Agreement lay in the 'imbrication' of the normative ideal of sharing with the power struggle of separation and that view captured neatly the ambivalence of post-Agreement politics (Ruane and Todd 1998: 191). The Germans have a word for this ambivalent condition and that word is *Verschlimmbesserung*. If any single word could sum up the period after 1998, then *Verschlimmbesserung* is about as good as any. Its particular virtue is that it recalls to our attention the fact that nothing in politics is an unmixed blessing and that much of it involves a wager on the future. The wager of the Agreement was that benefits would ultimately outweigh losses and that the polarization of electoral politics was ultimately less of a problem than the destructive consequences of terrorist campaigns. The wisdom drawn upon in this narrative is not that of modern conflict resolution theory but of a much older tradition of conflict management found in the practice of the Austro-Hungarian Empire. Acknowledging that it was impossible to achieve a truly harmonious relationship between its component ethnic parts, there developed in the Viennese Chancellory what was known as a 'policy of simmering'. The resentments and grievances between national groups and between national groups and the state had to be acknowledged as a fact of life. The single imperative was to ensure that they would not be so volatile that they induced civil unrest and it was thought the best that policy could achieve was limited. In short, if the politics of 'ethnic rage' was unavoidable that rage should only simmer and not boil over. Those who thought politics could do more than this were dangerous idealists and likely to provoke disaster. Given the fate of the Austro-Hungarian Empire this may be taken to be an illustrative failing of imperial cynical realism, a realism whose very cynicism became its own undoing.

However, the normative and power-political 'imbrication' of the peace process implied a Northern Ireland version of that policy of simmering. Ending the major campaigns of violence was to be the first (or perhaps last) step to prevent the ethnic pot boiling over and if, subsequently, the heat could be slowly reduced in relations between unionists and nationalists then it was possible to envisage power-sharing devolution working. Lowering the temperature of communal politics would be the necessary condition for workable institutions. Since there had been no consensual Garden of Eden from which politics in Northern Ireland had fallen there was no promised land to which it would return. For all the grandiloquent language that had accompanied it, the Agreement in this view was only a contract to facilitate communal politics of a moderated, less murderous, sort since the blessing of the new would inevitably be mixed with a reformulation of the old. While themes from liberalism and pluralism were being absorbed into the discourse of unionism and nationalism, 'these same reconstructed ideologies are no less effective in articulating opposition than the irredentist nationalism or supremacist unionism of the past' (Ruane and Todd 1998: 182). Equally, the reconstructed paramilitarism of the peace process, loyalist and republican, was no less effective in maintaining its ability to threaten, manipulate and extort (McIntyre 2004). In other words, things would indeed get better but some things would probably get worse.

The important factor, however, was that the framework had changed. How might this changed framework be envisaged? In what way, according to this narrative, did the modification of circumstances define the new beginning? Arthur Schopenhauer's fable of the porcupines may suggest an answer.

A number of porcupines, Schopenhauer wrote, huddled together for warmth on a cold day but as they pricked one another they were forced to disperse. The cold drove them together again but the process of dispersal was repeated. After many turns of huddling and dispersing they discovered that a comfortable relationship involved maintaining a little distance from one another. It is only when we discover such a moderate distance, Schopenhauer believed, that life becomes tolerable: our mutual needs can be reasonably satisfied and, as far as possible, we can avoid pricking one another. He used an English expression to capture the wisdom of this sort of social arrangement: 'Keep your distance' (Schopenhauer 1892: 142). Schopenhauer's concern was with relations between individuals but his fable may be used to convey a vision of political association and its implications for Northern Ireland are obvious in terms of the three narratives. If porcupinal warmth stands for sharing and porcupinal pricking stands for separation, then the following readings can be made. According to the narrative of progress, the Agreement's promise lay in the solidarity of working together and the collective warmth that would be generated by acting according to the principle of conciliation. Unionist and nationalist porcupines would be able constantly to adjust their relationship without violence or instability and their relationship would promote an environment friendly to those who thought themselves to be neither unionist nor nationalist but 'other'. According to the narrative of regress, the reality of the Agreement has been the increasing distance between the communities as well as the sectarian pricking that has continued to afflict politics and to define governance. Moreover, some would argue that the warmth is unevenly distributed and that Northern Ireland has now become a 'cold house' for unionists, not nationalists. Schopenhauer thought that a porcupine of some self-generated heat would prefer to remain aloof from this sort of political huddle, neither pricking nor being pricked. That ideological role in Northern Ireland was traditionally played by those who claimed that there was an alternative to nationalism and unionism and after 1998 there appeared to be little role for them any longer. All that mattered was the relative strength between and the balance of power amongst the largest porcupines. In the third narrative, so long as the communities *did* keep their distance (sectarian violence is kept within bounds), so long as the temperature *did* not get too hot (the politics of simmering), and so long as ends and means *were* kept in proportion (the priority of democratic procedure), then an imperfect association of mitigated ethnic rage was about as good as it could get. It was the balance between a sense of improvement and a sense of deterioration that counted, what one journalist described as that curious state in which 'the aspirational co-exists with the precautionary' (McKittrick 2003). That, in short, is the realism of *Verschlimmbesserung*.

From this perspective, the notion that the Assembly election results of November 2003 either represented some benign logic or some malignant corruption was misconceived. Paramilitary violence in some form was likely to continue whatever the election result and 'the authorities (however hypocritcally) don't seem to mind'. Moreover, the prospect of political stalemate did not appear to be significantly more dangerous than the experience of an on-off Assembly (Breen 2003). That people in Northern Ireland appeared to be comfortable with the knowledge that things had just got worse (political polarization) may actually have been a consequence of their realization that things had also got better (there was little likelihood of a return to terrorist violence). Even the highly critical IMC First Report acknowledged that the level of paramilitary murder, though still disturbingly serious, had significantly reduced. And if you were determined to look on the bright side then perhaps Balfour's presupposition of a people that could safely afford to bicker and no longer so dangerously disturbed by the never-ending din of political conflict was imaginable now in Northern Ireland. The major exception was that one could never conceive of this people being either fundamentally at one or quite so sure of their own moderation. This was certainly not the vision of deep reconciliation that some like Porter had wished for but it could be taken as an acceptable, if not particularly honourable, settling of historical and political accounts. The realistic core of *Verschlimmbesserung* – that there would be some rough with the smooth – was not that exceptional. What distinguished it from the narratives of progress and regress was its equanimity. It appeared to eschew either optimism or pessimism in favour of scepticism, refusing to accept that this was the best of all possible worlds and also refusing to accept that it had become the worst. In many ways this confirmation of the actual was quite refreshing.

On the other hand, the danger of this third narrative had already been identified by Crick. As he had suggested, this understanding of Northern Ireland could be both patronizing and ingenuous and was all the more debilitating for being a pervasive self-understanding. In certain circumstances, it was important to expect more of politics rather than a mere confirmation of prejudice (see Chapter 2). Unfortunately, this narrative of the new Northern Ireland itself had difficulty holding the two stories together and gave itself to rather ironic conclusions. On the one hand, the proposition that the confirmation of electoral polarization had not brought the end of the world, only confirmed what everyone knew and so provided a better guide to what was possible, had some force. It was true that there was little point 'in continuing to pretend the UUP and SDLP spoke for a majority of unionists and nationalists when they clearly didn't' (Breen 2003). Though this was not the writer's intention, it was possible to conclude on the basis of this argument that everything was fine and that things were bound to sort themselves out. If we were confronted with the inescapable facts nothing but good could come of it. Of course, that was just as optimistic in its reading of events as the narrative of progress. On the other hand, the assertion that 'rest assured there will be more "IRA activity" over which no-one has any control' could be substantiated by reference to Irish history and it was a useful corrective to both apolitical moralizing and political point-scoring. It was important to remind people that self-righteousness was not a useful disposition in politics. To acknowledge the force of that argument did not mean that one was forced to accept, in the name of realism, that allowances should always be made for paramilitary infringements of justice. It did not mean that one had to accept every extenuating circumstance permitting IRA activity to continue for years 'until republicans can endorse a police service'. To do so really avoided having to address the central anxiety of the narrative of regress. Indeed, it actually confirmed it. The notion that, for example, Sinn Fein leaders were 'damned if they do' for trying to end IRA activity (they admitted responsibility) and 'damned if they don't' (they were irresponsible) may have been a fair summary of the dilemma (Feeney 2004b). However, to conclude that it was fine if the Sinn Fein leadership did nothing contributed little to the development of a conciliatory political culture.

Conclusion

By 2004, a decade after the publication of *Northern Ireland: The Choice* and six years after the Belfast Agreement, what conclusions could be drawn about the alternatives of sharing and separation? While the experiment in devolution was briefly operative the ironic impression was that the sharing of power actually helped to serve the purposes of separation. The Executive functioned not as a collectivity accepting common purposes but as an arrangement of distinct party fiefdoms as O'Leary had suspected would be the case. If it were indeed true that the communal porcupines were shifting their association into a more comfortable and less vicious shape then it was also true that a pattern of balkanization was also detectable. Indeed, policing reforms that emphasized local accountability could well comple-ment those political, residential and cultural shifts already detectable and this would dramatically enforce rather than erode social boundaries. This would confirm Schopenhauer's aphorism: 'No rose without a thorn'. For those who subscribed to the narrative of progress the bloom of the rose was the important thing and a politics of sharing would be the ground upon which it would be nourished. For those who subscribed to the narrative of regress, Schopenhauer's qualification was the important thing. No rose without a thorn, yes. 'But many a thorn without a rose' and as the bloom of the Agreement wilted, the thorn of sectarianism would remain as visible as ever (Schopenhauer 1970: 235). As one outspoken Catholic cleric, Monsignor Faul, put it succinctly: 'Things are worse than they were in

1968' and the country was now ruled by paramilitaries who continued to kill, exile and intimidate people from their homes (O'Neill 2004). In the perspective of *Verschlimmbesserung*, however, acknowledging the thorn and the rose was the beginning of wisdom, wisdom capable of holding the two stories of progress and regress together in a soundly political way.

11 Afterword

By the summer of 2004, Northern Ireland presented yet another interesting paradox. The first side of the paradox was revealed in the outcome of the European Parliament election of 10 June. The result of that election confirmed the polarizing trend that had been clear since at least the Westminster elections of 2001. The DUP topped the poll with 32 per cent of first preference votes (175,761), up 3.6 per cent on its 1999 performance, and secured the return of its novice candidate, Jim Allister. Sinn Fein came second with 26.31 per cent of first preferences (144,541), up 9 per cent on 1999 and its candidate, Bairbre de Brun, won the party's first European seat in Northern Ireland. The UUP came third on 16.6 per cent (91,164), down 1 per cent, securing a seat on DUP transfers. The SDLP got 16 per cent of the vote (87,559), down 12 per cent and lost the seat held since 1979 by its former leader John Hume. On the unionist side, the European elections have always delivered a large vote for the DUP and that party's former MEP, Ian Paisley, consistently topped the poll. In 2004 the UUP slipped back only slightly on its 1999 vote and at least it could live in hope of better performances in the future. However, the immediate future of unionism was now firmly in the hands of the DUP leadership. On the nationalist side, the position of the SDLP was particularly serious, leading one nationalist newspaper to editorialize that it was now more or less dead as a political force and 'as relevant as an ice cube at the north pole' (*Sunday Business Post* 2004). The long-term future of Northern nationalism now belonged to Sinn Fein, underpinned by its advances in the Republic of Ireland where it won a European Parliament seat in Dublin. On 8 per cent of first preference votes, Sinn Fein had become the fourth most popular party in the Southern state and it was well poised to make further gains in the next Dail elections (for the most intelligent analysis see Feeney 2004c).

The election results confirmed that Northern Ireland politics would continue as a familiar trial by mandate now focused on the conditions for the revival of devolution. This trial by mandate had its own internal contradiction. On the one hand, the DUP argued that *its* mandate set the limits of the possible. It would make clear to Sinn Fein (though not directly) what was required of it and, as Robinson argued, 'they'll have to deliver or walk away' (cited in Murray 2004). Unfortunately for Robinson, there appeared to be no incentive for Sinn Fein either to listen or to take heed. Sinn Fein claimed that *its* mandate to speak for the majority of nationalists on its own terms could not be denied. That a majority of Northern nationalists and a section of the Southern electorate were prepared to vote for a party still inextricably linked to the IRA endorsed an inflexible position on republican inclusion. Moreover, both leaderships gave the impression of returning to an older sort of rhetoric. The DUP spoke of driving the final nail into the coffin of the Agreement while Adams declared Sinn Fein's performance in the south 'a vote to get the Brits out of Ireland' (cited in King 2004). On the other hand, more emollient signals were also being sent that held out the familiar prospect of a historic compromise between the two parties and this encouraged the two governments to sustain a political culture of wishful thinking. However, the timescales were awry. The DUP was talking about a deal that was at least three years away while Sinn Fein was demanding – ironically so, given the title of the DUP's own policy document – devolution now.

The second part of the paradox was revealed in the results of the Northern Ireland Life and Times Survey published in the same week as the result of the European poll. It found that 66 per cent of Protestants either did not want or did not care for the return of devolution while 50 per cent of Catholics felt the same way. Power-sharing continued to return high levels of support amongst respondents in both communities but the deep scepticism of the practicalities or viability of power-sharing under the Agreement appeared well founded in experience after 1998 (Northern Ireland Life and Times Survey 2003). This widespread popular indifference to the centrepiece of the Agreement's institutional architecture suggested either continued suspicion of the integrity of the political process (see Chapter 9) or satisfaction with the prolongation of direct rule with (relative) peace and stability. As one academic noted, 'as long as hospital waiting lists are low, unemployment is way down and there is relative peace on the streets then people are generally content with the status quo' (Wilford, cited in McDonald 2004). Both the SDLP and the UUP found some comfort in the abstention rate and could speculate that a re-mobilization of 'middle Ulster' was not impossible. However, the reasons for satisfaction and abstention were quite different and it was here that the paradox is partly if not entirely resolved.

For a number of reasons, unionists could look with some equanimity at the crisis of devolution. They could take satisfaction from the fact that the IRA's 30-year military campaign had failed, that Articles 2 and 3 of the Republic's Constitution had gone and that the border, for the moment at least, had been taken out of Irish politics. Direct rule from London, then, was psychically more acceptable than having republicans in government while the IRA continued to exist. Under direct rule, unionists might expect the Union to remain stable if not exactly to prosper, but this positive expectation, however, covered a deep and very old anxiety. As the *Ballymoney Free Press* had put it on 8 May 1912, 'The statement of Unionist Ulster is that it merely wants to be let alone.' Unfortunately, 'since Satan entered the Garden of Eden good people will not be left alone' (cited in Bew 1994: 47). Indeed, this disposition was also part of Trimble's character. Once asked what he wanted for his people he had replied, 'To be left alone' (Godson 2004: 807). The paradoxical intersection of unionist expectation that things might get worse and anxiety that republicans in office would make their lives a misery produced a partial disengagement from serious politics on the assumption that direct rule would best leave them alone. It also encouraged the unionist electorate to take out a protection policy against the nationalist swing to Sinn Fein by voting in greater numbers for the DUP. The principle was clear enough. Assertive nationalism required an equally assertive unionism but this communal assertiveness was best kept out of government.

For a number of reasons, nationalists were more likely to calculate that the absence of devolution would marginalize unionist influence further and increase the leverage of the republican movement on the governments in London and Dublin to deliver more in their favour. The material advancements they expected as a community appeared to depend not on seats in an Executive at Stormont but on the British Government's continued willingness to respond favourably to their grievance claims. A strengthened mandate for Sinn Fein (and a shadowy IRA) was a wager on that strategy of advancement just as much, if not more so, than a vote for the return of devolved government. Indeed, a correspondingly strengthened unionist mandate for the DUP was to be welcomed since it appeared to confirm unionism as irredeemably backward and thus to clinch the nationalist case. This new triumphalism, however, only faintly obscured the old anxiety about the 'unionist veto' on nationalist advancement. The paradoxical intersection of nationalist expectation of success and anxiety about the possible frustration of that success produced a partial disengagement from serious politics also based on the assumption that direct rule would favour them. Northern nationalists also took out an investment policy in Sinn Fein as the party best equipped and most committed to promote their communal advantage, devolution or no devolution (see Feeney 2004c).

To emphasize the positive in such circumstances appeared to be an act of simple faith rather than an act of political analysis. It seemed to ignore what one seasoned commentator called that 'fabulous beast', the elephant on the doorstep, a metaphorical beast that can be taken to signify 'a very large problem which, despite its great size, some people manage to ignore'. What did some people (especially British and Irish ministers) choose to ignore? First, they chose to ignore that the conflict was not over and that there still existed 'heavily armed illegal armies linked to political parties, still active, still engaging in acts of terror and frighteningly widespread criminality'. Second, they chose to ignore that the very nature of the problem, despite all the talk of a new beginning, remained an open question and was not resolved. The basis for trust and cooperation had never been established (Kennedy 2004). In other words, Northern Ireland six years after the Belfast Agreement continued to be trapped between the impossible and the not possible. It was *impossible* in the foreseeable future for terrorist organizations like the IRA to return to their systematic campaigns of widespread violence. It was *not possible* for devolved institutions to be restored since, as Bew had argued, the very building blocks of political accommodation had been knocked down one by one (see Chapter 10). One faintly optimistic interpretation of this condition was that politics in Northern Ireland remained in neutral, neither negative nor positive, neither constructive nor destructive, and that this was about as good as it could get given that we already know how bad it can get. This was not the best of all possible worlds but the necessary evil of a 'politics of simmering'. A pessimistic interpretation was that this view is a comforting illusion. Rather, the situation was like a local version of Fukuyama's second thoughts about the common destination of world history. We cannot know, argued Fukuyama, 'provided a majority of the wagons eventually reach the same town, whether their occupants, having looked around a bit at their new surroundings, will not find them inadequate and set their eyes on a new and more distant journey' (1992: 339). In Northern Ireland the majority of the electorate was brought to the new surroundings of the Belfast Agreement but there is little evidence that they have found those surroundings entirely adequate. That may have been, as Chapter 7 suggested, because unionists and nationalists were in the habit of looking at different things. And when they set their eyes on a new future the prospect is different too.

Even though it is unlikely to prove as violent as the years between 1969 and 1996 or as politically dramatic as the years after 1998, the more distant journey that beckons for Northern Ireland is also unlikely to be a comfortable one.

References

Adams, D. (1995) 'A rational region?', *Fortnight*, 343 (October): 16.

Adams, G. (1995) *Free Ireland: Towards a Lasting Peace*, Dingle: Brandon.

Adams, G. (2003a) 'The peace process', *Guardian*, 24 January.

Adams, G. (2003b) *Hope and History: Making Peace in Ireland*, Dingle: Brandon.

Adams, G. (2004) 'Dublin must stand up and defend Agreement', *Derry Journal*, 23 April.

Akenson, D. (1991) *Small Differences. Irish Catholics and Irish Protestants 1815–1922*, Dublin: Gill and Macmillan.

Akenson, D. (2000) 'New Scriptures Needed', in D. Kennedy (ed.) *Forging an Identity. Ireland at the Millennium: The Evolution of a Concept*, Belfast: The Irish Association.

Amery, J. (1999) *At the Mind's Limits*, trans. S. Rosenfeld and S. P. Rosenfeld, London: Granta Books.

Anderson, J. and Shuttleworth, I. (1994) 'Sectarian readings of sectarianism: interpreting the Northern Ireland Census', *Irish Review*, 16: 74–93.

Archard, D. (1995) 'Myths, lies and historical truth: a defence of nationalism', *Political Studies*, 43: 472–81.

Arendt, H. (1958) *The Human Condition*, Chicago: University of Chicago Press.

Arendt, H. (1972) *Crises of the Republic*, Harmondsworth: Penguin Books.

Arthur, P. (1995) 'Dialogue between Sinn Fein and the British government', *Irish Political Studies*, 10: 185–91.

Arthur, P. (1996a) 'The Heath Government and Northern Ireland', in S. Ball and A. Seldon (eds) *The Heath Government 1970–74*, London: Longman.

Arthur, P. (1996b) 'Time, territory, tradition and the Anglo-Irish "peace" process', *Government and Opposition*, 31: 426–40.

Aughey, A. (1988) 'Political Violence in Northern Ireland', in H. H. Tucker (ed.) *Combating the Terrorists: Democratic Responses to Political Violence*, New York: Facts on File.

Aughey, A. (1989) *Under Siege: Ulster Unionism and the Anglo-Irish Agreement*, London: Hurst.

Aughey, A. (1993) 'Irresistible Force?', *Fortnight*, 321 (October): 14–17.

Aughey, A. (1997a) 'Back from Sabbatical: Irish Terror, Self-sacrifice, and the Pursuit of the Impossible', in G. Frost (ed.) *Loyalty Misplaced: Misdirected Virtue and Social Disintegration*, London: The Social Affairs Unit.

Aughey, A. (1997b) 'A state of exception: the concept of the political in Northern Ireland', *Irish Political Studies*, 12: 1–12.

Aughey, A. (1998) 'Fukuyama, the end of history and the Irish question', *Irish Studies in International Affairs*, 9: 85–92.

Aughey, A. (2000) 'The 1998 Agreement: Unionist Responses', in M. Cox, A. Guelke and F. Stephen (eds) *A Farewell to Arms? From 'Long War' to Long Peace in Northern Ireland*, Manchester: Manchester University Press.

Aughey, A. (2001) 'Learning from "The Leopard"', in R. Wilford (ed.) *Aspects of the Belfast Agreement*, Oxford: Oxford University Press.

Avineri, S. (1972) *Hegel's Theory of the Modern State*, Cambridge: Cambridge University Press.

Barker, C. and Galasinski, D. (2001) *Cultural Studies and Discourse Analysis: A Dialogue on Language and Identity*, London: Sage.

Baudrillard, J. (1994) *The Illusion of the End*, trans. C. Turner, London: Polity Press.

Bean, K. (1995a) 'Between the lines', *Fortnight*, 345 (December): 37.

Bean, K. (1995b) 'The new departure? Recent developments in republican strategy and ideology', *Irish Studies Review*, 10: 2–6.

Beck, U. (1997) *The Reinvention of Politics. Rethinking Modernity in the Global Social Order*, trans. M. Ritter, London: Polity Press.

Beckett, J. C. (1966) *The Making of Modern Ireland 1603–1923*, London: Faber and Faber.

Beetham, D. (2003) 'Human Rights and Democracy', in R. Axtmann (ed.) *Understanding Democratic Politics: An Introduction*, London: Sage.

Beggan, D. and Indurthy, R. (2002) 'Explaining why the Good Friday Accord is likely to bring a lasting peace in Northern Ireland', *Peace and Change*, 27: 331–55.

Bellamy, R. and Baehr, P. (1993) 'Carl Schmitt and the contradictions of liberal democracy', *European Journal of Political Research*, 23: 163–85.

Bennett, R. (1998) 'Marching Orders', *London Review of Books*, 30 July.

Berki, R. N. (1972) 'The Distinction between Moderation and Extremism', in B. Parekh and R. N. Berki (eds) *The Morality of Politics*, London: Allen and Unwin.

Berki, R. N. (1981) *On Political Realism*, London: Dent.

Berki, R. N. (1983) *Insight and Vision: The Problem of Communism in Marx's Thought*, London: Dent.

Bew, P. (1994) *Ideology and the Irish Question: Ulster Unionism and Irish Nationalism 1912–1916*, Oxford: Oxford University Press.

Bew, P. (1998) 'The unionists have won, they just don't know it', *Sunday Times*, 17 May.

Bew, P. (2000) 'The Belfast Agreement of 1998: From Ethnic Democracy to a Multicultural, Consociational Settlement', in M. Cox, A. Guelke and F. Stephen (eds) *A Farewell to Arms? From 'Long War' to Long Peace in Northern Ireland*, Manchester: Manchester University Press.

Bew, P. (2002) 'At last we know the human cost of Gerry Adams', *Daily Telegraph*, 2 October.

Bew, P. (2003) 'Why agree to meet when you know they won't show?', *The Sunday Times*, 26 October.

Bew, P. and Gillespie, G. (1999) *Northern Ireland: A Chronology of the Troubles 1968–1999*, Dublin: Gill and Macmillan.

Bew, P. and Patterson, H. (1987) 'The New Stalemate: Unionism and the Anglo-Irish Agreement', in P. Teague (ed.) *Beyond the Rhetoric*, London: Lawrence and Wishart.

Bew, P., Gibbon, P. and Patterson, H. (2002) *Northern Ireland 1921–2001: Political Forces and Social Classes*, London: Serif.

Billen, A. (2003) 'If the IRA went away, there'd be another IRA the day after' (interview with Gerry Adams), *The Times*, 7 October.

Birnie, E. (2001) 'Down the Aisle or Down the Isles? Norman Davies' Prophecy of the Break-up of the United Kingdom', in R. Hanna (ed.) *The Union: Essays on Ireland and the British Connection*, Newtownards: Colourpoint Books.

Birnie, E. (2003) 'The Future of Unionism', *Guardian*, 5 July.

Blair, T. (1999) 'Keynote speech by the Prime Minister, Mr Tony Blair at Stranmillis University College, Belfast, 15 June', http://cain.ulst.ac.uk/events/peace/docs/tb15699.htm

Blair, T. (2002) 'Speech by the Prime Minister Tony Blair in Belfast, Northern Ireland, 17 October', http://labour.org.uk/tbnisspeech/

Blaug, R. (1997) 'Between fear and disappointment: critical, empirical and political uses of Habermas', *Political Studies*, 45: 100–17.

Bogdanor, V. (1999) 'The British-Irish Council and devolution', *Government and Opposition*, 34: 287–98.

Bok, S. (1978) *Lying: Moral Choice in Public and Private Life*, London: The Harvester Press.

Borges, J. L. (1999) *Selected Non-Fictions*, trans. E. Allen, S. J. Levine and E. Weinberger, New York: Viking Penguin.

Bourke, R. (2003) *Peace in Ireland: The War of Ideas*, London: Pimlico.

Boyce, D. G. and O'Day, A. (1996) *The Making of Modern Irish History: Revisionism and the Revisionist Controversy*, London: Routledge.

Boyce, D. G., Eccleshall, R. and Geoghegan, V. (eds) (1993) *Political Thought in Ireland since the Seventeenth Century*, London: Routledge.

Boyle, K. and Hadden, T. (1994) *Northern Ireland: The Choice*, Harmondsworth: Penguin.

Boyle, K. and Hadden, T. (1995) 'The peace process in Northern Ireland', *International Affairs*, 71: 269–83.

de Breadun, D. (2001) *The Far Side of Revenge: Making Peace in Northern Ireland*, Cork: The Collins Press.

Breen, S. (1994) 'Wrong again', *Fortnight*, 329 (June): 8.

Breen, S. (1995) 'Sword in the stone', *Fortnight*, 340 (June): 7.

Breen, S. (1997) 'The chuck elite', *Fortnight*, 364 (September): 7.

Breen, S. (1998) 'Is the talks game up?', *Fortnight*, 368 (February): 7.

Breen, S. (2000) 'On the one road', *Fortnight*, 388 (September): 18–19.

Breen, S. (2003) 'The people's right to choose', *News Letter*, 4 December.

British Council Ireland (2003) *Through Irish Eyes: Irish Attitudes towards the UK*, Dublin: British Council Ireland.

Bruce, S. (1992) *The Red Hand: Protestant Paramilitaries in Northern Ireland*, Oxford: Oxford University Press.

Bruton, J. (2000) 'Has Politics Failed?', speech to the Irish Association, 2 September, http://www.Irish-association.org/archives/index.html

Bubner, R. (ed.) (1997) *German Idealist Philosophy*, Harmondsworth: Penguin.

Burchell, D. (1995) 'The attributes of citizens: virtue, manners and the activity of citizenship', *Economy and Society*, 24: 540–58.

Burke, J. (1999) 'On Walzer's hermeneutics of justice, Gadamer's criterion of openness and Northern Ireland's Belfast Agreement', *Irish Political Studies*, 14: 1–22.

Burns, J. H. (2003) 'Majorities: an exploration', *History of Political Thought*, 24: 66–85.

Cadogan Group (2003) *Picking up the Pieces: Northern Ireland after the Belfast Agreement*, Belfast: The Cadogan Group.

Campbell, F. (1991) *The Dissenting Voice: Protestant Democracy in Ulster from Plantation to Partition*, Belfast: The Blackstaff Press.

Campbell, G. (2002) 'Negotiating a new Agreement', *Belfast Telegraph*, 21 October.

Campbell, G. (2003) 'Campbell spells out new rules for talks', DUP Press Release, 12 November.

Campbell, G. (2004) 'Speech delivered by East Londonderry MP and MLA Gregory Campbell to the World Economic Forum in Davos, Switzerland, 22 January 2004', DUP Press Release, 22 November.

Canovan, M. (1990) 'On being economical with the truth: some liberal reflections', *Political Studies*, 38: 5–19.

Canovan, M. (2000) 'Patriotism is not enough', *British Journal of Political Science*, 30: 413–32.

Carmola, K. (2003) 'Noble lying: justice and intergenerational tension in Plato's *Republic*', *Political Theory*, 31: 39–62.

Christiansen, T. (2000) 'A Region among Regions: The Wider View', in D. Kennedy (ed.) *Living with the European Union*, Basingstoke: Macmillan.

Christie, C. J. (1992) 'Partition, separatism and national identity: a reassessment', *Political Quarterly*, 63: 68–78.

Clarke, L. (2004) 'Drifting peace process needs a plan B', *The Sunday Times*, 21 March.

Clohesy, A. M. (2000) 'Provisionalism and the (Im)possibility of Justice in Northern Ireland', in D. Howarth, A. J. Norval and Y. Stavrakakis (eds) *Discourse Theory and Political Analysis: Identities, Hegemonies and Social Change*, Manchester: Manchester University Press.

Coakley, J. (2001) 'The Belfast Agreement and the Republic of Ireland', in R. Wilford (ed.) *Aspects of the Belfast Agreement*, Oxford: Oxford University Press.

Collins, J. (2002) 'The unionist numbers do not add up', *Irish News*, 12 December.

Collins, J. (2003) 'Voters face "tempting" possibilities', *Irish News*, 13 November.

Collins, J. (2004a) 'How many mountains are left?', *Irish News*, 29 April.

Collins, J. (2004b) 'Irish eyes aren't losing sight of unity', *Irish News*, 19 February.

Condren, C. (1997) *Satire, Lies and Politics: The Case of Dr Arbuthnot*, Basingstoke: Macmillan.

Connolly, C. (2001) 'Theorising Ireland', *Irish Studies Review*, 9: 301–15.

Cooke, M. (2000) 'Five arguments for deliberative democracy', *Political Studies*, 48: 947–69.

Cowan, R. (2003) 'IRA condemns "unrealistic ultimatums"', *Guardian*, 9 January.

Cox, M. (1997) 'Bringing in the "international": the IRA ceasefire and the end of the Cold War', *International Affairs*, 73: 671–93.

Cox, W. H. (1991) 'Uphill all the way: constitution-making for Northern Ireland', *Parliamentary Affairs*, 44: 521–30.

Crick, B. (1994) 'Review essay', *The Political Quarterly*, 63: 371–4.

Cunningham, M. (1997) 'The political language of John Hume', *Irish Political Studies*, 12: 13–22.

Delanty, G. (1996) 'Habermas and post-national identity: theoretical perspectives on the conflict in Northern Ireland', *Irish Political Studies*, 11: 20–32.

Democratic Dialogue (1997) *Reconstituting Politics*, Belfast: Democratic Dialogue.

Democratic Unionist Party (1997) 'Democracy – not Dublin Rule', DUP Press Release, May.

Democratic Unionist Party (1998a) '10 steps on the "road to Dublin"', DUP Press Release, May.

Democratic Unionist Party (1998b) 'Step by step guide of the Trimble/Adams deal', DUP Press Release, May.

Democratic Unionist Party (2004) 'Devolution Now: The DUP's Concept for Devolution', http://www.dup.org.uk/default.asp

Devine, P. and Schubotz, D. (2004) 'What our 16-year-olds think about the divide', *Belfast Telegraph*, 6 April.

Dickson, B. (2003) 'A Cold House', *Fortnight*, 416: July/August.

Dixon, P. (1997) 'Paths to peace in Northern Ireland (1): civil society and consociational approaches', *Democratization*, 4: 1–27.

Dixon, P. (2001) *Northern Ireland: The Politics of War and Peace*, London: Palgrave.

Dixon, P. (2003) 'No point in pretending any more', *Fortnight*, 410 (January): 5.

Dodds, N. (2004) 'Speech by Nigel Dodds MP, MLA to the Party Conference, Ramada Inn, Belfast', DUP Press Release, 8 May.

Dombrowski, D. (1997) 'Plato's "Noble Lie"', *History of Political Thought*, 18: 565–78.

Donaldson, J. (1995) 'Practising politics', *Fortnight*, 338 (April): 20.

Donaldson, J. (2001) 'Extracts from a speech to the AGM of Lagan Valley Unionist Association', 18 January, http://www.uup.org/newsroom/

Donaldson, J. (2003) 'The Future of Unionism', *Guardian*, 5 July.

Dryzek, J. (1990) *Discursive Democracy: Politics, Policy, and Political Science*, Cambridge: Cambridge University Press.

Dryzek, J. (2000) *Deliberative Democracy and Beyond: Liberals, Critics, Contestations*, Oxford: Oxford University Press.

Dryzek, J. and List, C. (2003) 'Social choice theory and deliberative democracy: a reconciliation', *British Journal of Political Science*, 33: 1–28.

Durkan, M. (2003) 'The Future of Nationalism', Speech to the Irish Association, 26 April, http://www.Irish-association.org/archives/index.html

Eames, R. (1992) *Chains to Be Broken: A Personal Reflection on Northern Ireland and its People*, London: Weidenfeld and Nicolson.

Edelman, M. (1977) *Political Language: Words that Succeed and Policies that Fail*, New York: Academic Press.

Edelman, M. (1988) *Constructing the Political Spectacle*, Chicago: University of Chicago Press.

Elliott, M. (2001) *The Catholics of Ulster*, New York: Basic Books.

Ellis, S. G. (1996) 'Writing Irish History: Revisionism, Colonialism, and the British Isles', *The Irish Review*, 19: 1–21.

Encounter (2002) *Round Table: Assessing the Devolution Experience*, London: Encounter.

English, R. (1996) 'Reflections on republican socialism in Ireland: Marxian roots and Irish historical dynamics', *History of Political Thought*, 28: 553–70.

English, R. (1997) 'Challenging peace', *Fortnight*, 362 (June): 24–5.

English, R. (2002a) 'Losing the peace?', *The Salisbury Review*, 21: 28–30.

English, R. (2002b) 'The chucks have no choice', *Fortnight*, 408 (November): 5.

English, R. (2003) *Armed Struggle: A History of the IRA*, London: Macmillan.

Equality Commission for Northern Ireland (2003) *2002 Monitoring Report No. 13. A Profile of the Northern Ireland Workforce*, Belfast: Equality Commission.

Ervine, D. (2003) 'Unionism', paper presented at the Virginia Foundation for the Humanities Conference on Re-Imagining Ireland, Charlottesville, May 2003.

Evans, G. and O'Leary, B. (2000) 'Northern Irish voters and the British-Irish Agreement: foundations of a stable consociational settlement?', *Political Quarterly*, 71: 78–101.

Evans, J. A. J. and Tonge, J. (2003) 'The future of the "radical centre" in Northern Ireland after the Good Friday Agreement', *Political Studies*, 51: 25–50.

Farren, S. (2000) 'The SDLP and the Roots of the Good Friday Agreement', in M. Cox, A. Guelke and F. Stephen (eds) *A Farewell to Arms? From 'Long War' to Long Peace in Northern Ireland*, Manchester: Manchester University Press.

Farren, S. and Mulvihill, B. (1996) 'Beyond self-determination towards co-determination in Ireland', *Etudes Irlandaises*, 21: 183–91.

Farry, S. (2002) 'The Morning After: An Alliance Perspective on the Agreement', in J. Neuheiser and S. Wolff (eds) *Peace at Last? The Impact of the Good Friday Agreement on Northern Ireland*, New York: Berghahn Books.

Fealty, M. (2003) 'Will rights for all secure the peace?', *Fortnight*, 416 (July/August): 8.

Fearon, K. (2000) 'Whatever Happened to the Women? Gender and Peace in Northern Ireland', in M. Cox, A. Guelke and F. Stephen (eds) *A Farewell to Arms? From 'Long War' to Long Peace in Northern Ireland*, Manchester: Manchester University Press.

Feeney, B. (2003a) 'Trimble still afraid of the bogeyman', *Irish News*, 30 April.

Feeney, B. (2003b) 'Another case of the emperor's new clothes', *Irish News*, 10 September.

Feeney, B. (2003c) 'Just another hoop for SF to jump through', *Irish News*, 2 July.

Feeney, B. (2003d) 'Inching along to nowhere with Trimble', *Irish News*, 12 February.

Feeney, B. (2003e) 'Republicans get blame game wrong', *Irish News*, 7 May.

Feeney, B. (2003f) 'Census shows that change will be rapid', *Irish News*, 1 January.

Feeney, B. (2004a) 'DUP angling for "unionist" assembly', *Irish News*, 11 February.

Feeney, B. (2004b) 'Damned if you do, and if you don't', *Irish News*, 17 March.

Feeney, B. (2004c) 'Absent middle ground gives extremes huge boost', *Sunday Tribune*, 20 June.

Feldman, A. (1997/98) 'Retaliate and punish: political violence as form and memory in Northern Ireland', *Eire-Ireland*, 33: 195–235.

Festenstein, M. (2000) 'Cultural Diversity and the Limits of Liberalism', in N. O'Sullivan (ed.) *Political Theory in Transition*, London: Routledge.

Finlay, A. (2001) 'Defeatism and Northern Protestant 'identity'', *Global Review of Ethnopolitics*, 1: 3–20.

Finlay, F. (1998) *Snakes and Ladders*, Dublin: New Island Books.

Finlay, F. (2003) 'They choose the words but we are the losers in their zero-sum game', *Irish Examiner*, 3 April.

Fischer, D. H. (1970) *Historians' Fallacies: Towards a Logic of Historical Thought*, New York: Harper Torchbooks.

Foster, A. (2003) 'Protestants need rights', *Fortnight*, 411 (February): 12–16.

Foster, J. W. (1991) *Colonial Consequences: Essays in Irish Literature and Culture*, Dublin: The Lilliput Press.

Foster, J. W. (2002) 'Icy winds blow through Stormont', *Fortnight*, 403 (March): 20–2.

Foster, S. (2003) 'Some speak with forked tongue …' (letter), *Belfast Telegraph*, 21 November.

Freeman, M. (1995) 'Are there collective human rights?', *Political Studies*, 43: 23–40.

Fukuyama, F. (1992) *The End of History and the Last Man*, Harmondsworth: Penguin Books.

Gadd, B. (2004) 'Findings of report should not surprise', *Irish News*, 17 February.

Gambetta, D. (1998) '"Claro!": An Essay on Discursive Machismo', in J. Elster (ed.) *Deliberative Democracy*, Cambridge: Cambridge University Press.

Gamble, A. (2000) *Politics and Fate*, London: Polity.

Garland, R. (2003a) 'Only mutual togetherness brings peace', *Irish News*, 26 May.

Garland, R. (2003b) 'Imposed unity cannot be the final solution', *Irish News*, 29 September.

Garland, R. (2004a) 'Courageous DUP is finally facing realities', *Irish News*, 9 February.

Garland, R. (2004b) 'Taking risks not always good politics', *Irish News*, 2 February.

Garvin, T. (1987) *Nationalist Revolutionaries in Ireland, 1858–1928*, Oxford: Oxford University Press.

Gellner, E. (1964) *Thought and Change*, London: Weidenfeld and Nicolson.

Giddens, A. (1994) *Beyond Left and Right: The Future of Radical Politics*, London: Polity Press.

Gilchrist, S. (2002) 'Go surrender? Unionism and decommissioning', *The Blanket*, 26 February, http://lark.phoblacht.net

Gkotzaridis, E. (2001) 'Irish revisionism and continental theory: an intellectual kinship', *Irish Review*, 27: 121–39.

Godson, D. (2003) 'Meeting of the extremes', *Spectator*, 6 December.

Godson, D. (2004) *Himself Alone: David Trimble and the Ordeal of Unionism*, London: HarperCollins.

Goodin, R. (1998) 'Review article: communities of enlightenment', *British Journal of Political Science*, 28: 531–58.

Goodin, R. (2003) *Reflective Democracy*, Oxford: Oxford University Press.

Gorz, A. (1989) *The Traitor*, trans. R. Howard, London: Verso.

Graham, W. (2003) 'Adams urges unionists to make quantum leap and vote for SF', *Irish News*, 15 November.

Gray, J. (1998) 'Global utopias and clashing civilizations: misunderstanding the present', *International Affairs*, 74: 149–64.

Gray, J. (2000) *Two Faces of Liberalism*, London: Polity Press.

Grogan, D. (1995) 'Trimble win is a blow to hopes of compromise', *Irish Times*, 9 September.

Guelke, A. (1996) 'Consenting to consent', *Fortnight*, 353 (September): 14–15.

Guelke, A. (1997) 'Consenting to agreement', *Fortnight*, 366 (November): 12–13.

Guelke, A. (2002) 'Civil Society and the Northern Ireland Peace Process', paper presented at the annual conference of the Political Studies Association of Ireland, Belfast, 18–20 October.

Guelke, A. (2003) 'Who really wants an alliance of the extremes?', *Fortnight*, 413 (April): 6.

Gwynn, S. (1924) *Ireland*, London: Ernest Benn.

Hadden, T. (2000) 'You say you want a constitution ...', *Fortnight*, 388 (September): 24–5.

Hadfield, B. (1998) 'The Belfast Agreement, sovereignty and the state of the Union', *Public Law* (Winter): 599–616.

Hampton, J. (1995) 'The Moral Commitments of Liberalism', in D. Copp, J. Hampton and J. E. Roemer (eds) *The Idea of Democracy*, Cambridge: Cambridge University Press.

Harding, T. (2003) 'Sinn Fein fails to give clarity on IRA standing down', *Daily Telegraph*, 1 May.

Harding, T. (2004) 'The security wall on our doorstep', *Daily Telegraph*, 25 February.

Harris, E. (2004) 'We've got to stop lying to ourselves', *Sunday Independent*, 4 January.

Harvey, C. (2001a) 'A New Beginning: Reconstructing Constitutional Law and Democracy in Northern Ireland', in C. Harvey, *Human Rights, Equality and Democratic Renewal in Northern Ireland*, Oxford: Hart Publishing.

Harvey, C. (2001b) 'Northern Ireland in Transition: An Introduction', in C. Harvey, *Human Rights, Equality and Democratic Renewal in Northern Ireland*, Oxford: Hart Publishing.

Harvey, C. (2003a) 'Stick to the terms of the Agreement', *Fortnight*, 416 (July/August): 9.

Harvey, C. (2003b) 'Building blocks of the GFA are central to progress', *Derry Journal*, 31 October.

Hayes, B. and McAllister, I. (1996) 'British and Irish public opinion towards the Northern Ireland problem', *Irish Political Studies*, 11: 61–82.

Hayes, B. and McAllister, I. (2001) 'Who voted for peace? Public support for the 1998 Northern Ireland Agreement', *Irish Political Studies*, 16: 73–93.

Hazelkorn, E. and Patterson, P. (1994) 'The new politics of the Irish Republic', *New Left Review*, 207: 49–71.

Hazleton, W. A. (2000) 'Devolution and the diffusion of power: the internal and transnational dimensions of the Belfast Agreement', *Irish Political Studies*, 15: 25–38.

Heath, J. (1995) 'Review essay: Habermas and speech-act theory', *Philosophy and Social Criticism*, 21: 141–7.

Hegel, G. W. F. (1952) *Hegel's Philosophy of Right*, trans. T. M. Knox, Oxford: The Clarendon Press.

Hegel, G. W. F. (1966) *The Phenomenology of Mind*, trans. J. Baillie, London: Allen and Unwin.

Hennessey, T. (2000) *The Northern Ireland Peace Process: Ending the Troubles?*, Dublin: Gill and Macmillan.

HMSO (1995) *Frameworks for the Future*, Belfast: HMSO.

Holland, J. (1999) *Hope Against History: The Ulster Conflict*, London: Hodder and Stoughton.

Hollis, M. (1998) *Trust within Reason*, Cambridge: Cambridge University Press.

Honohan, I. (2002) *Civic Republicanism*, London: Routledge.

Horowitz, D. L. (2001) 'The Northern Ireland Agreement: Clear, Consociational and Risky', in J. McGarry (ed.) *Northern Ireland and the Divided World: Post-Agreement Northern Ireland in Comparative Perspective*, Oxford: Oxford University Press.

Horowitz, D. L. (2002) 'Explaining the Northern Ireland Agreement: the sources of an unlikely constitutional consensus', *British Journal of Political Science*, 32: 193–220.

Hutchinson, B. (1995) 'Citizen 2000', *Fortnight*, 343 (October): 17.

Ignatief, M. (1999) 'Human rights: the midlife crisis', *New York Review of Books*, 46 (May): 58–62.

International Monitoring Commission (IMC) (2004) *First Report of the International Monitoring Commission*, London: The Stationery Office.

Ivory, G. (1999) 'Revisions in nationalist discourse among Irish political parties', *Irish Political Studies*, 14: 84–103.

Jackson, A. (1996) 'Irish Unionism', in D. G. Boyce and A. O'Day (eds) *Modern Irish History: Revisionism and the Revisionist Controversy*, London: Routledge.

Jackson, A. (2003) *Home Rule: An Irish History 1800–2000*, London: Weidenfeld and Nicolson.

Johnson, J. (1998) 'Arguing for Deliberation: Some Skeptical Considerations', in J. Elster (ed.) *Deliberative Democracy*, Cambridge: Cambridge University Press.

Johnston, J. (2003) 'Inside the private life of Gerry Adams', *Daily Mirror*, 18 October.

Johnston, P. (2003) 'Predictable outcome in land of half-promises and mutual mistrust', *Daily Telegraph*, 22 October.

Kearney, H. (2001) 'Visions and revisions: views of Irish history', *Irish Review*, 27: 113–20.

Kearney, R. (2000) 'Towards a postnational archipelago', *Edinburgh Review*, 103: 21–34.

Kearney, R. and Wilson, R. (1994) 'Northern Ireland's future as a European region', *The Irish Review*, 15: 51–69.

Kelly, D. (2000) 'Multicultural citizenship: the limitations of liberal democracy', *Political Quarterly*, 71: 31–41.

Kennedy, D. (1994) 'The European Union and the Northern Ireland Question', in B. Barton and P. Roche (eds) *The Northern Ireland Question: Perspectives and Policies*, Aldershot: Avebury.

Kennedy, D. (2000) 'Europe and the Northern Ireland Problem', in D. Kennedy (ed.) *Living with the European Union*, Basingstoke: Macmillan.

Kennedy, D. (2004) 'The Murphy law ignores elephants on our doorstep', *Belfast Telegraph*, 16 June.

Kennedy, L. (1996) *Colonialism, Religion and Nationalism in Ireland*, Belfast: The Institute of Irish Studies.

Kent, G. (1998) 'Peace train or warpath', *Fortnight*, 371 (June): 13–14.

King, S. (2003) 'Passionate nationalists are selling their country short', *Belfast Telegraph*, 19 November.

King, S. (2004) 'Tactical voting might ward off illiberalism in province', *Belfast Telegraph*, 16 June.

Knowles, D. (2001) *Political Philosophy*, London: Routledge.

La Rochefoucauld, F. de (1959) *Maxims*, trans. with an intro. by Leonard Tancock, Harmondsworth: Penguin Classics.

Laborde, C. (2002) 'From constitutional to civic patriotism', *British Journal of Political Science*, 32: 591–612.

Laclau, E. (1996) *Emancipation(s)*, London: Verso.

Lee, S. (1993) 'Lost for words', *Fortnight*, 316 (April): 22–5.

Levy, J. T. (2000) *The Multiculturalism of Fear*, Oxford: Oxford University Press.

Lichtenberg, G. C. (1990) *Aphorisms*, trans. R. J. Hollingdale, Harmondsworth: Penguin.

Lijphart, A. (1977) *Democracy in Plural Societies: A Comparative Exploration*, New Haven: Yale University Press.

Little, A. (2002) 'Feminism and the politics of difference in Northern Ireland', *Journal of Political Ideologies*, 7: 163–77.

Little, A. (2003) 'The problems of antagonism: applying liberal political theory to conflict in Northern Ireland', *British Journal of Politics and International Relations*, 5: 373–92.

Little, A. (2004) *Democracy and Northern Ireland: Beyond the Liberal Paradigm?*, Basingstoke: Palgrave.

Livingstone, S. (2000) 'The Northern Ireland Human Rights Commission', *Irish Political Studies*, 15: 163–71.

Lloyd, J. (1998) 'Still on the edge of terror', *New Statesman*, 22 May.

Lloyd, J. (1999) 'Ulster: why the left must think again', *New Statesman*, 13 September.

Longley, E. (1993) 'Challenging complacency', *Fortnight*, 315 (March): 22–5.

Longley, E. (1994a) 'A Northern "turn"?', *The Irish Review*, 15: 1–13.

Longley, E. (1994b) *The Living Stream: Literature and Revisionism in Ireland*, Newcastle: Bloodaxe Books.

Longley, E. (1997) 'Review article: What do Protestants want?', *Irish Studies Review*, 20: 104–20.

Longley, E. (1999) 'Postcolonial versus European (and post-Ukanian) frameworks for Irish literature', *The Irish Review*, 25: 75–94.

Longley, E. (2000a) *Poetry and Posterity*, Tarset: Bloodaxe Books.

Longley, E. (2000b) 'An Irish Kulturkampf', in D. Kennedy (ed.) *Forging an Identity. Ireland at the Millennium: The Evolution of a Concept*, Belfast: The Irish Association.

Luby, T. (2003) 'Lies, the lying liars who tell them – and the law of unintended consequences', *The Blanket*, 24 October, http://lark.phoblacht.net

Lynch, J. (1994) 'Ceasefire in the Academy?' (interview with Professor Paul Bew), *History Ireland*, 2: 11–14.

McCall, C. (1999) *Identity in Northern Ireland: Community, Politics and Change*, Basingstoke: Macmillan.

McCall, C. (2001) 'The protean British identity in Britain and Northern Ireland', *Soundings*, 18: 154–68.

McCall, C. (2002) 'Political transformation and the reinvention of the Ulster-Scots identity and culture', *Identities: Global Studies in Culture and Power*, 9: 197–218.

McCarney, J. (2000) *Hegel on History*, London: Routledge.

McCartney, J. (2003) 'Northern Ireland's past has become its future', *Sunday Telegraph*, 30 November.

McCartney, R. (1995) 'Talks that won't do the Union any good', *Parliamentary Brief Northern Ireland*, December: xiv–xv.

McCartney, R. (1999) 'North's hope of a bright future is fast becoming a nightmare', *The Irish Times*, 12 January.

McCartney, R. (2001) *Reflections on Liberty, Democracy and the Union*, Dublin: Maunsel.

McCartney, R. (2002) 'Counting the cost of the "Agony Aunt"', *Belfast Telegraph*, 22 October.

McCartney, R. (2003a) 'Investigating the Inquiry', *Belfast Telegraph*, 2 October.

McCartney, R. (2003b) 'Trimble was sold a baby elephant, not a pup', *Belfast Telegraph*, 23 October.

MacDermott, E. (2003) 'Saville fails to grasp republican culture', *Sunday Business Post*, 9 November.

McDonald, H. (2000) *Trimble*, London: Bloomsbury.

McDonald, H. (2002) 'Gerry Adams's travelling circus is relying on sleight of hand', *Observer*, 3 March.

McDonald, H. (2003) 'IRA ready to declare war is over', *Observer*, 21 September.

McDonald, H. (2004) 'More voters want direct rule than Stormont', *Observer*, 13 June.

McDonald, P. (1997) *Mistaken Identities: Poetry and Northern Ireland*, Oxford: The Clarendon Press.

McDonnell, J. (2003) 'Why I stood up for Bobby Sands', *Guardian*, 3 June.

McDowell, L. (2002) 'Grim reality and make-believe', *Belfast Telegraph*, 18 January.

McDowell, L. (2003) 'Masking the stench won't rid society of terrorist scourge', *Belfast Telegraph*, 31 October.

McGarry, J. (ed.) (2001) *Northern Ireland and the Divided World: Post-Agreement Northern Ireland in Comparative Perspective*, Oxford: Oxford University Press.

McGarry, J. and O'Leary, B. (eds) (1990) *The Future of Northern Ireland*, Oxford: The Clarendon Press.

McGarry, J. and O'Leary, B. (1995) *Explaining Northern Ireland: Broken Images*, Oxford: Blackwell.

McGimpsey, M. (1995) 'No stepping stone', *Fortnight*, 343 (October): 18–19.

McGonagle, S. (2003) 'Survey reveals schism between communities', *Irish News*, 5 March.

McGurk, T. (2003) 'Another night with cannibals of the Union', *Sunday Business Post*, 7 September.

McIntyre, A. (1994) 'Waking up to reality', *Fortnight*, 332 (September): 17.

McIntyre, A. (1995) 'Modern Irish republicanism: the product of British state strategies', *Irish Political Studies*, 10: 97–121.

McIntyre, A. (1999) 'Republican leadership excludes republicans', *Sunday Tribune*, 14 November.

McIntyre, A. (2000) 'New Republic', *Fortnight*, 386 (June): 8–9.

McIntyre, A. (2001) 'Modern Irish Republicanism and the Belfast Agreement: Chickens Coming Home to Roost, or Turkeys Celebrating Christmas?', in R. Wilford (ed.) *Aspects of the Belfast Agreement*, Oxford: Oxford University Press.

McIntyre, A. (2002a) 'The great divide – numberism', *The Blanket*, 28 February, http://lark.phoblacht.net

McIntyre, A. (2002b) 'Time has run out for an armed IRA', *Observer*, 20 October.

McIntyre, A. (2003a) 'Who knew – who knows – who will tell?', *The Blanket*, 15 May, http://lark.phoblacht.net

McIntyre, A. (2003b) 'Pulling the guns over their eyes', *The Blanket*, 27 October, http://lark.phoblacht.net

McIntyre, A. (2003c) 'The rite of passage', *The Blanket*, 3 October, http://lark.phoblacht.net

McIntyre, A. (2003d) 'A tale of two writers', *The Blanket*, 11 February, http://lark.phoblacht.net

McIntyre, A. (2004) 'A subtle but brilliant use of the IRA', *The Blanket*, 11 January, http://lark.phoblacht.net

McKearney, T. (1999) 'In reality, IRA has little room for manoeuvre', *Sunday Tribune*, 7 March.

McKearney, T. (2004) 'It is decision time for republicanism', *Irish News*, 27 February.

McKeown, C. (2003) 'Fantasy politics', *News Letter*, 18 October.

McKittrick, D. (2003) 'How others see us', *Belfast Telegraph*, 25 November.

McMichael, G. (1999) *An Ulster Voice: In Search of Common Ground in Northern Ireland*, Boulder: Roberts Rinehart.

Maginnis, K. (1998) 'Way forward for unionism is a yes vote', *Belfast Telegraph*, 5 May.

Mallie, E. and McKittrick, D. (1997) *The Fight for Peace: The Secret Story of the Irish Peace Process*, rev. edn, London: Mandarin.

Mansergh, M. (1996) 'Manufacturing consent', *Fortnight*, 350 (May): 13–15.

Marcus, L. (1992) '"An invitation to life": Andre Gorz's *The Traitor*', *New Left Review*, 194 (January): 114–20.

Martin, G. (1998) 'Wavering unionists fear havoc a strong no vote could cause', *Irish Times*, 20 May.

Meehan, E. (1999) 'The Belfast Agreement – its distinctiveness and points of cross-fertilization in the UK's devolution programme', *Parliamentary Affairs*, 52: 19–31.

Michaelis, L. (1999) 'The deadly goddess: Friedrich Hölderlin on politics and fate', *History of Political Thought*, 20: 225–49.

Milosz, C. (1981) *The Captive Mind*, Harmondsworth: Penguin Books.

Minogue, K. (1996a) 'Machiavelli and the duck/rabbit problem of political perception', *Government and Opposition*, 81: 216–26.

Minogue, K. (1996b) 'A war of everyone', *Times Literary Supplement*, 20 September.

Mitchell, C. (2003) 'From victims to equals? Catholic responses to political change in Northern Ireland', *Irish Political Studies*, 18: 51–71.

Mitchell, E. (1999) 'What will political life in Northern Ireland be like if George Mitchell clinches a deal?', *Sunday Tribune*, 31 October.

Mitchell, P. (2001) 'Transcending an Ethnic Party System? The Impact of Consociational Governance on Electoral Dynamics and the Party System', in R. Wilford (ed.) *Aspects of the Belfast Agreement*, Oxford: Oxford University Press.

Mitchell, P., O'Leary, B. and Evans, G. (2001) 'Northern Ireland: flanking extremists bite the moderates and emerge in their clothes', *Parliamentary Affairs*, 54: 725–42.

Moloney, E. (1998a) 'Nationalists advance inexorably, making love not war', *Sunday Tribune*, 12 April.

Moloney, E. (1998b) 'Nos lose despite better campaign', *Sunday Tribune*, 24 May.

Moloney, E. (1999) 'Choreographed events created this week's events', *Sunday Tribune*, 4 July.

Moloney, E. (2000a) 'Mansergh doubts the GFA will lead to unity', *Sunday Tribune*, 1 October.

Moloney, E. (2000b) 'IRA defying "logic" on decommissioning', *Sunday Tribune*, 30 January.

Moloney, E. (2001a) 'It's not over yet', *Sunday Tribune*, 28 October.

Moloney, E. (2001b) 'SF's southern strategy depends on decommissioning', *Sunday Tribune*, 30 September.

Moloney, E. (2002) *A Secret History of the IRA*, London: Allen Lane.

Moloney, E. (2004) 'With the "war" decisively over, Adams has little to bargain with', *Irish Times*, 1 May.

Montesquieu (1993) *Persian Letters*, trans. C. J. Betts, Harmondsworth: Penguin.

Morgan, A. (2000) *The Belfast Agreement: A Practical Legal Analysis*, London: The Belfast Press.

Morgan, V. (2002) 'Women and a "New" Northern Ireland', in J. Neuheiser and S. Wolff (eds) *Peace at Last? The Impact of the Good Friday Agreement on Northern Ireland*, New York: Berghahn Books.

Morley, B. (2004) 'The process of "constitutionalisation"', *The Blanket*, 11 January, http://lark.phoblacht.net

Morrison, D. (2002) 'Irish republicans do not like the assembly, but they want to work it', *Guardian*, 14 October.

Mosher, M. (1983) 'Civic identity in the juridical society: on Hegelianism as discipline for the romantic mind', *Political Theory*, 11: 117–32.

Mouffe, C. (1993) *The Return of the Political*, London: Verso.

Mouffe, C. (2000) 'For an Agonistic Model of Democracy', in N. O'Sullivan (ed.) *Political Theory in Transition*, London: Routledge.

Mulholland, M. (2000) *Northern Ireland at the Crossroads: Ulster Unionism in the O'Neill Years 1960–9*, Basingstoke: Macmillan.

Murphy, J. A. (2003) 'Republicans the ones rewriting history', *Sunday Independent*, 7 September.

Murphy, P. (2003) 'Out of the barrel of a silenced gun', *Irish News*, 14 October.

Murray, A. (2004) 'Deal with SF not close: Robinson', *Sunday Life*, 13 June.

Murray, G. (2002) 'The Good Friday Agreement: An SDLP Analysis of the Northern Ireland Conflict', in J. Neuheiser and S. Wolff (eds) *Peace at Last? The Impact of the Good Friday Agreement on Northern Ireland*, New York: Berghahn Books.

Myers, K. (2002) 'The war is over: and the IRA has won it', *Sunday Telegraph*, 4 July.

Nairn, T. (2000) *After Britain: New Labour and the Return of Scotland*, London: Granta.

Needham, R. (1998) *Battling for Peace*, Belfast: The Blackstaff Press.

Neumann, P. (2003) *Britain's Long War: British Strategy in the Northern Ireland Conflict*, Basingstoke: Palgrave.

Newey, G. (1997) 'Political lying: a defense', *Public Affairs Quarterly*, 11: 93–116.

Newey, G. (2002) 'Discourse rights and the Drumcree marches: a reply to O'Neill', *British Journal of Politics and International Relations*, 4: 75–97.

News Letter (2003) 'Trimble launches scathing attack on DUP talks record', 1 October.

Nic Craith, M. (2002) *Plural Identities, Singular Narratives: The Case of Northern Ireland*, New York: Berghahn Books.

Noel, S. J. R. (2001) 'Making the Transition from Hegemonic Regime to Power-sharing: Northern Ireland and Canada in Historical Perspective', in J. McGarry (ed.) *Northern Ireland and the Divided World. Post-Agreement Northern Ireland in Comparative Perspective*, Oxford: Oxford University Press.

Nolan, P. (2000) 'The plump Cinderella; or politics without politics', *Fortnight*, 388 (September): 28–30.

Norris, P. (2000) 'The 1998 Northern Ireland Assembly Election', *Politics*, 20: 39–42.

Northern Ireland Human Rights Commission (2001) *Making a Bill of Rights*, Belfast: NIHRC.

Northern Ireland Life and Times Survey (2003) http://www.ark.ac.uk/nilt/2003/

Norton, P. and Aughey, A. (1981) *Conservatives and Conservatism*, London: Temple Smith.

Novak, M. (1997) 'Truth and liberty: the present crisis in our culture', *The Review of Politics*, 59: 5–24.

Oakeshott, M. (1975) *On Human Conduct*, Oxford: The Clarendon Press.

Oakeshott, M. (1983) *On History and Other Essays*, Oxford: Blackwell.

Oakeshott, M. (1991) *Rationalism in Politics and Other Essays*, Indianapolis: Liberty Fund.

O'Brien, B. (1993) *The Long War: The IRA and Sinn Fein 1985 to Today*, Dublin: The O'Brien Press.

O'Brien, C. C. (1988) *God Land: Reflections on Religion and Nationalism*, Cambridge: Harvard University Press.

O'Brien, C. C. (1993) *The Great Melody*, London: Minerva.

O'Brien, C. C. (1994) *Ancestral Voices: Religion and Nationalism in Ireland*, Dublin: Poolbeg Press.

O'Brien, C. C. (1999) 'Malign Changes and Benign Labels', speech to the Annual Conference of the Irish Association, Carrickfergus, 12 November, http://www.Irish-association.org/archives/index.html

O'Callaghan, S. (2003) 'Walk tall, walk free', *Observer*, 28 September.

O'Connor, F. (2002) *Breaking the Bonds: Making Peace in Northern Ireland*, London: Mainstream Publishing.

O'Doherty, M. (1995) 'Community charged', *Fortnight*, 342 (September): 12–13.

O'Doherty, M. (1998) *The Trouble with Guns: Republican Strategy and the Provisional IRA*, Belfast: The Blackstaff Press.

O'Doherty, M. (2002a) 'Where now for Northern Nationalism?', speech to the Irish Association, Mansion House, Dublin, 22 March, http://www.Irish-association.org/archives/index.html

O'Doherty, M. (2002b) 'If peace was a breeze', *Fortnight*, 406 (July/August): 5.

O'Doherty, M. (2003a) 'Pick your Trimble', *Fortnight*, 413 (April): 3.

O'Doherty, M. (2003b) 'The piffle of the IRA', *Fortnight*, 415 (June): 6–7.

O'Doherty, M. (2003c) 'The "Nixon in China" theory . . . was there too much faith in Trimble?', *Belfast Telegraph*, 26 November.

O'Doherty, M. (2003d) 'Collapse of faith in an ability to agree', *Guardian*, 29 November.

O'Doherty, M. (2004) 'Sinn Fein and SDLP must come to terms with reality', *Belfast Telegraph*, 12 January.

O'Dowd, N. (2000) 'Trimble selling a pig in a poke', *Ireland on Sunday*, 30 January.

O'Farrell, J. (1998) 'First among equals', *Fortnight*, 374 (November): 11–12.

O'Farrell, J. (2000) 'Making history', *Fortnight*, 382 (January): 5.

O'Hagan, D. (1998) 'The Concept of Republicanism', in N. Porter (ed.) *The Republican Ideal: Current Perspectives*, Belfast: The Blackstaff Press.

O'Halloran, C. (1987) *Partition and the Limits of Irish Nationalism: An Ideology under Stress*, New Jersey: Humanities Press International, Inc.

O'Hanlon, E. (2003) 'Lest we forget our real history', *Sunday Independent*, 31 August.

O'Leary, B. (1989) 'The limits to coercive consociationalism in Northern Ireland', *Political Studies*, 39: 562–88.

O'Leary, B. (1992) 'Public opinion and Northern Irish futures', *Political Quarterly*, 63: 143–70.

O'Leary, B. (1999) 'The nature of the British-Irish Agreement', *New Left Review*, 233: 66–96.

O'Leary, B. (2001a) 'The Character of the 1998 Agreement: Results and Prospects', in R. Wilford (ed.) *Aspects of the Belfast Agreement*, Oxford: Oxford University Press.

O'Leary, B. (2001b) 'Comparative Political Science and the British-Irish Agreement', in J. McGarry (ed.) *Northern Ireland and the Divided World: Post-Agreement Northern Ireland in Comparative Perspective*, Oxford: Oxford University Press.

O'Leary, B. (2001c) 'The protection of human rights under the Belfast Agreement', *Political Quarterly*, 72: 353–65.

O'Leary, B. and McGarry, J. (1996) *The Politics of Antagonism*, 2nd edn, London: Athlone.

O'Leary, P. (1993) 'The poverty of Irish nationalism', *The Equal Citizen*, 2 (October): 11–16.

Oliver, T. (2004) 'Streets of shame that lead to despair', *Daily Telegraph*, 18 February.

O'Neill, B. (2002) 'How the peace process divided', *The Blanket*, 25 July, http://lark.phoblacht.net

O'Neill, Shane (1994) 'Pluralist justice and its limits: the case of Northern Ireland', *Political Studies*, 42: 363–77.

O'Neill, Shane (1996) 'The idea of an overlapping consensus in Northern Ireland: stretching the limits of liberalism', *Irish Political Studies*, 11: 83–102.

O'Neill, Shane (2000) 'Liberty, equality and the rights of cultures: the marching controversy at Drumcree', *British Journal of Politics and International Relations*, 2: 26–45.

O'Neill, Shane (2001) 'Mutual Recognition and the Accommodation of National Diversity: Constitutional Justice in Northern Ireland', in A-G. Gagnon and J. Tully (eds) *Multinational Democracies*, Cambridge: Cambridge University Press.

O'Neill, Shane (2002) 'Democratic theory with critical intent: reply to Newey', *British Journal of Politics and International Relations*, 4: 98–114.

O'Neill, Sharon (2004) '"Life worse now than 1968" says Mgr Faul', *Irish News*, 8 June.

Osborne, R. (2004) *Fair Employment in Northern Ireland*, Belfast: The Blackstaff Press.

O'Sullivan, N. (1983) *Fascism*, London: Dent.

O'Sullivan, N. (1992) *Santayana (Thinkers of Our Time)*, London: The Claridge Press.

Parry, G. (1997) 'Opposition questions', *Government and Opposition*, 32: 457–61.

Patterson, H. (1989) *The Politics of Illusion: Republicanism and Socialism in Modern Ireland*, London: Hutchinson Radius.

Patterson, H. (1994) 'Wishful thinking', *Fortnight*, 327 (April): 14–17.

Patterson, H. (2002) 'How clever was Adams?', *Fortnight*, 389 (November): 26.

Patterson, H. (2003) 'The defeat of compromise', *Observer*, 30 November.

Paxman, J. (2003) *The Political Animal*, London: Penguin.

Pensky, M. (2001) 'Editor's Introduction', in J. Habermas, *The Postnational Constellation: Political Essays*, trans. M. Pensky, London: Polity.

Pocock, J. G. A. (1984) 'Verbalizing a Political Act: Toward a Politics of Speech', in M. J. Shapiro (ed.) *Language and Politics*, Oxford: Blackwell.

Pollak, A. (ed.) (1993) *A Citizen's Inquiry: The Opsahl Report on Northern Ireland*, Dublin: The Lilliput Press.

Porter, N. (1996) *Rethinking Unionism: An Alternative Vision for Northern Ireland*, Belfast: The Blackstaff Press.

Porter, N. (2003) *The Elusive Quest: Reconciliation in Northern Ireland*, Belfast: The Blackstaff Press.

Power, P. (1990) 'Revisionist "consent", Hillsborough, and the decline of constitutional republicanism', *Eire-Ireland*, 25: 20–39.

Pridham, G. (2000) *The Dynamics of Democratization: A Comparative Approach*, London: Continuum.

Richards, S. (1991) 'Field Day's Fifth Province: Avenue or Impasse?', in E. Hughes (ed.) *Culture and Politics in Northern Ireland*, Milton Keynes: Open University Press.

Roberts, Sir I. (2003) 'New Relationships within and between These Islands', lecture to the Irish Association, 28 February, http://www.Irish-association.org/archives/index.html

Robinson, P. (2003a) 'We need to find a form of administration which can survive any election or the bad behaviour of any political party', *Belfast Telegraph*, 23 October.

Robinson, P. (2003b) 'Only a deal that embraces DUP can stick and last', *Irish News*, 24 November.

Robinson, P. (2004) 'Speech by Deputy Leader to the Party Conference, Ramada Inn, Belfast', DUP Press Release, 8 May.

Roche, P. J. (1994) 'Northern Ireland and Irish nationalism. A Unionist perspective', *The Irish Review*, 15: 70–8.

Rodgers, B. (2002) 'Is the "New Ireland" Now a Real Possibility?', speech to the Irish Association, Mansion House, Dublin, 22 March, http://www.Irish-association.org/archives/index.html

Rorty, R. (1989) *Contingency, Irony and Solidarity*, Cambridge: Cambridge University Press.

Rose, R. (1971) *Governing Without Consensus: An Irish Perspective*, London: Faber and Faber.

Rose, R. (1976) *Northern Ireland: A Time of Choice*, London: Macmillan.

Rowan, B. (1995) *Behind the Lines: The Story of the IRA and Loyalist Ceasefires*, Belfast: The Blackstaff Press.

Ruane, J. (1994a) 'Ireland, European integration, and the dialectic of nationalism and postnationalism', *Etudes Irlandaises*, 19: 183–93.

Ruane, J. (1994b) 'Colonial legacies and cultural reflexivities', *Etudes Irlandaises*, 19: 107–19.

Ruane, J. (1999) 'The End of (Irish) History? Three Readings of the Present Conjuncture', in J. Ruane and J. Todd (eds) *After the Good Friday Agreement*, Dublin: University College Dublin Press.

Ruane, J. and Todd, J. (1991) 'Why Can't You Get Along with Each Other? Culture, Structure and the Northern Ireland Conflict', in E. Hughes (ed.) *Culture and Politics in Northern Ireland*, Milton Keynes: Open University Press.

Ruane, J. and Todd, J. (1996) *The Dynamics of Conflict in Northern Ireland: Power, Conflict and Emancipation*, Cambridge: Cambridge University Press.

Ruane, J. and Todd, J. (1998) 'Peace Processes and Communalism in Northern

Ireland', in W. Crotty and D. E. Schmitt (eds) *Ireland and the Politics of Change*, London: Longman.

Ruane, J. and Todd, J. (1999) 'The Belfast Agreement: Content, Context, Consequences', in J. Ruane and J. Todd (eds) *After the Good Friday Agreement*, Dublin: University College Dublin Press.

Santayana, G. (1951) *Dominations and Powers: Reflections on Liberty, Society, and Government*, New York: Charles Scribner's Sons.

Schmitt, C. (1976) *The Concept of the Political*, trans. G. Schwab, New Jersey: Rutgers University Press.

Scholz, S. J. (2002) 'Dyadic deliberation versus discursive democracy', *Political Theory*, 30: 746–50.

Schopenhauer, A. (1892) *Essays*, selected and trans. by T. Bailey Saunders, London: Swann and Sonnenschein.

Schopenhauer, A. (1970) *Essays and Aphorisms*, trans. R. J. Hollingdale, Harmondsworth: Penguin.

Schopenhauer, A. (1988) *Manuscript Remains: Volume 1 – Early Manuscripts (1804–1818)*, ed. A. Hubscher and trans. E. F. J. Payne, New York: Berg.

Schopflin, G. (2000) *Nations, Identity, Power*, London: Hurst.

Schulze, K. (1997) 'The Northern Ireland political process: a viable approach to conflict resolution?', *Irish Political Studies*, 12: 92–110.

Schwab, G. (1985) 'Introduction', in C. Schmitt, *Political Theology*, trans. G. Schwab, Cambridge: MIT.

Sciascia, L. (2001) *Sicilian Uncles*, London: Granta.

Sebald, W. G. (2003) *On the Natural History of Destruction*, London: Hamish Hamilton.

Seldon, A. (1997) *Major: A Political Life*, London: Phoenix.

Shils, E. and Grosby, S. (1997) *The Virtue of Civility: Selected Essays on Liberalism, Tradition, and Civil Society*, Indianapolis: Liberty Fund.

Shirlow, P. (2000) 'Fear, loathing and intimidation', *Fortnight*, 388 (September): 37–8.

Shirlow, P. (2001) 'It's grim up north', *Fortnight*, 398 (September): 12–13.

Shirlow, P. (2003) 'Ethno-sectarianism and the reproduction of fear in Belfast', *Capital and Class*, 80: 77–93.

Simon, S. (1999) 'Trimble a Moses, not a Judas', *Daily Telegraph*, 29 November.

Sinclair, T. (1970) 'The Position of Ulster', in S. Rosenbaum (ed.) *Against Home Rule*, Port Washington: The Kennikat Press.

Slagstad, R. (1988) 'Liberal constitutionalism and its critics: Carl Schmitt and Max Weber', in J. Elster and R. Slagstad (eds) *Constitutionalism and Democracy*, Cambridge: Cambridge University Press.

Smith, M. L. R. (1997) *Fighting for Ireland? The Military Strategy of the Irish Republican Movement*, London: Routledge.

Smith, M. L. R. (1999) 'The intellectual internment of a conflict: the forgotten war in Northern Ireland', *International Affairs*, 75: 77–97.

Smyth, J. (1995) 'Poking at the entrails', *Fortnight*, 344 (November): 35.

Spectator (2002) 'End the charade' (leader), *Spectator*, 12 October: 4.

Spencer, P. and Wollman, H. (2002) *Nationalism: A Critical Introduction*, London: Sage.

Stevenson, J. (1996) *'We Wrecked the Place': Contemplating an End to the Northern Irish Troubles*, New York: Free Press.

Stewart, A. T. Q. (1977) *The Narrow Ground: Patterns of Ulster History*, London: Faber and Faber.

Stewart, A. T. Q. (1993) *A Deeper Silence: The Hidden Origins of the United Irishmen*, London: Faber and Faber.

Stewart, A. T. Q. (2001) *The Shape of Irish History*, Belfast: The Blackstaff Press.

Stewart, B. (2000) 'On the necessity of de-hydifying Irish cultural criticism', *New Hibernia Review*, 4: 23–44.

Sunday Business Post (2004) 'All changed, changed utterly for SDLP and UUP' (editorial), *Sunday Business Post*, 13 June.

Taylor, P. (1999) *Loyalists*, London: Bloomsbury.

Taylor, R. (2001) 'Northern Ireland: Consociation or Social Transformation', in J. McGarry (ed.) *Northern Ireland and the Divided World: Post-Agreement Northern Ireland in Comparative Perspective*, Oxford: Oxford University Press.

Teague, P. (1994) 'Approved border road', *Fortnight*, 332 (October): 31–4.

Tester, K. (1992) *Civil Society*, London: Routledge.

Thody, P. (1993) *The Conservative Imagination*, London: Pinter.

Todd, J. (1995) 'Beyond the community conflict: historic compromise or emancipatory process', *Irish Political Studies*, 10: 161–78.

Todd, J. (1999) 'Nationalism, Republicanism and the Good Friday Agreement', in J. Ruane and J. Todd (eds) *After the Good Friday Agreement*, Dublin: UCD Press.

Tonge, J. (2002) *Northern Ireland Politics: Conflict and Change*, Harlow: Longman.

Tonge, J. and Evans, J. A. J. (2001) 'Faultlines in unionism: division and dissent within the Ulster Unionist Council', *Irish Political Studies*, 16: 111–31.

Tonge, J. and Evans, J. A. J. (2002) 'Party members and the Good Friday Agreement in Northern Ireland', *Irish Political Studies*, 17: 59–73.

Townshend, C. (1988) 'Synergy and Polarity in Ireland: Historical Elements of the Problem of Consensus', in C. Townshend (ed.) *Consensus in Ireland: Approaches and Recessions*, Oxford: The Clarendon Press.

Trimble, D. (1998) 'Speech by the Rt. Hon. David Trimble MP to the Northern Ireland Forum', Ulster Unionist Party Press Statement, 17 April.

Trimble, D. (1999) 'The commitment to peace and democracy', Ulster Unionist Party Press Statement, 22 May.

Trimble, D. (2000a) 'Speech to the British-Irish Association at Oxford', September, http://www.uup.org/current/index.shtml

Trimble, D. (2000b) 'Statement to a fringe meeting at the Labour Party Conference, 28 September', http://www.uup.org/current/index.shtml

Trimble, D. (2001) *To Raise up a New Northern Ireland*, Belfast: The Belfast Press.

Trimble, D. (2002a) 'Sinn Fein irresponsibility still threatens peace in Ulster', *Daily Telegraph*, 25 July.

Trimble, D. (2002b) 'Leader addresses party conference in Londonderry', 19 October, http://www.uup.org/current/index.shtml

Trimble, D. (2003a) 'Words, words, words', *Times Literary Supplement*, 18 April.

Trimble, D. (2003b) 'Leader's speech at the Annual Party Conference in Armagh', Ulster Unionist Party Press Statement, 18 October.

Trimble, D. (2003c) '"Ourselves Alone" is not the motto of the Ulster Unionist Party', address to the Inverness Presbytery of the Church of Scotland, Ramada Hotel, Inverness, 8 September.

Trimble, D. (2003d) 'Unionism back in from the window ledge', speech to the East

Belfast Ulster Unionist Association, La Mon House, Belfast, 11 June, http://www.uup.org/current/index.shtml

Trimble, D. (2004) 'Why the war on terror is one single struggle', *Belfast Telegraph*, 22 March.

Tudor, H. (1972) *Political Myth*, London: Pall Mall.

Vargas Llosa, M. (1991) 'A Fish out of Water', in *Vargas Llosa for President: A Novelist's Personal Account of his Campaign for the Presidency of Peru*, *Granta*, 36, June.

Vernon, R. (1998) 'Liberals, democrats and the agenda of politics', *Political Studies*, 46: 295–308.

Walker, B. (1989) *Ulster Politics: The Formative Years 1868–86*, Belfast: The Ulster Historical Foundation and The Institute of Irish Studies.

Walker, B. (1996) *Dancing to History's Tune: History, Myth and Politics in Northern Ireland*, Belfast: The Institute of Irish Studies.

Walker, B. (2000) *Past and Present: History, Identity and Politics in Ireland*, Belfast: The Institute of Irish Studies.

Walker, G. (2001) 'The British-Irish Council', in R. Wilford (ed.) *Aspects of the Belfast Agreement*, Oxford: Oxford University Press.

Whitehead, L. (1997) 'Bowling in the Bronx: The Uncivil Interstices between Civil and Political Society', in R. Fine and S. Rai (eds) *Civil Society: Democratic Perspectives*, London: Frank Cass.

Whyte, J. (1991) *Interpreting Northern Ireland*, Oxford: The Clarendon Press.

Wilford, R. (2000) 'Designing the Northern Ireland Assembly', *Parliamentary Affairs*, 53: 577–90.

Wilford, R. (2001) 'The Assembly and the Executive', in R. Wilford (ed.) *Aspects of the Belfast Agreement*, Oxford: Oxford University Press.

Williams, H. (1994) 'Democracy and right in Habermas's theory of facticity and value', *History of Political Thought*, 15: 269–82.

Wilson, R. (1993) 'Pavlovian politicos', *Fortnight*, 319 (July/August): 5.

Wilson, R. (1994) 'Spare us the homilies', *Fortnight*, 329 (June): 5.

Wilson, R. (1997) 'Forum or farce? The failure of political dialogue in Northern Ireland', *Etudes Irlandaises*, 22: 183–92.

Wilson, R. (2002) 'The apartheid thinking of the Agreement', *Fortnight*, 409 (December): 6.

Wilson, R. (2003) 'Reforms can breathe life into faltering Agreement', *Belfast Telegraph*, 2 September.

Wolf, C. (1993) *The Author's Dimension: Selected Essays*, trans. J. Van Heurck, New York: Farrar, Straus and Giroux.

Wolff, S. (2001) 'Context and Content: Sunningdale and Belfast Compared', in R. Wilford (ed.) *Aspects of the Belfast Agreement*, Oxford: Oxford University Press.

Wolff, S. (2002) 'Conclusion: The Peace Process in Northern Ireland since 1998', in J. Neuheiser and S. Wolff (eds) *Peace at Last? The Impact of the Good Friday Agreement on Northern Ireland*, New York: Berghahn Books.

Wood, A. (1990) *Hegel's Ethical Theory*, Cambridge: Cambridge University Press.

Young, I. M. (2002) *Inclusion and Democracy*, Oxford: Oxford University Press.

Zamoyski, A. (1999) *Holy Madness: Romantics, Patriots and Revolutionaries 1776–1871*, London: Weidenfeld and Nicolson.

Zizek, S. (1996) 'Fantasy as political category: a Lacanian approach', *Journal for the Psychoanalysis of Culture and Society*, 1: 77–85.

Index